Applied Cognitive and Behavioural Approaches to the Treatment of Addiction

A Practical Treatment Guide

Luke Mitcheson
Jenny Maslin
Tim Meynen
Tamara Morrison
Robert Hill
Shamil Wanigaratne

WILEY-BLACKWELL

A John Wiley & Sons, Ltd., Publication

This edition first published 2010
© 2010 John Wiley & Sons Ltd.

Wiley-Blackwell is an imprint of John Wiley & Sons, formed by the merger of Wiley's global
Scientific, Technical, and Medical business with Blackwell Publishing.

Registered Office
John Wiley & Sons Ltd, The Atrium, Southern Gate, Chichester, West Sussex, PO19 8SQ, UK

Editorial Offices
The Atrium, Southern Gate, Chichester, West Sussex, PO19 8SQ, UK
9600 Garsington Road, Oxford, OX4 2DQ, UK
350 Main Street, Malden, MA 02148-5020, USA

For details of our global editorial offices, for customer services, and for information about how to
apply for permission to reuse the copyright material in this book please see our website at www.
wiley.com/wiley-blackwell.

Library of Congress Cataloging-in-Publication Data

Applied cognitive and behavioural approaches to the treatment of addiction : a practical treatment
guide / Luke Mitcheson ... [et al.].
      p. cm.
   Includes bibliographical references and index.
   ISBN 978-0-470-51062-9 (cloth) – ISBN 978-0-470-51063-6 (pbk.)   1. Substance abuse–
Treatment.   2. Compulsive behavior–Treatment.   3. Cognitive therapy.   4. Behavior
therapy.   I. Mitcheson, Luke.
   RC564.A65 1010
   616.86–dc22

                                                                                  2009053118

A catalogue record for this book is available from the British Library.

Set in 10 on 12 pt Galliard by Toppan Best-set Premedia Limited
Printed in Singapore by Markono Print Media Pte Ltd.

1   2010

Applied Cognitive and Behavioural Approaches to the Treatment of Addiction

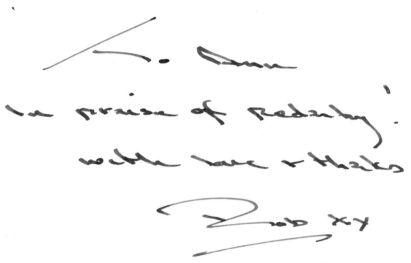

'The ways in which we interact with our clients are the essential tools of our trade. The National Institute for Clinical and Health Excellence has already published rigorous analyses of the evidence for various psychological approaches. But, until now, we have not had an authoritative guide to the relevant cognitive and behavioural therapeutic techniques. This book fills that void. It is easy to read and draws on the authors' wealth of experience of working with clients with drug and alcohol problems. I expect this book rapidly to become a well-thumbed and widely-borrowed book which will help us all to improve the competence and quality of the interventions that we deliver.'

Professor John Strang, Director, National Addiction Centre, London

Contents

About the Authors

Luke Mitcheson BSc, MSc, D.Clin.Psych. has 15 years' experience working as a Clinical Psychologist in substance misuse services. He is a Consultant Clinical Psychologist and is the lead psychologist in the South London and Maudsley NHS Foundation Trust, Lambeth addictions services. He is also an accredited psychotherapist with the British Association for Behavioural and Cognitive Psychotherapies. He has developed services for stimulant drug users and has been involved in research projects looking at applied psychosocial interventions for the treatment of substance use problems. He is also involved in training and supervision of staff to develop their psychosocial skills and practice. He is seconded to the National Treatment Agency as part of the clinical team and holds an honorary lecturership at the Institute of Psychiatry, Kings College, London.

Jenny Maslin is a Clinical Psychologist who has worked in Substance Misuse Services for South London and Maudsley NHS Foundation Trust, Lambeth for the last five years. She works with clients at varying stages of their substance use career, who use a variety of substances and experience a range of psychological problems. She also provides training, along with her co-facilitators, in the use of cognitive and behavioural therapy for clients with substance use and co-morbid difficulties.

Tim Meynen is a Chartered Clinical Psychologist who has worked in Community and Criminal Justice Substance Misuse Services for South London and Maudsley NHS Foundation Trust, Lambeth for the last six years. He provides cognitive and behavioural therapy training and supervision to both addictions and adult mental health staff for clients with substance use and co-morbid difficulties.

Tamara Morrison BSc Hons, D.Clin.Psych has worked in clinical and research posts in a number of South London mental health services since completing a degree in Human Psychology at Aston University in 1999. She qualified as a Clinical Psychologist in 2005 from University College, London, and has since been working as a Clinical Psychologist in Lambeth Community Drug and Alcohol Team. She has worked with both statutory and non-statutory drug services. Since 2009, Tamara has also been working in the Islington Psychology Assessment and Treatment Service, which became a site for Improving Access to Psychological Therapies in September 2009.

Robert Hill BSc, MSc, MA, PhD, Psych.D has worked in the field of mental health since 1983. Since 1999 he has worked as lead Clinical Psychologist for inpatient addictions at the South London and Maudsley NHS Foundation Trust, Lambeth. He has also worked as a Senior Lecturer at Middlesex University, jointly managing a three-year European project focusing on the reduction of patient violence, stress and burnout among community and inpatient mental health personnel in Denmark, Finland, Norway, Poland and the UK. He has a particular interest in philosophy and holds an MA in Modern European Philosophy.

Shamil Wanigaratne BSc, D.Clin.Psych, C.Psychol, AFBPsS is Consultant Clinical Psychologist and Head of Clinical Psychology of the Addictions Division at the South London and Maudsley NHS Foundation Trust, Lambeth. He is also Honorary Senior Lecturer at the Institute of Psychiatry, Kings College, London. Throughout his career he has worked to combine clinical practice with academic research. He is currently involved in a number of research collaborations. His clinical and research interests include cognitive and neuropsychological aspects of addictions, initiation and maintenance of behaviour change, outcome measurement, culture and substance misuse, psychological impact of trauma and the association between trauma and addictive behaviours.

He has acted as a consultant to various UK government bodies. He has also acted as an international consultant in a number of countries and was one of the founding members of the British Psychological Society's Special Interest Group in Addictions, which is now the Faculty of Addiction.

He co-founded the UK–Sri Lanka Trauma Group in 1996 and was the first chair. He was also involved in setting up the first clinical psychology training course in Sri Lanka, at the University of Colombo.

Foreword

Traditionally there has been a divide between health care professionals who do and those who do not specialise in the treatment of addictions. Addiction specialisation certainly has its advantages for those dedicated to working full-time with these issues. These difficulties occur on a continuum; people who experience severe addictions often need specialised medical, psychological and psychosocial help. Clients struggling with addiction also often need help with a myriad of other issues such as depression, anxiety, relationship difficulties and even psychosis. Some addiction specialists are not trained to treat these problems and it would be beneficial for their clients if they were more knowledgeable about effective treatments for common co-occurring conditions.

On the other hand, health care providers who are not addiction specialists often fail to recognise substance use problems or behavioural addictions and therefore may not include these in treatment planning. Given the widespread use of alcohol, prescription medications and other drugs it is unlikely there are many health care workers, therapists or counsellors who do not have clients who might beneficially work on issues related to substance use. However, when therapists lack specialisation in addictions yet have expertise in treating mood disorders, relationship difficulties and other common therapy issues, it is understandable that these latter issues are identified for focus in treatment rather than substance use. A therapist may conjecture, *My client's overuse of alcohol, prescription medication, or street drugs is simply self-medication for anxiety and it will go away as the anxiety improves.* Sometimes it does and sometimes it doesn't.

The historical division between addiction specialists and non-specialists artificially divides clients into categories of addicts and non-addicts when the human reality is not this clear-cut at all. There is no way to know how many serious addictions might have been prevented if health care workers had more eagerly helped clients manage the early stages of substance misuse. Similarly, we do not know how many 'treatment failures' in psychotherapy are, at least in part, due to missed opportunities to explore a reliance on addictive behaviours or chemical use. Nor do we know how many people 'fail' in treatment of their addiction because other psychological difficulties are not effectively treated.

In my experience as a CBT instructor and consultant, I have learned that health care providers rarely neglect treatment areas in which they are knowledgeable and confident in their abilities. We all want to help our clients in the best ways possible. Thus, one important antidote to all these missed opportunities is to build a knowledge bridge so addiction specialists and non-specialist therapists can all become better educated about effective treatment approaches for addictions and their co-existing psychological problems.

Applied Cognitive and Behavioural Approaches to the Treatment of Addiction: A Practical Treatment Guide elegantly constructs this bridge. Readers who are addiction specialists and yet relatively unfamiliar with cognitive behavioural therapy (CBT) will appreciate the simple and practical explanations of CBT's principles and methods. The authors clearly illustrate how CBT can be integrated with other treatment approaches that may be more familiar to addiction specialists such as motivational interviewing, relapse prevention and pharmacologically assisted recovery. At the same time, therapists and counsellors without a speciality in addictions will learn to artfully apply the therapy methods they already understand to addiction problems. In addition, therapists without addiction expertise learn to integrate CBT with key methods from motivational interviewing and other addiction therapies to help many client problems, not only addictions.

Chapter by chapter, readers learn good questions to ask that help provide therapeutic focus to the assessment and treatment of addictions. Detailed examples show how to tailor CBT homework and behavioural experiments to help these problems. In addition, the authors educate readers how to implement a non-judgemental, compassionate treatment framework that emphasises and enhances client optimism, resilience, social integration and choice.

As a CBT-specialist who is not an addictions specialist, I appreciate the personable non-academic writing style adopted by these authors. The lives of clients with substance use problems can sometimes seem messy and chaotic. It is reassuring to read a therapy guide for helping these clients that is clear, organised and empathic to both therapists and clients. The authors are highly experienced in treatment of addictions and their expertise is reflected in the calm guidance they offer on how to foster personal development in clients no matter where their struggles fit along the addiction continuum. At the same time, the authors acknowledge a deep understanding of the pressures and challenges therapists face, especially those of us without addiction expertise. They address common therapist fears and beliefs as well as social and moral values that can impact the treatment choices we make. The shadows these concerns can cast on treatment are slowly dispelled by the practical and, at times, inspirational guidance offered.

In the end, this book captures how rewarding it can be to help clients engaged in this very human struggle. The authors not only destigmatise addiction, they show how therapists in all practice settings can approach and help clients manage these issues. As each chapter unfolds, readers are likely to notice their own optimism, resilience and choices increase as they begin to practise the methods described and integrate these with current knowledge and skills.

Now it is time for you to dip into this inviting book or take a deep plunge, whichever approach suits your current learning needs. Whether you are an addictions specialist already, a therapist wary of addictions, or someone in between, your clients will benefit from the time you spend with this practical treatment guide.

Christine A. Padesky, Ph.D.
www.padesky.com
Co-author, *Mind Over Mood*

Preface

As a group of clinical psychologists, we have over 60 years' experience of working in the field of substance misuse. This is a significant period of time and this book is born out of a desire to capture some of the essence of this work and share some of the lessons we have learnt. Most of our experience has been working in NHS treatment services in the UK, both community and residential programmes and within multidisciplinary teams with our colleagues from nursing, psychiatry, occupational therapy and social work as well as with drug workers, some of whom have no formal therapeutic training.

Our roles in these teams can be split between direct work with clients and work with staff to develop treatment programmes and their practice in the use of psychosocial interventions. Over the years we have sought to enable staff to think psychologically about what might be going on with their clients and to use psychological ideas to unpick the sometimes baffling and demoralising aspects of addictive behaviour. We have run numerous types of supervision groups, provided one-to-one supervision for staff, developed treatment pathways and interventions for drugs such as cocaine and cannabis for which there is no pharmacological intervention, and implemented comprehensive treatment programmes within inpatient settings.

In all these aspects of our work we have drawn on cognitive and behavioural therapy (CBT) interventions and the conceptualisation process that underpins these interventions as a central way of thinking about what and how things should be done. Through running training workshops we have seen how staff are enthused when enabled to use an approach which has an explicit and understandable conceptual basis linked to practical and useful tools which can be incorporated into their day to day work.

This book represents our attempt to set out how we have adapted CBT to work in a substance misuse setting and focus specifically on substance-using behaviour. With this at the heart of the book we hope it will be of interest outside specialist treatment services to practitioners who come across substance-using clients in the context of their clinical work. We are not presenting a new CBT theory of addiction or attempting to validate the approach through experimental research. Rather, we set out to present a pragmatic approach that is theoretically consistent with a cognitive and behavioural framework and interventions.

Whilst we are indebted to the many staff who have travelled alongside our learning, it is the clients we have worked with who have been, perhaps, our most significant teachers. It is a privilege to have worked with and experienced clients who have gone on to achieve recovery from problem substance use, often in the face of years of abuse, neglect and marginalisation from social resources. It is the part that CBT has played in their recovery journeys that has convinced us of the value of the approach and given us the audacity to write a book like this.

List of Abbreviations

AA	Alcoholics Anonymous
BEs	behavioural experiments
CBT	cognitive behavioural therapy
CM	contingency management
CORE	Centre for Outcomes, Research and Effectiveness
DAAT	Drug and Alcohol Action Team
DOH	Department of Health
HRS	high risk situation
IAPT	Improving Access to Psychological Therapies
IDS	Inventory of Drinking Situations
IDTS	Inventory of Drug-taking Situations
ITEP	International Treatment Effectiveness Programme
LFT	low frustration tolerance
MI	motivational interviewing
NA	Narcotics Anonymous
NICE	The National Institute for Health and Clinical Excellence
NTA	National Treatment Agency
ORIC	optimism, resilience, integration or reintegration and choice
PIG	problem of immediate gratification
PRIME	plans, response, impulses/inhibitory forces, motives, evaluations
RCTs	randomised controlled trials
REBT	rational emotive behaviour therapy
RET	rational emotive therapy
SAMHSA	Substance Abuse and Mental Health Services Administration
SCQ	Situational Confidence Questionnaire
SIDs	seemingly irrelevant decisions
SMART	Specific, Measurable, Achievable, Realistic and Time-based
TOP	Treatment Outcomes Profile
UKATT	UK Alcohol Treatment Trial

Acknowledgements

Thanks to Ann McDonnell for her many suggestions, both literary and therapeutic, and to Paul de Mornay Davies, Nicola Meynen, Susan Sallas, Jane Tooke and Lee Wilson for their patience, advice and support.

Finally, thanks to Esmerelda Claessen for permission to use her father's painting.

Chapter 1

Introduction to CBT for Substance Use Problems

In this book we set out a comprehensive cognitive behavioural therapy (CBT) approach for the treatment of drug and alcohol problems. We explain how CBT makes sense of substance use problems and introduce a range of interventions for workers and therapists to use with clients to enable them to achieve control and, if appropriate, abstain from substance use altogether. We have aimed to make this book accessible not only to people who have no professional therapy training but also to health professionals and cognitive behaviour therapists wishing to develop their competencies in working with people with substance use problems. It is intended for people working in general health and mental health services as well as specialist substance misuse treatment services.

CBT is one of a number of psychosocial interventions used in the field of substance misuse and for which there is an emerging evidence base in Europe and North America. As with many evidence-based interventions, a gap remains between research findings and actual clinical practice. We hope this book provides a platform to develop the practice of CBT in the field and to address this theory/practice gap. We are advocates of CBT as a result of our clinical experience and work with multi-professional staff groups. We believe CBT has unique qualities which are of direct relevance to substance use problems and that the CBT emphasis on collaborative work and building skills is well suited to addressing the needs of clients. Our work with staff groups in both community and inpatient settings has demonstrated how CBT can provide them with a way of thinking about substance use problems instead of feeling overwhelmed and confused by them. This

Applied Cognitive and Behavioural Approaches to the Treatment of Addiction: A Practical Treatment Guide By Luke Mitcheson, Jenny Maslin, Tim Meynen, Tamara Morrison, Robert Hill and Shamil Wanigaratne
Copyright © 2010 John Wiley & Sons, Ltd.

understanding empowers workers to start to do things with clients as well as engage in critical discourse about the relative efficacy of different interventions. Essentially, we believe CBT helps workers to think psychologically about their clients and clinical work.

CBT and recovery

One of the emerging ideas influencing service developments in mental health and substance misuse is the notion of recovery and from the outset we believe it is important to ground our vision of CBT within this broader context. The UK Drug Policy Commission Consensus Group (UK Drug Policy Commission Recovery Consensus Group, 2008) developed the following definition of recovery to clarify this concept.

> The process of recovery from problematic substance use is characterised by voluntary sustained control over substance use which maximises health and wellbeing and participation in the rights, roles and responsibilities of society.

This definition is a challenge to the structure and focus of current treatment services. We believe that CBT will be part of the solution in adopting a more recovery-focused approach. One criticism of addiction treatment is that it is primarily concerned with acute care aimed at stabilisation rather than the longer-term changes required to sustain recovery (White, 2008). White cogently argues that whilst there have been many advances in the knowledge and treatment of addictions, not least in the field of CBT, limitations remain in the efficacy of these treatments. Thus some clients, generally those whose substance use is part of a broader cluster of problems, typically relapse. This outcome has led to a call for a reorientation of treatment away from an acute care model to a recovery management model (White, 2008).

Acute care is defined in terms of crisis-intervention and symptom suppression with the aim of cure or permanent problem resolution. However, White and other commentators have noted that addiction has characteristics similar to chronic health problems (e.g. type-2 diabetes, hypertension and asthma). Whilst not all addiction problems are chronic, as some people respond to a brief period of treatment and never return to problem substance use, a number of service users, particularly those in contact with specialist treatment agencies, have a range of needs for which a chronic care model is more appropriate. A chronic care model focuses more on empowering service users to self-manage their condition and locates resources to managing well-being and sustaining recovery within social networks and the broader community. White describes this as a recovery management model which focuses on addressing the range of issues associated with substance use problems, such as educational underachievement and vocational, legal and housing difficulties, as well as co-occurring mental health problems (e.g. trauma and depression). The aim is to build 'recovery capital' to overcome social exclusion and to enable our clients to participate in society.

We believe that CBT, as described in this book, is relevant to both the acute and chronic care models as both have a part to play in enabling clients to achieve recovery from substance misuse problems. An episode of acute care can be the trigger to initiate recovery, to help a service user to understand and gain control over his or her substance use behaviour. This would then shift into a chronic care or recovery management focus in which the service user learns to self-manage his difficulties or, as White describes it, 'focus on the lived solution'. In this context CBT involves helping clients to address obstacles in their life that stand in the way of change as well as build resources that will sustain long-term recovery from problem substance use.

We think that adopting a CBT approach within services bridges the gap between acute and chronic care models. In particular, our vision of CBT is one that is strongly grounded in an environmental context and recognises that factors outside treatment are more important for recovery maintenance. CBT enables professionals to collaborate with clients in order to help them in their recovery. Addressing both the acute and chronic aspects of substance use problems, recovery can be thought of as a two-stage process: recovery from drugs or alcohol and recovery related to wider social and personal opportunities. We call these two senses of recovery: *recovery from* and *recovery for*. Recovery from could mean abstaining from substances altogether, harm minimisation or substance stabilisation. Recovery for refers to the stage beyond substance use when clients are looking for positive things in their lives, such as social reintegration. Of course, these two elements are rarely that clear-cut, nor do they occur in such a neat, sequential manner. Indeed, the impetus or desire for a life beyond alcohol or drugs is often the initial reason for change. Sadly, such a desire or willingness to change substance-using behaviour is rarely successful on its own. Something else is needed – the skills to succeed. This is the primary focus of this book and although we mainly focus on *recovery from*, we hope that we do not lose sight of the fact that it is *recovery for* that is probably the more meaningful to both clients and staff in the long run.

As clinicians we are interested in both recovery from substance use and recovery for life more generally. Although CBT may appear to the uninitiated to be a highly technical exercise unrelated to wider social issues, it is clear that there are underlying principles at work in all good CBT interventions. We have identified four that we believe are particularly important when working with clients who have substance use difficulties. These are: increased client optimism, resilience, integration (or reintegration) and choice (ORIC). Through the considered application of CBT principles and techniques we believe clients will be more optimistic, have more resilience, be more socially included and utilise choices in their lives that enhance their sense of identity and connection with those around them. Another way of looking at this is to ask yourself what it is that is often lacking in the lives of clients with substance use difficulties. Often clients report pessimism about their ability to change, underestimate their own abilities, feel that they have very few social connections outside their using behaviour and feel trapped, as if real choice has been taken away from them. We think that a focus on optimism, resilience, integration and choice captures some of the essence of recovery and what a client needs if he is to be successful. We deal with these in more depth in Chapter 13 where we look in detail at the important issue of recovery. At this stage, when one is beginning a treatment episode with a client or reviewing where one has got, it is important that one is attentive to the development of these four areas and that they are considered as important as the particular treatment intervention itself.

Overview of chapter 1

This chapter is divided into four key areas:

1. What is CBT?
2. What is CBT for addictions?
3. Why we use CBT in the treatment of addictions.
4. Ways of using this book.

This chapter provides a basic understanding of CBT and an orientation to the following chapters. At this stage we make a practice-based case for this therapeutic approach, highlighting both its philosophical basis and our experiences with it. Throughout this book we refer to three hypothetical clients who exemplify some of the key issues we have experienced in our clinical work. These clients are used to illustrate the general approach outlined in this book and the specific use of a range of cognitive and behavioural techniques. To illustrate the application of various techniques we introduce new information about the clients as if it has emerged through the process of clinical work as and when this is required. We introduce the first client, Paul, below, Sally in Chapter 5 and Simon in Chapter 6. By introducing Paul at this early stage we hope that you will be willing to consider your reactions to the information presented – specifically, your thoughts, emotional reactions and how these might make you respond. At this point, we envisage that this may raise more questions and answers for you; we also prompt you with specific questions to facilitate this process. However, we hope that this will create a desire to answer these questions and inspire you to read on.

Paul

Paul is 35 years old and has recently presented to your clinic as low in mood. He has asked for a methadone prescription. At assessment you find out that he is injecting £40 of heroin daily and also injects crack cocaine with heroin when he has money available. He started smoking heroin at the age of 19 and injecting daily from the age of 22. He began smoking crack regularly five years ago. You have also gathered some information that indicates that Paul has experienced a number of traumatic life experiences and that most of his social life involves contact with other drug users. He engages in some criminal activity to fund his use.

What might be your initial feelings about Paul? Even for an experienced drugs worker this presentation might engender wariness. Thoughts that might be contributing to this are that this entrenched pattern of drug use will be hard to shift and that Paul's life experiences will not have equipped him with many resources to change. Equally, Paul's involvement in criminal activity and his social network do not inspire confidence that there is much around him to support his initial steps in seeking recovery from his drug use. If you are not working in the field of substance use, this presentation may seem very distant from what you are used to seeing in your day-to-day working life. Your concerns might centre on Paul's criminality and you may have concerns about the drugs he is using and how he uses them. It would not be unusual to draw on your own attitudes and beliefs about drugs and the people who use them and for this to influence what you do next. Indeed, the service you work in might actively encourage passing him on to another service and terminating your work with him.

However, let us assume that you are supported to work with Paul; indeed, let us attend to the fact that Paul has voluntarily sought treatment and that this is something you wish to nurture and find out more about. You may see this as the first step towards social reintegration and that his talking to you could facilitate this process. You may recognise that, as a professional, you have access to information and resources that Paul may at some stage benefit from. You may also be interested in Paul's resourcefulness and how he has managed to get through life so far. We make these assumptions because you are reading this book, which suggests you have at least some curiosity and are seeking guidance in working with the chaos and uncertainty problem substance use can often bring. At the very least, we hope this book will inspire you to look beyond the presenting drug problem and see Paul as more than just a 'junkie'.

After Paul has been in treatment for a month, he has entered the induction phase and has attended two of the four appointments you have made with him. He is on an 80 ml daily supervised dose of methadone, which has been increasing with the aim of reducing his heroin use. Paul reports he is still spending up to £20 on heroin and £20 on crack cocaine once a week. You have successfully completed the clinic's full assessment and have got to know Paul a little better. You have begun the complex and often subtle task of engaging him in treatment. Consequently, you have begun to get to know him and have found out he does little to occupy his time and reports that he often feels bored. Paul has confided that his entire social network consists of long-term users like himself and he has found it difficult to make new, non-drug-using friends.

Through reading this book, we hope to encourage you to ask specific questions about drug and alcohol use, to seek to understand such behaviour. Let us assume that your contact with Paul has enabled you to elicit the following information. The usual pattern of his weekly use is that on the day he receives his state benefits one of his drug-using friends visits him at home and suggests that they use drugs together. Paul described what happened the last time he used drugs. His friend came round and suggested that they score, 'just for old times' sake'. Paul started to experience cravings. Although he tried to say 'no', his friend reminded him of the times when he had helped him in the past when Paul had no money and needed to score. Although part of him didn't want to use any drugs, he was worried that if he said no, this would mean he was a lousy friend. He also worried that if he said no, he would lose this friendship, would be entirely friendless and that his boredom would become unbearable. This made Paul feel low and hopeless, and his cravings intensified. So, Paul agreed to score some drugs.

Perhaps now you have some initial hypotheses about what is maintaining his drug use and how this relates to Paul's low mood. You might think that because of his drug use Paul never has any money to engage in activities that might overcome his boredom. You see how he has become so unhappy and why he feels stuck. Through reading this book we also hope to develop your ability to understand how drug problems emerge over time and the context of substance use. Perhaps you have been able to get the following information. Paul tells you that he began smoking heroin when he was 14 years old. Having been abused by his family when he was younger, he had become withdrawn and socially isolated. You find out that using heroin helped him to cope with the emotional consequences of the abuse and also meant that he was part of a group of drug users who supported each other.

Whether you work in a specialist drug treatment service, a primary care service or service for people with common mental health problems, if you have got to this level of understanding, then you will be well on the way to engaging Paul and there is a real possibility that your relationship with him could help him. However, you may have some anxiety about what to do next and may think that you do not know how to organise the information you have gathered in any particular way. You may still feel concerned about Paul's capacity to engage in treatment and remain uncertain about his continuing a behaviour which to you (and Paul) is clearly damaging. You may even dread the next session with Paul and feel you are in the dark about what to do next.

This book is written to address issues such as these, to enable you as the therapist or worker to feel better equipped to assist clients like Paul to manage their drug and alcohol use problems. Central to this is an understanding of the relationship between thoughts, feelings, behaviours and social context, which then leads to understanding the functions that drug use serves for individuals. Using this book will help you to use CBT thinking to direct an assessment, formulate a client's substance-using behaviour, plan, implement and evaluate the effectiveness of interventions with the goals of gaining control and preventing relapse. This should increase your confidence and enable you to develop an effective working relationship with clients like Paul.

What is CBT?

CBT is now established as a major psychotherapeutic approach. It has a strong empirical basis for a range of difficulties, particularly some of the anxiety disorders and depression (Beck *et al.*, 1979). It is being adapted and utilised to treat many more problems, including addictive behaviour, for which there is an emerging evidence base (Beck *et al.*, 1993).

The central tenet of CBT is that there are thinking biases implicit in and maintaining specific problematic emotions and behaviours. By using techniques to make these thoughts explicit and assisting clients to develop alternative, more useful and realistic ones, emotions can be changed and behaviours managed or brought under control. CBT generally focuses on difficulties that are manifest in the here and now. It is an explicit collaboration between therapist and client and aims to teach clients skills to self-manage their difficulties as well as maintain improvements. Thus, CBT is defined by its empirical foundations, its explicit theory base as well as its approach to understanding individuals' difficulties.

Within this broad way of understanding human behaviour and emotions, models have been developed to guide treatment for specific disorders including addiction. Chapter 2 introduces these cognitive and behavioural addiction models. These inform the treatment for each individual through the use of formulations to conceptualise that person's specific problems. Formulations may be highly circumscribed by the model for a specific disorder, such as social anxiety (Clark &

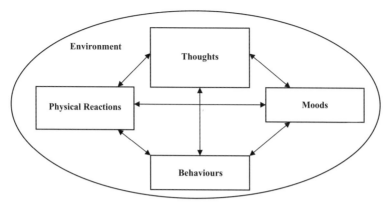

Figure 1.1 Padesky & Mooney's Five-part Generic Cognitive Model (© 1986 Center for Cognitive Therapy, www.padesky.com)

Wells, 1995), or may be idiosyncratic and individually tailored, but still within the broad cognitive and behavioural framework that links thoughts, emotions and behaviour within an environmental context. We take a broad approach to formulation, but one that is used to plan and evaluate interventions and may also be adapted according to how the client responds to treatment. Formulation is the central organising aspect of a CBT approach and is explained in detail in Chapter 5.

In our clinical and teaching experience we have found it helpful to use Padesky & Mooney's (1990) five-part generic cognitive model, which outlines five domains: thoughts, physical reactions, moods, behaviours and the environment (Figure 1.1). This model was devised by Padesky and Mooney as a way to explain the cognitive model in their clinical work. It is developed further in *Mind over Mood* (Greenberger & Padesky, 1995), which is an excellent general cognitive therapy resource for clients. The model is grounded on the assumption that each element is an important aspect of life experience and that all are interconnected. This means that each area affects the others and that changes in one can lead to changes in all. We use this five-part model as a formulation tool to illustrate how an individual's substance use can be understood, along with why a particular intervention is used. The model can be used to incorporate all the information utilised in the specific addictions models described in Chapter 2 and has the advantage of being easy for clients to understand and for practitioners to use.

What is CBT for addiction?

CBT for addictive behaviour is a development within the general CBT tradition. It has given rise to a number of conceptual models and treatment manuals. Kouimtsidis *et al.* (2007) is a good example of a treatment manual based on a specific addictions model, in this case Beck *et al.*'s (1993) cognitive model of substance abuse. CBT for addiction understands substance-using behaviour within the broad framework described in the previous section and uses this understanding to inform a range of interventions. Carroll (1998) states in her cognitive and behavioural manual designed to treat cocaine addiction that CBT attempts to help patients *recognise* the common situations in which they use cocaine, *avoid* these as appropriate and *cope* with them if necessary, as well as cope with a range of addictions-associated problems. In other words, CBT for substance use problems helps develop insight and control over addictive behaviour.

A quick note on terminology. We have already used a number of terms to describe drug and alcohol use and one of the consequences of this behaviour: addiction. There is a great deal of debate about the meaning of the term 'addiction'. It is used in academic circles as well as in everyday discourse. In acknowledgement of this broad use we have used it in the title of our book. However, as psychologists, wherever possible we seek to describe behaviour and therefore also use the term 'addictive behaviour'. To be more specific, we also use the term 'substance use problems' to indicate that the focus of this book is on the problematic use of substances, not substance use *per se*. The term 'substance use problems' includes a range of substance-related difficulties, including addiction and all the generally used diagnostic criteria for dependency and misuse. By substances we mean all psychoactive drugs, including alcohol. We also use the term 'substance misuse' in the context of describing services and with reference to the treatment field as this term is commonly used in these contexts. Other terms, such as substance abuse, are used with reference to their use in original texts. Whatever you prefer or your own service uses, always remember that it is the language the client uses that is key. Language, even when technically accurate, can alienate and confuse, and medical descriptions in particular can stand in the way of sharing intimate experiences.

As a therapist it is important to know and to be able to share with clients three particularly important assumptions underlying the CBT approach to treating substance use problems.

1   Addiction is a learnt behaviour

Substance dependence emerges over time with repeated use of drugs or alcohol. In this way it could be described, perhaps controversially, as a learnt behaviour. Although substance dependence is clearly complicated by biological/psychopharmacological events and social contexts it is useful to think about it in terms of the principles of learning theory.

CBT has its origins in behavioural theory and therapy. Key concepts are classical and operant conditioning. Classical conditioning describes how a stimulus produces a particular response through association. A neutral stimulus can produce a conditioned response through this learning process. This is commonly reported by substance-dependent clients. Items associated with using drugs, such as injecting equipment or foil, can trigger a desire to use. Operant conditioning describes how the consequences of a particular behaviour come to moderate the frequency of that behaviour. Behaviour can be increased through the removal of negative consequences (negative reinforcement) or by providing a reward (positive reinforcement). Behaviour can also be reduced through punishment or withdrawal of rewards (extinction). Operant conditioning is useful to understand why the euphoric or mood-altering consequences of behaviour can reinforce continued use (positive reinforcement) and why substance-dependent clients seek to avoid withdrawal through continued substance use (negative reinforcement). The behavioural theories of classical and operant conditioning provide some explanation as to how addictive behaviour can develop and be maintained through what happens before substance-using behaviour (what the person is doing, thinking or feeling) as well as what happens after the ingestion of a substance (how the substance makes the person think, feel and behave). These concepts are explained more fully in Chapter 2. Therapies based on these ideas have also been developed to enable the addictive behaviour to be changed. The most effective of these is contingency management. Contingency management uses the principle of positive reinforcement to change substance-using behaviour by reinforcing abstinence from a specific drug. This is done through the provision of a reward that has some meaning to a client. These can be considered as motivational incentives and may be household goods, shop vouchers or prizes. Reward schedules can be constructed so that continued and sustained abstinence from a substance can be encouraged. The National Institute for Health and Clinical Excellence guideline on psychosocial interventions for drug misuse (NICE, 2007) recommends that contingency management is implemented in drug treatment services in the UK and implementation studies are currently being trialled.

Although a behavioural perspective on addiction suggests that where behaviour is learnt it can also be unlearnt, it does not ignore the biological origins of addiction or the social context in which substance use develops and occurs. This understanding enables a variety of treatment goals to be negotiated with clients and worked towards in addition to total abstinence. These may include controlled use or goals informed by a harm reduction approach. These behavioural changes may be more acceptable to clients, enable early successes in treatment and may in themselves be important steps towards achieving abstinence.

2 Addiction emerges in an environmental context

CBT recognises the environment and the client's experience within this context. It is suggested that the availability of substances is a key factor in determining levels of dependency within specific populations. The influence of others and learning from peers and parents can influence substance use and dependence. Environmental factors, including numerous markers of social deprivation, are strongly associated with developing substance dependency. The way clients understand their world needs to be recognised as emerging from their developmental and social context. This will help inform the interventions and enable the necessary sensitivity required to undertake CBT and develop a collaborative relationship.

3 Addiction is developed and maintained by particular thought patterns and processes

Thinking processes are central to the development and maintenance of addictive behaviour as well as to the relapse process. Whilst thought patterns and processes are not always readily accessible to clients, recognising the cognitive components of addictive behaviour is essential in helping clients gain an understanding of and control over the behaviour. Cognitions related to addictive behaviour include thoughts related to outcome expectancies, often with an aspect of relief from negative emotional states, as well as thoughts that give permission to use, such as minimising the consequences of using. These thoughts can often reinforce and maintain thinking patterns related to other psychological or psychiatric problems such as those associated with low mood or feelings of anxiety.

Why cognitive behavioural therapy for addictive behaviour?

Cognitive and behavioural interventions have a strong evidence base for specific disorders, especially anxiety disorders and depression. However, the picture is not as clear for addictive behaviour. In Chapter 2 we introduce the principal cognitive and behavioural models that have sought to explain the development of addictive behaviour, its progression and the relapse process. However, these models have not given rise to a package of interventions that produce results above and beyond other therapeutic modalities (NICE, 2007).

Why might this be? Some reasons for this are outlined below:

1. Addiction is a profoundly complex phenomenon. The nature of addiction is contested by academics and some would question whether addiction or the other terms used (e.g. dependence) are helpful constructs to advance its understanding. Advances in brain science are unravelling the underlying biological aspects of addiction, yet any comprehensive theory must also incorporate social and psychological aspects. The cognitive therapy developments that have revolutionised the treatment of anxiety disorders are only now beginning to touch the addiction field.

2. Any search for *the* superior treatment approach in the field of addiction may be misplaced. Recent studies have indicated that different approaches tend towards similar outcomes. Project Match (Project Match Research Group, 1997) examined three interventions for alcohol dependence in a multi-site, randomised control trial. These were: motivational enhancement therapy, CBT and 12-step facilitation. Each was found to be equally effective in reducing alcohol use and few specific patient treatment matches were found. UKATT (2005), a UK alcohol treatment trial, compared motivational enhancement therapy and social network therapy and similarly found both to be as effective as treatment for alcohol misuse. These results suggest that there may be common factors to therapy that lead to change and that research may be better focused on seeking to understand common change processes rather than the relative merits of one approach over another.

If addiction is such a complex phenomenon for which definitive psychosocial treatments have yet to emerge, why might CBT still be regarded as a useful approach in this area? Some of our reasons are outlined below:

1. Paradoxically, the very complexity of addiction is a powerful reason why we advocate CBT. We need conceptual models to help us unravel the phenomenon. CBT not only provides a developmental perspective, but also grounds

this in each individual's social and environmental context, and has models to draw on that explain motivation as well as the maintenance of substance use and relapse processes. CBT encompasses a broad range of psychological approaches which are clinically useful and amenable to ongoing theory testing research.

2. CBT is useful for clients and adds value for therapists and other workers involved in care coordination and key working relationships. It consequently meets a clinical need. People need practical and pragmatic frames to understand what they do and why they do it and terminology to discuss and describe how they do it. CBT fosters a structured and collaborative approach and can inform the use of specific interventions without the need for comprehensive training. It can be adapted to a range of treatment goals, from harm reduction or controlled use to abstinence. It can also be used by more experienced therapists to develop individually tailored interventions.

3. Contingency management has been shown to be highly effective in the United States and is recommended as a key treatment intervention for stimulant drug users in the UK (NICE, 2007). Contingency management as a behavioural intervention provides motivational incentives to help reward-attaining goals such as abstinence from a specific drug. Any historical account of CBT will refer to its behavioural roots and theoretical foundations in learning theory. Thus, CBT shares a theoretical foundation with a widely validated and recommended intervention.

4. Although contingency management (CM) says nothing about internal change processes that may be occurring during a period of change, it is likely that clients are reflecting on the consequences, both positive and negative, of their behaviour. One can therefore surmise that cognitions at least mediate behaviour change. Developing cognitive interventions that maximise the changes an individual can make through a CM programme may be worthwhile. This is supported by research that shows that if the programme of motivational incentives is withdrawn, relapse rates increase (Epstein *et al.*, 2003). We argue that paying attention to the cognitive change processes is a valuable exercise and an important source of information to help individuals sustain changes made in their substance use and achieve lasting recovery.

5. Many substance-dependent clients have comorbid mental health problems, particularly depression and anxiety disorders. The Co-morbidity of Substance Misuse and Mental Illness Collaborative Study (Weaver *et al.*, 2003) found that most substance-dependent clients had a psychiatric disorder, with an affective or anxiety disorder identified in 67.6 per cent of drug clients and 80.6 per cent of alcohol clients. CBT is recommended as the treatment of choice for these problems and is explicitly recommended in the NICE guidelines (NICE, 2007). This is an important statement as, historically, substance-dependent clients have often been denied psychological treatment merely by virtue of their substance use. However, we do not yet know whether substance-dependent clients do well with generic CBT interventions or whether clinicians in generic mental health services have the capabilities, will or capacity to work with them. We argue that for these clients we are likely to need to adapt aspects of CBT for anxiety and depression treatment programmes, for example by including the substance use itself within their formulation of

their difficulties. Integrating a therapeutically congruent approach is relatively simple and this book is written with this in mind.

6. CBT can be integrated well with other approaches. Whilst CBT is explicit in its theory of distress and change, it overlaps with other approaches, at least at a basic level of intervention. Take, for example, a 12-step approach in which addiction is understood as a disease and offers a spiritual recovery programme through the 12-step fellowship. Whilst this is a fundamentally different understanding of addiction, the 12-step approach still recognises the importance of addressing negative thought patterns (also known as 'stinking thinking'). The International Treatment Effectiveness Programme (ITEP) also integrates well with CBT (Simpson & Joe, 2004). There are specific cognitive components to some of the maps and the process of nodal link mapping that are clearly related to understanding thoughts, feelings and behaviour. Motivational interviewing is another approach that sits comfortably alongside CBT and can be effective when used as a precursor or as an adjunct to CBT (Arkowitz *et al.*, 2008), or as a fallback when treatment is not progressing.

7. CBT is often criticised for being too formulaic and insular, yet it can be used to examine process and relational issues. One of the key reasons addicted clients may be excluded from standard mental health services is that they may be deemed too chaotic to engage in therapy. It is certainly the case that some clients may miss appointments, present intoxicated or be in withdrawal and that these behaviours can interfere with other therapeutic activities. There is also a high prevalence of comorbid personality disorders. However, we argue that if therapists can step back from the issues of substance use *per se*, these issues may be more helpfully construed as therapy-interfering behaviours and dealt with accordingly. Any therapist versed in the principles and approach of CBT would be able to use CBT to address these issues with clients. Moreover, therapists can use CBT to reflect effectively on their own beliefs in working with addicted clients.

8. As indicated in the introduction, a debate currently emerging in the UK field of addictions treatment is the meaning of recovery and how services may be able to promote recovery. This represents a convergence with mental health debates and draws on definitions of recovery used in mental health. Recovery is a process resulting in a change in attitudes, values and goals to achieve meaning and maximise individual potential. Services need to support people in these individual aspirations and shift from a strict focus on managing addiction. We believe that both the collaborative process of doing CBT and its adaptability to individual goals make it relevant to the process of recovery and fits well with the longer-term recovery focus required in treatment. Indeed, whilst CBT may appear to be simply concerned with the removal of distress, whether this be anxiety, depression or substance dependence, it is just as much about living more effectively so that clients can achieve what it is they want from life.

9. Finally, we argue that there are intrinsic qualities of CBT which make it especially relevant to the treatment of addictive behaviour. Beck (1995) describes 10 principles that underlie cognitive therapy which highlight certain qualities and which are also relevant to CBT. We understand cognitive therapy to be a form of CBT, albeit with a more explicit and narrow focus on modifying

beliefs. The approach we describe in this book includes a number of elements of cognitive therapy in addition to some interventions focused directly on changing behaviour.

a) *Cognitive therapy is based on a constantly evolving formulation of the patient and her problems in cognitive terms.* The emphasis on evolving learning and understanding within CBT is helpful with substance-using clients who may be sceptical about approaches imposed externally. Developing a shared cognitive formulation with a client sets out the therapy as a collaborative approach which respects the independence and expertise of the client. This is a very useful therapeutic stance for clients who may be ambivalent about changing their behaviour. CBT is also a flexible, individualised approach that can be adapted to a wide range of clients as well as a variety of settings (inpatient, outpatient) and formats (group, individual).

b) *Cognitive therapy requires a sound therapeutic alliance.* Clients with substance use problems may have experienced negative interactions with professionals in the context of related health issues or in other areas of their life. Whilst this may simply reflect their difficulties and/or thinking errors, it is also possible that it genuinely reflects the negative stigma attached to addiction in wider social discourse. Clients may thus approach treatment with preconceptions about what their drug worker will think of them. Treatment itself can also be set up as an unequal power dynamic, particularly when the worker is responsible for providing a prescription of controlled drugs such as methadone or benzodiazepines. The practice of CBT can be applied to thinking about these issues, in order to identify and evaluate thoughts about the therapy, the relationship and service. By bringing these to the fore, the relationship can be enhanced in a productive way.

c) *Cognitive therapy emphasises collaboration and active participation.* CBT is ideally suited to clients who, by the nature of their difficulties, may be ambivalent about changing their behaviour and who may have a preconceived idea about treatment involving a loss of autonomy. A cognitive perspective on managing resistance, drawing on ideas from the motivational interviewing literature, enables these issues to be brought into the body of the therapeutic approach. Focusing on building a collaborative relationship that harnesses the client's expertise, values and beliefs will always be useful and often becomes the platform on which new ways of managing addictive behaviour can be developed.

d) *Cognitive therapy is goal-oriented and problem-focused.* In our experience many clients with substance use problems also have impaired problem-solving skills. CBT models an approach to managing life difficulties. It can also be focused on the problems that are explicit and clients bring to the sessions, in particular, the problem of continued substance use despite intentions to desist from this behaviour. CBT is also adaptable to a range of substance use goals tailored to the individual client. These goals may be understood in terms of harm reduction and controlled use, not just abstinence. Equally, CBT can focus on one or more substances when clients have a poly-drug-using profile.

e) *Cognitive therapy initially emphasises the present.* Addicted clients are generally best served by focusing on current active use. This is often the source of distress, particularly loss of control resulting in problems in relationships. CBT's emphasis on building control in the here and now is highly relevant to addiction. It is our experience that clients' ability to resolve past difficulties, often those associated with the development of addictive behaviour, is generally limited unless they are first able to utilise skills to manage substance use day by day, including attending sessions in a sober state. We argue that it could even be damaging to clients to focus on past issues without first giving them the skills to manage their substance use in the present.

f) *Cognitive therapy is educative, aims to teach the patient to be her own therapist and emphasises relapse prevention.* Clients with substance use problems are often baffled by their addictive behaviour. CBT provides a framework which can lead to better understanding. This in turn becomes the basis for developing control. Central to CBT is the practice of testing new ways of thinking and being. The emphasis in therapy is what the client does outside the consulting room. Practitioners in the substance misuse field will recognise the value of this approach. It is how clients apply themselves in the real world that makes the difference in their recovery. Practitioners will also appreciate the relevance of relapse prevention. This refers to the goals of therapy as well to as a theoretical model and intervention package (discussed in Chapter 2). As a goal of therapy, relapse prevention underpins most addiction treatments, including that described in this book. The longer-term focus on managing recovery can be assisted by a set of generalisable problem-solving skills and strategies for dealing with daily hassles and setbacks.

g) *Cognitive therapy aims to be time-limited.* Therapy needs to be focused on immediate problems from which clients are seeking relief and may be utilised in contexts where there may be only limited time to work. These settings may be determined by treatment care pathways devised to move people through the treatment system, but also be within other contexts, such as short inpatient admissions or day programmes. CBT can be targeted at these episodes of acute care, but is also relevant to developing skills for longer-term recovery management.

h) *Cognitive therapy sessions are structured.* As indicated above, some clients with substance use problems have difficulties problem-solving and lack experience in basic self-management. The structure of CBT sessions models a way of being and thinking that can be helpful to clients outside the consulting room. The structure can also assist the process of therapy, it provides space for clients' concerns, is democratic in how time is allocated and allows the therapist to be explicit in how time can be best utilised. This is useful when trying to engage a client who is ambivalent about treatment and sensitive to the power hierarchies explicit in being, or having to be, in treatment.

i) *Cognitive therapy teaches patients to identify, evaluate and respond to their dysfunctional thoughts and beliefs.* This is the unique defining element of CBT. The following chapters demonstrate how this can be useful in work with people with substance use problems. At this point, the relevance of this is the idea of empowering clients to be their own therapist, to take what is learnt in therapy and apply that in their everyday lives, learning an approach to difficulties that will become an ingrained and effective way to respond to ongoing and new life problems. If one accepts that addiction is a chronic relapsing condition, then the idea of learning skills to generalise across new situations and experiences is essential to long-term recovery.

j) *Cognitive therapy uses a variety of techniques to change thinking, mood and behaviour.* We believe you will find things in this book to help you in your work with clients with addictive behaviours. We have included a variety of techniques that can be described as behavioural and cognitive. We have also included mindfulness, which is showing promise in the treatment of depression. One strength of CBT is that it is broad-ranging, giving rise to a variety of tools and techniques. However, this may also be a weakness as it makes testing CBT in addictions settings and comparing across treatment trials problematic, as what is called CBT is quite varied. For the clinician, however, this is an opportunity as it provides great diversity in what can be drawn on in therapeutic work. We envisage this book will facilitate bringing together these ideas into a coherent form when planning and evaluating CBT with individual clients.

Overview and ways of using this book

The aim of this book is to build competence in understanding and working with addictive behaviour. We outline a complete package of treatment from assessment to formulation and through to intervention. The book is designed to be relevant to clinicians working in different contexts, with different remits and different levels of experience in working with substance use as well as experience of using CBT. Throughout, we use the terms practitioner, clinician or therapist to encompass a wide range of roles in which therapeutic activities occur. This includes key workers, case or care coordinators working in drug and alcohol treatment services. We have set out to make this book relevant to workers with no specific therapy training but with access to appropriate supervision in which they can present and discuss the work they are doing. The approach and techniques are relevant to assist with the principal tasks of the treatment process: engaging clients, helping them to make changes in substance use and developing strategies to prevent relapse. This book can be used to identify and use specific targeted interventions as part of a care plan across the treatment journey. It can also be used by workers with CBT therapy training or a professional background to develop client-specific, formulation-based interventions. A brief overview of the chapters in this book is outlined, followed by suggestions on how you might use the book, according to your experience and knowledge of CBT.

Chapter 2: Cognitive and motivational theories of addiction

Chapter 2 describes the theoretical background to the treatment approach described in this book. This chapter provides a conceptual framework for understanding addiction and presents a synthesis of various biological, psychological and social perspectives of addictive behaviour as well as theories of motivation, including

West's (2006) PRIME theory. We also introduce the main cognitive and behavioural models for substance-using behaviour, Marlatt & Gordon's (1985) original cognitive model of the relapse process as well as Witkiewitz & Marlatt's (2004) new dynamic model of relapse, which reflects recent findings from psychological research and attempts to accommodate the range of variables and ways in which these interact in the relapse process. We also introduce Annis & Davis's (1988b) relapse prevention model and Beck *et al.*'s (1993) cognitive therapy model of substance misuse, which also sets out a framework for understanding substance misuse from a developmental perspective. Finally, we briefly outline the evidence base for CBT with substance use problems. We envisage this chapter to be particularly relevant to those studying CBT as well as to experienced CBT practitioners interested in the conceptual and theoretical underpinnings of CBT in the area of addictive behaviour.

Chapter 3: Fundamentals of treatment

In this chapter we set out the foundations of therapy on which our CBT approach should be placed. We describe the key tasks of treatment – assessment and formulation, engagement, intervention and relapse prevention – and represent these as processes which develop through therapy rather than as discrete elements that occur in sequence. We place these within the need for a positive therapeutic relationship, which may be thought of as the vehicle for the key tasks of treatment. When thinking about the therapeutic relationship we find it helpful to include two areas: (i) what we call therapist attitudes, which include how you as a worker think about your work and your clients, as well as how you might understand cultural difference and issues of diversity; and (ii) what we call therapy structure, which is the responsibilities you have as a therapist to structure the time you have with clients in a way that maximises the productivity and keeps the work on track. We believe that attention to these two aspects is essential in developing an effective therapeutic alliance. This chapter will be most relevant to workers who have not had specific therapy training and are looking for some accessible frameworks in which to develop their thinking and use of CBT interventions.

Chapter 4: Enhancing motivation to change

This chapter addresses a fundamental aspect of working with addictive behaviour – namely, enhancing motivation to change. We describe how basic counselling skills can be used to help initiate a therapeutic alliance with clients. We draw on a number of ideas and techniques based on Miller & Rollnick's (2002) motivational interviewing approach and place this communication style within a CBT framework. This chapter may be of particular interest to CBT practitioners who have less experience in working with clients with substance use problems and wish to develop skills in managing ambivalence about behaviour change.

Chapter 5: Assessment and introducing CBT to clients

In this chapter we introduce assessment and socialisation to the CBT approach. Assessment in CBT is a targeted activity and needs to be organised in such a way that the necessary information is collected to develop a formulation. This activity is crucial for you as a therapist to understand your clients' substance-using behaviour. This is also the time in which you begin to socialise, or help the clients to understand their substance use from a cognitive and behavioural perspective. CBT is done *with* clients not *to* clients, so engaging them with the basic model and process needs to occur right at the start of treatment. As with Chapter 3, this chapter should be required reading for workers less familiar with CBT.

Chapter 6: Formulation

This chapter sets out what we mean by formulation. This is the central organising construct that underpins CBT. It is the means by which you as a therapist organise the assessment information in a way that enables you and your clients to understand their substance-using behaviour. It then becomes the organising framework for selecting and evaluating the impact of specific interventions. This chapter is essential reading for workers less familiar with CBT.

Chapters 7–10: Cognitive interventions and behavioural experiments

In these four chapters we introduce a range of interventions designed to change the thoughts and thinking patterns – or cognitions – that are maintaining substance-using behaviour. In Chapter 7 we focus specifically on these cognitions and break them down into nine categories. In Chapter 8 we look at some of the standard cognitive therapy approaches to challenging beliefs and how they may be applied to substance-using behaviour. In Chapter 9 we develop these ideas and highlight a further range of techniques and interventions. Chapter 10 is devoted to behavioural experiments. These are tasks set with clients that are designed to test specific cognitions. Done well, they can be powerful in helping clients see things differently. Behavioural experiments should not be confused with behavioural interventions (Chapter 11), which are directly focused on changing behaviour as opposed to testing cognitions. These four chapters will all be useful to experienced CBT therapists to develop their practice. For less experienced workers we recommend starting at Chapters 7 and 8 and utilising these techniques under the guidance of an appropriately qualified supervisor.

Chapter 11: Behavioural interventions

In this chapter we focus on changing behaviour directly, on enabling clients to do something different. We have defined these as behavioural as opposed to cognitive interventions. This distinction is somewhat arbitrary as behaviour and cognitive changes are intrinsically linked. We introduce five interventions which are aimed at helping clients gain control over areas of their lives, including craving management and problem-solving. These interventions can be used as standalone, single interventions and are recommended for workers just beginning their practice.

Chapter 12: Working with emotions

In this chapter we focus on a third key area of intervention: helping clients manage emotions. Emotions are often triggers to substance-using behaviour and many clients have not developed effective alternatives to managing the way they feel. In this chapter we show how the importance of emotions can be explained to clients, how the links between emotions and substance use may be understood and how they may be identified, labelled and managed. This chapter will be useful to both inexperienced workers and CBT practitioners wishing to develop their competence working with people with substance use problems.

Chapter 13: CBT and pathways to recovery

In the final chapter we bring together the various elements of the CBT approach described in this book and outline how this fits with a view of the client's long-term recovery from substance use problems. We also make some suggestions for how you as a therapist might develop your CBT practice. This chapter will be of interest to all those working in the substance misuse treatment area and enable them to integrate CBT into their practice and with the broader recovery agenda.

Workers in the field of substance misuse with relatively little exposure to formal CBT training

This book can be used to enhance a basic understanding of CBT and its relevance to clinical practice in drug and alcohol treatment settings. The book may be used as a resource to identify single interventions to be used in the context of key working and case coordination. Some of the ideas and language are likely to be familiar to those with some experience of working with the ITEP approach (Simpson & Joe, 2004). The visual maps to develop shared care plans and to problem-solve with clients can easily be integrated with a CBT approach and also complements some of the more cognitive-oriented aspects of ITEP.

This book may also be used to develop practice and competence in the CBT approach. For those without formal psychotherapy training, the key aspect that will be new is formulation (Chapter 6). Formulation is used to organise assessment information and to plan, evaluate and adapt interventions as required. Formulation becomes the central organising framework for work with clients. It is recommended that developing skills in using formulation be done under supervision. This may be one-to-one or in a group. Developing practice from the use of single interventions to a formulation-driven approach takes time and effort and can only occur in an organisation that supports this goal with time set aside to think reflectively about clients in a creative and constructive atmosphere. It is our experience that formulation is the key to thinking psychologically about clients and their wants, needs and aspirations.

CBT practitioners with limited experience in the field of substance misuse or some anxieties about working with clients with either past or present substance misuse problems

Drug and alcohol use is hard to avoid in any health or social care setting. The new UK Improving Access to Psychological Therapies (IAPT) initiatives have and will increase the number of potential clients being screened and offered CBT and other talking therapies for depression and anxiety disorders. It is highly likely that problematic drug and alcohol use will be present in the IAPT target populations. Clients with substance use problems have not traditionally been served well by psychological therapy departments. Substance use may either be ignored or lead to clients being denied access to relevant services. Neither serves workers or their clients well.

For current CBT practitioners, or for those in training, working in primary or secondary care with adult client groups, this book aims to bridge the gap between regular practice focused on mental health problems and CBT applied to substance-using behaviour. A quick scan of the book will reveal concepts and ideas familiar to those who have had a core CBT training. The central organising principles of assessment and formulation, and the integration of these into a specific focused approach, will also be familiar. What will be new is the application of the CBT approach to substance dependence, both at a theoretical level (Chapter 2) and also in terms of interventions. Using this book to understand what material is required to develop a CBT formulation will be useful, particularly so that the function of substance use can be clearly understood and appropriately conceptualised. This may aid clearer thinking and enable a better understanding of the relationship between substance use and mental illness, for example, recognising how substance use can often be a safety behaviour. Although working with beliefs and constructing behavioural experiments will be second nature, applying these interventions to specific aspects of substance use will be new. The explicit focus on motivation in Chapter 3 is likely to be of interest as the ambivalence to changing substance use that clients may present in therapy can often be a sticking point in progress and leave the therapist feeling unskilled and demoralised. This book should enable a constructive approach to these substance use related aspects of therapy-interfering behaviour. It is hoped that this will increase competence in staff and help to reduce some of the stigma and isolation from services that this population of clients experiences.

This book describes a psychological treatment approach to substance dependence and as such does not equip workers to be fully competent in the treatment of substance dependence. This requires some understanding of the biological risks and complications associated with dependence. As a rule, any advice on changing substance use requires consulting a general practitioner or addictions specialist doctor. If a client seems particularly unwell, especially if sedated, then admission to a local accident and emergency department may be required. In the UK, for workers wishing to develop their specific knowledge in this area, there are often drug awareness courses run locally by Drug and Alcohol Action Team (DAAT) partnerships.

Psychologists and therapists experienced in CBT and working in the field of substance use

This book may be useful not only as a reference point to develop practice but also to integrate different aspects of current CBT practice into a cohesive approach. Although the book is not intended to be used as a manual, it can be used as a handbook to plan individual sessions and care plans. For more experienced therapists it is likely to be used as a reference point for specific interventions. The book can also be used as a resource to develop protocol-based interventions and structured treatment programmes and groups. The book may also be an aid to the supervision of other staff without formal therapeutic qualifications.

We hope that this brief overview of what this book is about will instil some hope that you may be able to work with clients such as Paul. Some of the questions and thoughts that may now be running through your mind with regard to Paul are:

- I wonder what the function of his heroin use is?
- Given his drug using started when he was 19, I wonder what happened to him then?
- Is Paul's trauma something we could work on, or should I consult a specialist service?
- I wonder what motivated him to come into treatment now?
- I wonder which theory best explains Paul's current predicament?

Substance use problems are common in our society, yet our understanding and approaches to them are often limited. CBT has the potential to change this and we hope this book will assist this process.

Chapter 2

Cognitive and Motivational Theories of Addiction

Introduction

The adage 'nothing is more practical than good theory' certainly applies to interventions in the area of addictions. The interventions in this book, which come under the broad umbrella of cognitive behavioural therapy (CBT), are firmly grounded in theory. The theoretical models discussed in this chapter have been developed using research evidence and are subject to continuous scientific evaluation. Scientific evidence and theory help us continuously to increase our understanding of addiction and in turn develop interventions. In presenting a cognitive and behavioural approach to the treatment of addictive behaviour it is important first to outline how we understand addictive behaviour. This understanding provides a theoretical rationale for the treatment approach outlined in this book.

Using the analogy of a motor car, whilst it isn't strictly necessary to know how the engine works to drive the car, such knowledge could not only enhance your driving experience but even make you a better driver. For a practising clinician this chapter may not be essential reading, however it is recommended for those seeking to enhance their understanding of addictive behaviour and to understand the conceptual basis of the interventions described in later chapters.

The first chapter of West's *Theory of Addiction* (2006) is titled 'Journey to the Centre of Addiction'. We are not attempting to take you on this journey, but for a reader who is interested we strongly recommend this book. In 2001, West identified 98 theories and models of addiction and broadly categorised these into

Applied Cognitive and Behavioural Approaches to the Treatment of Addiction: A Practical Treatment Guide By Luke Mitcheson, Jenny Maslin, Tim Meynen, Tamara Morrison, Robert Hill and Shamil Wanigaratne

three main domains: psychological (behavioural); social; and biological. It is accepted that no theory or model in a single sphere can comprehensively explain addiction and that any understanding of addiction comes from looking at the interaction between the biological, psychological and social spheres. Hence there is general consensus that addiction is a biopsychosocial phenomenon (Wanigaratne, 2006). Although CBT theories and models are grounded in the psychological sphere, we adopt the rather more inclusive biopsychosocial approach in this book.

Components of the biopsychosocial understanding of addiction

The biological

At the biological level, apart from a genetic predisposition that may be expressed at the neuronal and physiological level, we also know that there is adaptation or change in the brain when an individual becomes addicted. Craving can be taken as one of the best examples to illustrate how the biological and psychological spheres interact. Incentive motivational theories (Robinson & Berridge, 2003) attempt to explain how substance-related stimuli elicit classically conditioned responses in substance users which are in both the physiological and cognitive domains (e.g. craving). Cognitive factors such as memory processes, expectancies (both positive and negative) and attentional processes have all been shown to be involved in craving. Recent findings of attentional bias in addicted individuals to substance-related cues or stimuli that trigger a response which includes motor preparation and a hyper-attentive state (craving) and cognitive processes that mediate between the stimulus and response, are relevant to CBT (Franken, 2003; Franken *et al.*, 2003). As our knowledge of phenomena such as craving increases, future interventions may include not only cognitive behavioural interventions that target cognitive and physiological domains as described in this book, but also pharmaceutical interventions, those for example that could mediate between attentional biases and craving. Future researchers will need to explore whether interventions such as mindfulness training and modified versions of cue exposure are effective in reducing attentional biases of substance users.

Our current knowledge of the underlying neurocircuit or cellular-level biological changes associated with addiction dictates that if interventions to change and maintain change are to be effective, they have to target these biological factors. The biological changes that occur when an individual becomes addicted can also be expressed in the psychological sphere as cognitive deficits. There is now a considerable body of evidence showing that individuals who have been misusing substances, particularly alcohol, for long periods have significant deficits in overall cognitive functioning, and more specifically, in executive functioning (Bates *et al.*, 2002, Crews *et al.*, 2005; Manning *et al.*, 2008). Executive functioning denotes the abilities involved in decision-making, planning and anticipating. These form the skills that are crucial in changing addictive behaviour and preventing relapse. There are other biological factors that contribute to, or are associated with, addiction. The autonomy of addiction, and the power of biological factors and cognitive biases over conscious efforts to change, are not fully acknowledged in CBT approaches to addiction (Ryan, 2006). Our current knowledge of the biology of addiction also tells us that addicted individuals have limited abilities to cope with stress. This is apparent from the high levels of stress hormones in clients undergoing detoxification or in withdrawal and also when these individuals are subject to subsequent stress (Goeders, 2002; Koob & Kreek, 2007).

The link between stress and craving has been known for more than 30 years (Litman, 1974), but scientists are now finding a neurobiological basis for this (Breese *et al.*, 2005). It is clear that stress reduction interventions and interventions that increase stress coping skills are critical in preventing relapse (Grüsser *et al.*, 2007; Kushner *et al.*, 2000). In the field of addiction the relapse prevention approach was the first to recognise the importance of such interventions (Marlatt & Gordon, 1985).

The psychological

The process of developing an addiction to substances, from experimentation and recreational use, to problematic use and dependence has been explained using three learning theories: classical conditioning; operant conditioning; and social learning theory. They are seen as over-learned habits that can be analysed and modified in much the same way as any other habit (Marlatt & Gordon, 1985; Wanigaratne, 2006).

1. Classical conditioning theories have been used to explain craving (Drummond, 2001). Environmental triggers such as drug paraphernalia, images of people drinking and smoking, or the smell of alcohol or tobacco are said to trigger craving in an addicted individual as a conditioned reflex. Cravings often lead to giving in to or indulging in the addicted behaviour unless the individual has learned skills to cope with this. Cue exposure is an intervention based on classical conditioning to reduce the conditioned response (Drummond, 2001).
2. Operant conditioning has also been shown to play a major role in the acquisition and maintenance of addiction. Psychoactive substances (e.g. alcohol, tobacco, cannabis, heroin, benzodiazepines), food and sex are all reinforcers in the conditioning process. A reinforcer, either positive or negative, increases the likelihood that a behaviour will be repeated. A positive reinforcer is rewarding; a negative reinforcer is the removal or reduction of an aversive state. This is often confused with punishment, which is an aversive event that reduces the likelihood of a behaviour being repeated. People get addicted to substances because they are highly reinforcing, at least in the early stages of use. If you take alcohol as an example, its central nervous system depressive effects initially make a person feel relaxed, sometimes resulting in a sense of euphoria, that can be seen as positive reinforcement. A socially anxious person whose anxiety is reduced by taking a drink before going out is negatively reinforcing this behaviour through his drinking as this reduces or eliminates the anxiety that occurs when social interaction takes place sober. A dependent individual taking alcohol or drugs to reduce withdrawal effects is another example of negative reinforcement. Hence operant conditioning could play a major part in developing and maintaining an addiction. By the same token, operant conditioning can be used to change and overcome addiction.

Contingency management, whereby clients are rewarded for positive behaviour, is an example of an intervention based on operant conditioning (Petry, 2006).

3. Social learning theory (Bandura, 1977a): this most recent of the learning theories introduces cognitive processes into learning. Cognitive processes such as anticipation, planning, expectancies, attributions, self-efficacy and decision-making have been shown to be integral to learning. All of these factors have been shown to be involved in the development and maintenance of addictive behaviours. The cognitive aspect of CBT comes from social learning theory and many of the interventions described in this book have their roots in this theory.

Psychological predispositions such as an addictive personality have also been thought to be a major factor in an individual becoming addicted. Although years of research have failed to identify a robust addictive personality trait (Zinberg, 1984), clusters of personality factors associated with addiction have been found; for example, Cloninger (1987) developed a tri-dimensional theory where the personality dimensions of novelty-seeking, harm avoidance and reward dependence interact to determine an individual's response to substances. This work has been further developed to identify and measure personality risk factors that could be associated with addiction (Sher *et al.*, 2000). Targeted CBT interventions for individuals with particular risk profiles (impulsivity, anxiety sensitivity, sensation-seeking) have been developed and initial evaluation of these have yielded promising results (Castellanos & Conrod, 2006).

For some individuals, childhood experience of trauma and neglect plays a major part in the development and maintenance of an addiction. The self-medication hypothesis of addiction (Khantzian, 1977) describes individuals using substances to reduce distress and feelings of deficit or loss. Once a particular substance, or combination of substances, helps an individual to reduce distress and cope with difficult emotions, it follows that the behaviour will be repeated, thus becoming an addictive behaviour. More importantly, it becomes less likely that the individual will learn more adaptive or less damaging ways of coping. Over a period of time both confidence and belief in the ability to cope with difficult emotions without the substance becomes low. Although the self-medication hypothesis was developed from a psychodynamic perspective, the implications for interventions based on it leave scope for a number of psychological or therapeutic approaches, including CBT. In fact, it could be argued that a 'stepped care approach' (see Figure 2.1) is best in tackling underlying psychological issues in addicted individuals (Wanigaratne & Keaney, 2002). Instead of attempting insight-oriented work in the first instance, a more targeted approach is advocated. Depending on how stable an individual is, different psychological interventions, ranging from behavioural (e.g. contingency management) to insight-oriented psychotherapy, could be used to help that individual. This pragmatic, stepped care approach has recently been adapted for all psychosocial work in the 'Psychosocial Tool Kit' published by the National Treatment Agency (NTA) for substance users in England and Wales (Pilling *et al.*, 2009).

Helping individuals develop or strengthen coping ('how to') skills is a major part of CBT and relapse prevention. Meditation, relaxation, distraction, self-

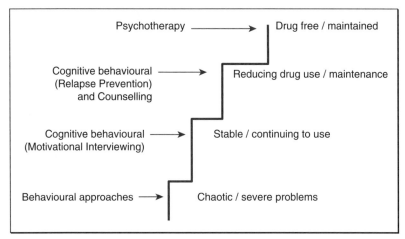

Figure 2.1 Stepped Care Model for Treatment of Substance Misuse Problems (Wanigaratne & Keaney, 2002)

soothing and impulse control are examples. More recent developments place greater emphasis on helping individuals discover their strengths and how to play to these strengths.

The social

Substance use always takes place in a context and often this is of a social nature. Initiation into substance use invariably happens in a social context and social factors often contribute to maintaining substance use. Cultures and subcultures are often associated with the presence or absence of particular substance use. Acceptability of substance use may determine both initiation and maintenance of substance use, as well as control its use. Harding & Zinberg (1977) argue that social controls, rituals and sanctions apply to the use of all drugs, including alcohol, and operate in a variety of social settings, from large social groups (weddings, parties, etc.) representative of the culture as a whole, to small, discrete groups (meeting friends, a family meal, etc.). The social pressures resulting from expectations in certain settings for the use of substances can make it very difficult for an individual not to conform. Interventions that do not take into consideration the social context of substance use are likely to fail. The focus on high-risk situations in relapse prevention programmes targets precisely these issues. There are also times when addictive behaviours, particularly substance use, have been confined to a particular context and are not transposed into different contexts. The classic example discussed is the work of Lee Robins and her colleagues with Vietnam veterans on heroin use. During the war heroin use was common and, of those who were addicted, almost 50 per cent used heroin after returning home, but only 12 per cent went on to become addicted again (Robins *et al.*, 1975). This research has led some to argue that the concept of addiction itself is entirely socially constructed (Peele, 1998).

Social deprivation has also been linked to substance misuse. Mental health problems and associated substance misuse in areas of social deprivation are well documented (Farrell *et al.*, 1998). Drink and drug culture-linked poverty are another example of the association of substance misuse and social deprivation (Baklien & Samarasinghe, 2003; Wanigaratne *et al.*, 2007). In cultures where substance use is not acceptable for religious or other reasons, there is a lower prevalence (Orford *et al.*, 2004). Early maladjustment also appears to be detrimental to treatment success (Hill *et al.*, 2006). Although changing cultural norms may be outside the scope of CBT, understanding their origin and manifestation in the individual is not. Cultural sensitivity and the appropriateness of interventions are crucial considerations in the application of CBT.

This brief outline of some of the key aspects of the biopsychosocial approach to understanding addiction sets the backdrop to the CBT models described below. Given the importance of adopting a developmental approach, the next section outlines a basic developmental model of addiction from a biopsychosocial perspective.

Developmental models of addiction

The first comprehensive psychological formulation of addiction, which includes a developmental perspective, was presented by Jim Orford in his excessive appetite theory (Orford, 2001). Integrating findings from a biopsychosocial perspective, the excessive appetite theory seeks to explain the process of addiction, covering areas such as: how an individual takes up an addictive behaviour; how factors within the individual may contribute to making that behaviour excessive; the breakdown of restraint; the strong attachment to the behaviour; internal conflict; decision-making; and self-control. This theory not only highlights the commonalities in different addictions but also helps formulate interventions from a broader, multidimensional perspective. It has influenced both the approach to treatment and theorising in the field (e.g. West, 2006).

The developmental model of addiction illustrated in Figure 2.2 indicates how the biological, psychological and social spheres influence the development and maintenance of addiction so it is imperative that interventions work on all three spheres. For example, from a biological perspective, genetic predispositions or gene expression may determine the distribution of dopamine receptors in different regions of the brain. This in turn may determine an individual's vulnerability to addiction as dopamine and the doperminergic system are seen as key mediators in the addiction process. Findings such as the association of poorer distribution of a particular type of dopamine receptor (D2) in the pre-frontal cortex with poor impulse control and stimulant addiction (e.g. Volkow *et al.*, 2001) are examples of how some explanation of behaviours may be linked to influences at the molecular level. As our knowledge and appreciation of biological influences in the development and maintenance of addiction grow, interventions should become more integrated and comprehensive rather than operating in separate spheres.

Looking at addiction from a psychological perspective, measurable constructs such as personality risk factors (e.g. impulsivity and anxiety sensitivity) may be expressions of molecular-level phenomena at the behavioural level. From a psychological perspective, emotion has been strongly associated with the development and maintenance of addiction. Negative and positive emotional states (Marlatt & Gordon, 1985) and the self-medication hypothesis (Khantzian, 1977) are examples. Using substances to cope with or enhance emotions and the cognitive factors associated with them (e.g. assumptions, beliefs, schemata and expectancies) are aspects of the addiction phenomenon. Developing skills to regulate emotions as an alternative to substance use, questioning assumptions and beliefs, and changing schemata and expectations can be described as the essence of CBT in addictions. The social and cultural influence on the development and maintenance of addiction is discussed in the previous section.

When assessing a client it is helpful to gather information about how each of these spheres may have contributed to that person developing an addiction problem (e.g. family history, personality and psychological make-up, social context of early drinking and drug use, etc.) and also how they might now be contributing to maintaining the problem (e.g. current emotional and social problems, context of current substance misuse, etc.). Chapter 5 on assessment and Chapter 6 on formulation explore the importance of working collaboratively with clients on these areas.

Figure 2.2 represents current thinking on the developmental factors associated with addiction.

The left side of the model describes those factors that may influence the development of an addictive behaviour. The right side describes how addiction may

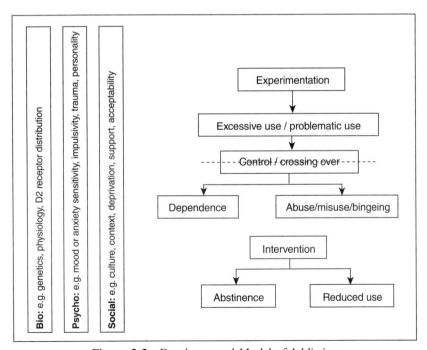

Figure 2.2   Developmental Model of Addiction

develop from experimentation to excessive or problematic use through to addiction (dependence or abuse/misuse in the case of substances). The box entitled 'Control/crossing over' has a line through it to indicate where, from a biological perspective, neuroadaptation, or changes in the neuronal or cellular structure of the brain, takes place (Koob & Le Moal, 2006). Whilst there is increasing evidence that crossing over to addiction involves changes at the biological level (molecular, neurocircuitry), understood as neuroadaptation, and at the psychological (cognitions and behaviour) and social (set and settings) levels, there is little information to help us understand different patterns of substance misuse. Although increased use and bingeing can lead to dependent use, it is also clear that bingeing and dependent use occur independently (Koob & Le Moal, 2006). It is a challenge to clinicians to find interventions that accommodate and address this difference.

Once someone has crossed the line and has become addicted, the critical question becomes why and how people change. An individual's readiness for change or his motivation is seen as the key factor in overcoming addiction. Some, perhaps the majority, of people who change or overcome addiction do so without intervention or help from services or professionals (Vaillant, 1983). With or without external help the decision to change, and maintaining the resolve to change, are undoubtedly the critical factors here. It can be argued that in the absence of a decision to change, intervention is most likely to fail. Motivational interviewing (Miller & Rollnick, 1986, 2002) is an intervention that aims to influence the decision to change and help strengthen the resolve to change.

Theories of motivation and change

A considerable amount of research has been carried out to answer the questions why and how people change. Prochaska & Di Clemente's (1983) trans-theoretical model of change was the result of research into why people quit smoking and has had an enormous impact in the field of addiction and beyond during the past 20 years. Prochaska & Di Clemente proposed that the process of change takes place in distinct stages; hence their model is called the 'Stages of Change Model'. These stages are: pre-contemplation – the period before the individual recognises or acknowledges that there is a problem; contemplation – when a person recognises/ acknowledges that there is a problem and considers doing something about it; decision – a preparation stage; action – when the individual attempts to change behaviour; and maintenance – where the change is maintained. Failure to maintain changes leads to the relapse stage where the individual may remain until they re-engage in the process. The model itself has undergone a few changes. The initial formulation was that of a cycle and if an individual exited a stage they would go back to pre-contempluition and start again. A more recent formulation (see Figure 2.3) structures the stages in a spiral where individuals exiting at one stage do not necessarily go back to the beginning but rejoin a previous stage (Prochaska & Di Clemente, 1996). Individuals move from one stage to the next by resolving their ambivalence to change. Whilst the trans-theoretical model has had a huge

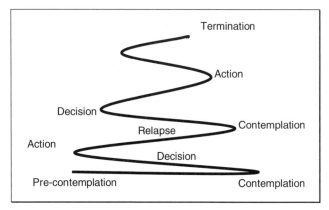

Figure 2.3   Stages of Change Model (Prochaska & Di Clemente, 1996, with kind permission of Springer Science and Business Media)

influence in the field of addiction the research evidence to support the theory of distinct stages of change has been poor. Readiness to change is currently viewed as a dynamic rather than a stable phenomenon.

The most recent theory of motivation that has been developed in the field of addiction is PRIME theory (West, 2006). PRIME theory attempts to integrate a number of theories of addiction and sets out an agenda for future research. West argues that to understand addiction we need to understand the human motivational system. He proposes that our motivational system operates at five levels in a complex manner and any one of them can function abnormally in an addicted individual. These five levels make up the PRIME:

P – plans (conscious mental representations of future actions plus commitment);
R – responses (starting, stopping or modifying actions);
I – impulses/inhibitory forces (which can be consciously experienced as urges);
M – motives (which can be consciously experienced as desires);
E – evaluations (evaluative beliefs).

It is proposed that adjacent elements of the system can influence each other (see Figures 2.4 and 2.5). Unlike other theories in the field of addiction, with the exception of Marlatt & Witkiewitz's (2005) model, this is not a linear or two-dimensional theory that enables simple predictions, but a multidimensional interactive system similar to weather systems and complex mathematical modelling based on catastrophe and chaos theories used to make predictions. It has not yet been tested scientifically and awaits clinical application.

Apart from motivational interviewing (Miller & Rollnick, 1986, 2002) and Prochaska & Di Clemente's trans-theoretical model, relapse prevention (Marlatt & Gordon, 1985) has had the greatest influence in the field in the past 20 years and a thorough understanding of this can be seen as essential for effective CBT work in addictions.

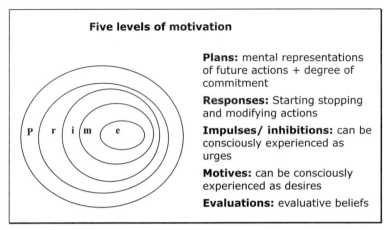

Figure 2.4   PRIME Theory (West, 2006)

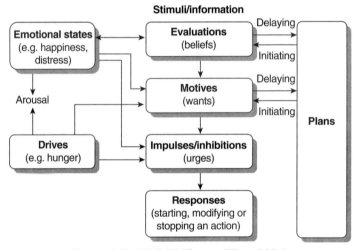

Figure 2.5   PRIME Theory (West, 2006)

Marlatt & Gordon's (1985) model of relapse

The cognitive behavioural model and interventions developed by Alan Marlatt and his colleagues is an integrative model. An important conceptual shift that Marlatt and Gordon introduced is that relapse is a 'process' and can take place over a long period of time and is not simply a reflex action like turning on a switch. Conceptually, it has brought together classical and operant conditioning, social learning theory, social psychology, cognitive psychology and Buddhist philosophy (Wanigaratne, 2003). The latter is responsible for some of the key concepts in the model. Avoidance of extremes (the middle path), the move away from the black or white abstinence/relapse dichotomy and the introduction of the concept of lapses or slips are all examples of this influence. The concept of lifestyle balance as a key factor in the maintenance of change in the longer term is another example of the influence of Buddhist thinking. Mindfulness-based therapies, in particular the mindfulness-based stress reduction work of Jon Kabat-Zinn, a scientist practitioner from the US, are becoming extremely influential in the field of addictions. Kabat-Zinn has been using mindfulness meditation since 1982, originally for chronic pain and anxiety. It has also been used successfully with depression, binge eating, psoriasis and cancer patients, and more recently has been adapted for use in relapse prevention of addictions in the US and the UK (Kabat-Zinn, 2001, 2004).

The essence of mindfulness in the context of substance misuse is about not being driven impulsively or on automatic pilot by emotions or cravings to use. Teaching mindfulness is a way of helping the individual to assume the stance of an impartial witness to become aware of his or her thoughts and feelings, learning to stand back from them and make a choice about whether or how to respond to them. Mindfulness gives choice and in effect disrupts old thinking, feeling and behaviour patterns, creating the opportunity for the client to think, feel and act differently (Chapter 12 discusses mindfulness in more detail).

Once an individual has resolved to change an addictive behaviour or has done so, this state of affairs holds until he encounters or experiences a high-risk situation (HRS). High-risk situations are defined as any situation or mood state that threatens the resolve to maintain change. These are likely to be situations that have previously been associated with relapse for that individual. The most common determinants are shown in Table 2.1.

The way an individual copes with an HRS determines whether and how he will increase his self-efficacy or reduce it (decreased self-efficacy). Where the individual copes well with the situation, an increase in self-efficacy will follow, with a subsequent decreased probability of relapse. The opposite happens if the person does not cope with the situation. According to the model, failure to cope with an HRS leads to a series of cognitive processes (thinking patterns) such as dissonance conflict (conflict between two positions or beliefs about oneself, e.g. 'I am weak – I could be strong'; 'I am an addict – I am an ex-addict'), rule violation effect (an example of all or nothing, or black and white, thinking, e.g. 'I have blown it, I had one cigarette, I am back to square one – I might as well finish the packet'), and positive outcome expectancies (distorted or filtered thinking, i.e. all the

Table 2.1 Intrapersonal and Interpersonal Determinants of High-risk Situations (Cummings *et al.*, 1980)

Intrapersonal determinants
- Negative emotional states
- Negative physical states
- Positive emotional states
- Testing personal control
- Urges and cravings

Interpersonal determinants
- Interpersonal conflict
- Social pressure
- Positive emotional states

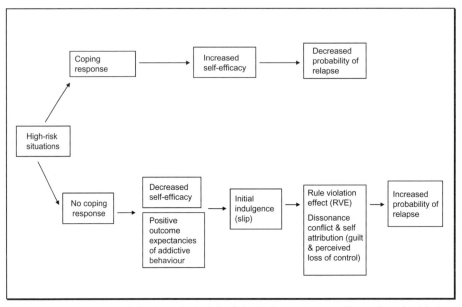

Figure 2.6   Cognitive Behavioural Model of the Relapse Process (Reproduced with permission from Marlatt, G. A. & Gordon, J. R., *Relapse Prevention: Maintenance Strategies in the Treatment of Addictive Behaviors.* New York, Guilford Press. ©1985)

negative or bad consequences of the addictive behaviour is filtered out and all the positives of the addictive behaviour are evoked or recalled, e.g. 'If only I had one drink, I would feel so much better'; 'One smoke of heroin will take all my aches and pains away') all leading to reduced confidence (self-efficacy) in the ability to resist. Together, these factors contribute to a relapse. The model emphasises that relapse is a process and that the initial indulgence, a 'slip' or a 'lapse', is not a relapse. The first part of Marlatt & Gordon's (1985) theory deals primarily with the period immediately following cessation or an intentional change in an addictive behaviour and is illustrated in Figure 2.6. This model has commonalities with Aaron Beck's model (described below), most notably in emphasising the key role of cognitive processes and outcome expectancies in determining substance use.

The second part of Marlatt & Gordon's theory deals with issues concerning the longer-term maintenance of change. Even if a person manages to cope with an HRS, builds confidence and manages to maintain changes for some time, there are factors that can contribute to relapse later. Marlatt & Gordon call these factors 'covert antecedents', highlighting their often cloaked and surreptitious nature. Examining the literature at the time Marlatt and his colleagues found that lifestyle imbalance was a key contributory factor in relapse in those who had developed skills to cope with HRSs in general. They found that when individuals did not manage everyday life stressors with adaptive coping mechanisms this gave rise to a build-up of stress that triggered a series of cognitive processors or thinking patterns. These include the problem of immediate gratification (PIG) where an individual feels 'hard done by' and argues in his mind for immediate compensation – justification of a treat regardless of the long-term negative consequences, positive outcome expectancies, denial (consciously arguing that he has got over the addiction problem 'it was a thing in the past') and seemingly irrelevant decisions (SIDs),

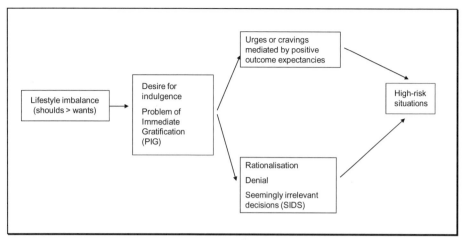

Figure 2.7 Covert Antecedents of Relapse (Reproduced with permission from Marlatt, G. A. & Gordon, J. R., *Relapse Prevention: Maintenance Strategies in the Treatment of Addictive Behaviors.* New York, Guilford Press. ©1985)

when one sets oneself up for a lapse by a series of decisions over a period of time. These thinking patterns, in combination with urges and cravings, increase the probability of relapse (see Figure 2.7).

It is these covert antecedents of relapse that are the key factors to look out for when clients report that after many years of sobriety or clean time they are using or drinking again. Indeed, it could be argued that the success of fellowship organisations such as AA and NA lies in the fact that there is constant exposure to other individuals able to articulate their own faulty thinking patterns. Thus participation in AA/NA may provide a form of vicarious learning of basic relapse prevention principles.

There is no doubt that Marlatt & Gordon's (1985) original work gave the field of addiction a clear framework in which to analyse patterns of relapse, identify weak points and, most importantly, intervene strategically. In essence, it prepares the person to anticipate HRSs and rehearse ways of coping similar to 'fire training' (Wanigaratne *et al.*, 1990).

Not only has the Marlatt & Gordon model had a huge impact on interventions in the field of addiction, it has also stimulated research to test the theoretical aspects of the model as well as the clinical effectiveness of the interventions based on it. Controlled and randomised control trials have demonstrated the effectiveness of relapse prevention. A meta-analytic review of the various trials by Irvin *et al.* (1999) shows that it is an effective intervention in general and is more effective with certain substances. Although relapse prevention has become one of the mainstays in CBT in addictions and has endured for more than 20 years it has not been without its critics (e.g. Edwards, 1987; Sutton, 1993; Donovan, 1996). The main criticisms and limitations of the model are:

- The lack of accommodation of potential influence of craving and withdrawal in the relapse process.
- Not accounting for the role of motivation.
- Not accounting sufficiently for the role of outcome expectancies.

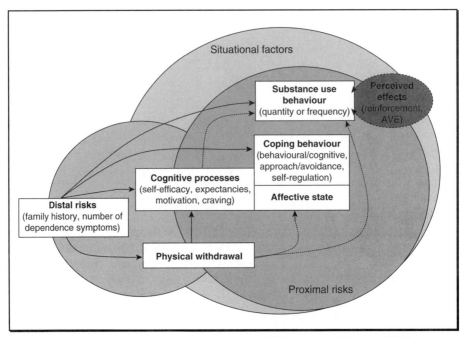

Figure 2.8   Dynamic Model of Relapse (Witkiewitz & Marlatt, 2004)

- Not adequately accounting for self-efficacy.
- Not adequately accounting for 'coping'.
- Discounting the importance of social support.
- Not accounting for diverse communities/cultural differences.
- Inadequate to deal with complex cases.

Taking these criticisms and perceived limitations on board, Witkiewitz & Marlatt (2004) have developed the dynamic model of relapse (see Figure 2.8).

This model shifts the conceptualisation of the relapse process from a linear, two-dimensional model to a complex, non-linear, multidimensional model. In this different factors at different levels interact dynamically to precipitate a relapse. Figure 2.8 shows how distal risk factors (the small circle) interact with proximal risk factors (the middle circle) which are both influenced by situational factors (the large circle) to form a self-organising system and the balance, or how the balance tips, ultimately determines the outcome (relapse or not). The key elements of this model are listed in Table 2.2.

Whilst the use of mathematical modelling based on chaos and catastrophe theories and conceptualisations such as tonic and phasic responses from neurophysiology to explain the mechanisms of the model make it difficult to grasp, the implications of the model for clinical practice follow intuition and could, like its predecessor, become one of the central planks in the addictions field. The previous model has not been abandoned or rejected; rather, the new model adds more dimensions to it. It enables real incorporation of biopsychosocial spheres that may

Table 2.2 Key Elements of the Dynamic Model of Relapse (Witkiewitz & Marlatt, 2004)

- Acknowledges the dynamic and complex nature of the relapse process
- In every situation the individual has the challenge of balancing multiple cues and possible consequences
- Self-regulating system
- Distal influences
- Proximal influences
- Situational influences
- Non-linear model
- Chaos/catastrophe theories

have contributed to the development of the addiction to the intervention process. In many ways it addresses a fundamental criticism of Edwards (1987), that the old relapse prevention model does not provide an adequate account of the idiosyncrasies of change, with the new model stressing the importance of highlighting the importance of relapse as an interactive, fluctuating process, which may never be interrupted in certain individuals (Marlatt & Witkiewitz, 2005). In other words, the earlier model represents an artificial slice of a continuous and dynamic process:

> the phrase Relapse Prevention may usefully stimulate thought, break old moulds, get the adrenaline flowing, give a title to a book, but at the end of the day it can be an invitation to artificial segmentation of the interaction, total and fluctuating process of change (Edwards, 1987, p. 319).

This critique also predicted what could be called the negative impact of relapse prevention, the perception that it is a discrete course of treatment like 'antibiotic treatment'. Such expectation among service users often leads to disappointment or false confidence that can put them at risk of relapse, thus undermining recovery.

The new model enables adjunctive treatments such as motivational interviewing, pharmacotherapies, contingency management (CM), family therapy, physical approaches such as acupuncture, as well as mindfulness meditation to be part of relapse prevention (Marlatt & Donovan, 2005). Tackling dual diagnosis in the form of mild to moderate mental illness (e.g. depression and anxiety disorders) could become part of relapse prevention and require combined CBT approaches. Low mood, anxiety, etc. are conceptualised more as situational factors than as enduring problems. CBT could also enable the latest findings from biological research (e.g. the discovery of the link between stress hormone cortisone releasing factors and craving) to be incorporated into relapse prevention work in a much more targeted way. Whilst stress management from a CBT perspective has always been part of relapse prevention, incorporation of medication that may dampen the stress response in the early stages of recovery as part of the overall relapse prevention strategy is made possible by this model. Most importantly, what the model allows is a comprehensive assessment of each individual (not dissimilar to what is done currently as a good clinical history), with particular reference to the pattern

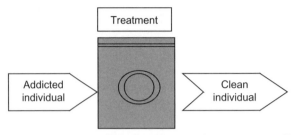

Figure 2.9   Representation of the Washing Machine Concept of Treatment

of interaction between factors for that individual. This could form a 'map' or basis of a recovery plan for that individual. Such an approach would enable the field to move away from the 'washing machine' model of treatment (see Figure 2.9), which traditional relapse prevention has also inadvertently become part of. Figure 2.9 represents the expectation of treatment which has become the dominant narrative in our times. Leading researchers (e.g. O'Brien & McLellan, 1996; O'Brien *et al.*, 2009) are campaigning to change this perception of treatment, with a broader focus on long-term recovery management.

Around the same time as Marlatt and his colleagues were developing their model in Seattle, Washington, Annis and colleagues in Toronto were applying CBT principles and developing relapse prevention interventions along similar, but not identical, lines.

Annis's model of relapse prevention

Bandura's (1977b) self-efficacy theory had a huge impact on applied psychology, particularly the development of cognitive behavioural interventions. Annis & Davis's (1988a) research into the relationship between self-efficacy and relapse led to the development of a relapse prevention model which can be seen as an expansion of one aspect of the Marlatt & Gordon model. The Annis & Davis (1988b) model of relapse prevention has its main focus on efficacy and outcome expectations in dealing with HRSs. Relapse prevention based on this model involves a detailed assessment of an individual's efficacy expectations in dealing with a range of potential high-risk situations. These are measured using standardised instruments (e.g. Inventory of Drug-taking Situations – IDTS; Inventory of Drinking Situations – IDS; and the Situational Confidence Questionnaire – SCQ) and an individualised cognitive-behavioural programme is devised to increase self-efficacy in vulnerable areas. If individuals do not succeed in their homework tasks, then the task is analysed further and broken down into what is more achievable. If they succeed, then the next situation in the hierarchy is set as the task. In everyday clinical work when there is no time to do more detailed and comprehensive relapse prevention work, this model offers the scope of doing effective CBT interventions focusing on an individual's reported HRSs (see Figure 2.10). This very practical intervention can be seen as a prime example of cognitive behavioural work, combining behavioural experiments with cognitive appraisal.

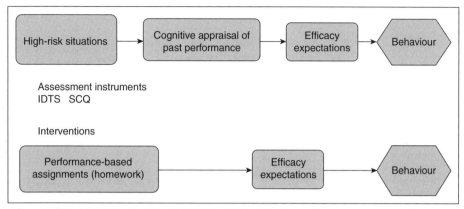

Figure 2.10 Annis & Davis's (1988b) Model of Relapse Prevention (Reproduced with permission from Annis, H. M. & Davis, C. S., *Assessment of Addictive Behaviors*. New York: Guilford Press. ©1988)

Aaron Beck's cognitive model of substance abuse

The application and adaptation of Beck's (1976) cognitive therapy model in the area of substance misuse is a landmark development in the field. The developmental aspect of Beck's work on substance dependence draws on his model of depression and the way in which core beliefs develop and predispose individuals to psychological problems. Beck *et al.*'s cognitive model (1993) describes addictive behaviours arising out of interplay between layers or levels of beliefs (see Figure 2.11). Core beliefs, which include substance-related beliefs that the person has developed as a result of life experience (as described in the developmental model of addiction), are activated by a critical incident. Critical incidents in Beck *et al.*'s model are the equivalent of HRSs in Marlatt & Gordon's (1985) model. Substance-related beliefs give rise to automatic substance-related thoughts, which trigger urges and cravings. In this cognitive model the decision to give in to the urge or craving is described as activation of permissive beliefs. Once the permissive belief is activated, the individual starts making plans for use. These plans are called instrumental strategies and, if not stopped, lead to using the substance. In this cognitive model the slip, or using, itself becomes an HRS and puts the person back into the cycle described above.

Interventions based on this model are mainly cognitive, although some behavioural strategies may also be utilised. The greater emphasis on cognitive interventions and strategies in this approach is the main difference between this and Marlatt & Gordon's approach. The key aspect of this model is that beliefs mediate the process that leads to addictive behaviour. Moderating these beliefs is central to the CBT treatment approach based on this model. For readers who wish to work in this way we recommend the excellent text by Kouimtsidis *et al.* (2007), which describes in detail how this model is applied. The focus of relapse prevention work within this framework is to modify an individual's core beliefs and schemata relating to his addictive behaviour. Hence this framework is more suitable for individual work, but could be adapted for group work.

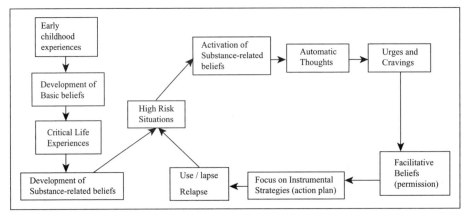

Figure 2.11   Beck *et al.*'s (1993) Cognitive Therapy Model of Substance Abuse (Reproduced with permission from Beck, A. T., Wright, F. D., Newman, C. F. & Liese, B. S., *Cognitive Therapy of Depression*. New York: Guilford Press. ©1993)

Beck *et al.*'s, Marlatt & Gordon's and Annis's models are all examples of cognitive models to explain aspects of addictive behaviour. Key to each is the dynamic interplay between an individual and the environment in which the individual's cognitions are the key mediators leading to substance use.

The evidence base for CBT with addictive behaviour

There is an emerging evidence base for the effectiveness of CBT in the treatment of substance misuse and other addictions. It is clear from reviews that the effectiveness of CBT in the case of substance dependence and misuse appears to be substance-specific. This means that CBT is differentially effective in the treatment of different substances. The appropriateness of randomised controlled trials (RCTs) as the gold standard of evidence for complex psychological interventions such as relapse prevention as well as the usefulness of meta-analytic reviews has been questioned (e.g. Charlton, 2000; Humphreys & Weisner, 2000; Westen *et al.*, 2004). An inherent weakness of reviews of evidence, particularly meta-analysis, is that CBT is viewed as a homogeneous treatment approach. The type, dose (duration and intensity), skill level of the therapist, severity of the client's addiction and a number of other confounding variables are not adequately considered in these reviews. The use of meta-analytic reviews in examining the effectiveness of psychological therapies which is particularly favoured by NICE in the UK, has been criticised by many. Charlton (2000, p. 13), for example, states:

> … an accumulation of inadequate data simply makes for a bigger pile of inadequate data, the statistical averaging of different trials, done in different places, by different people for different purposes merely generates a meaningless statistical artefact. To put it bluntly, meta-analysis is a logically incoherent technique of zero scientific credibility.

Nevertheless evidence from a broader perspective, including RCTs, does point to the effectiveness of CBT in the treatment of addiction. Reviews such as Morgenstern & Longabaugh (2000), Miller & Wilbourne (2002), Wanigaratne *et al.* (2005), Carroll *et al.* (2004) and Irvin *et al.* (1999) are all examples. The practitioner is also encouraged to gather practice-based evidence by systematic measurement of outcome and clear documentation of interventions. This approach, which is termed empirically grounded clinical intervention (Salkovskis, 2002), should yield more ecologically valid evidence than RCTs in the area of psychological interventions. Evidence from a series of single case studies would be an example of this approach.

Summary

Addiction theory is a fluid field and it is important to consider the value of a variety of different levels of explanation, including genetic predispositions, neurophysiological adaptation to substance use, personality factors, social norms and social context. This is particularly important where models can gain currency either because of their simplicity or because professional training is not up-to-date with more recent developments. For instance, it is not uncommon for therapists trained in addictions in the 1970s to hold on to models that focus on the client 'being in denial', despite the lack of empirical evidence for the existence of such a state.

This chapter started by drawing together a number of seemingly disparate ideas and presented them in terms of a broad paradigm. We do this without privileging a specific level of explanation and recognise that to view addiction across these dimensions is to start to appreciate the complexity of the behaviour. Hopefully, at each level of explanation we have begun to indicate what could be the focus for a clinical intervention. The more recent dynamic model of relapse (Marlatt & Witkiewitz, 2005) not only takes into consideration the biopsychosocial spheres, but also the dynamic interaction between them. It points to the importance of a comprehensive assessment and it is to this that we turn our attention in Chapter 5.

Chapter 3

Fundamentals of Treatment

In this chapter we provide an overview of the treatment journey explored in detail in Chapters 4–12. We have done this as an orientation aid and in order to provide an overview of the key tasks in the cognitive behavioural treatment of substance use. Figure 3.1 outlines four key building blocks of therapy: (i) engaging a client in treatment; (ii) undertaking an assessment and developing a formulation; (iii) applying techniques with a specific goal in mind (what we call intervention); and (iv) building a therapeutic relationship, something that happens from the moment you meet the client for the first time to the final follow-up session. For this reason, in Figure 3.1 we have overlapped all the other tasks with this therapeutic relationship. Chapters 4–12 are organised to reflect an idealised treatment journey through the tasks of engagement, assessment and intervention.

This journey starts with the aim of engaging clients in treatment and enhancing their motivation in order to undertake an assessment and gather information that can inform a cognitive and behavioural formulation of substance use. This formulation becomes the platform and rationale for CBT interventions. Although the book introduces these three tasks sequentially, real clinical work is rarely as neat as that. Indeed, having a useful conversation with a client as an engagement exercise can be hugely powerful and for some clients may tip the motivational balance for them to make changes in their life without further input from services. Conversely, work in the intervention phase may not go as planned and it may be necessary to review motivational issues and update assessments with new or emerging information. Throughout treatment the formulation is a key reference point,

Applied Cognitive and Behavioural Approaches to the Treatment of Addiction: A Practical Treatment Guide By Luke Mitcheson, Jenny Maslin, Tim Meynen, Tamara Morrison, Robert Hill and Shamil Wanigaratne

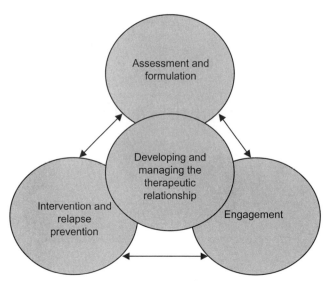

Figure 3.1   Key Tasks of Treatment

which is likely to be revised according to emerging information, including what happens in treatment. In reality, assessment, actively working with clients' motivations and intervening at appropriate points are in a dynamic and fluid relationship. We have also represented this interconnectedness between these three tasks in Figure 3.1.

These three broad tasks sit within a context which we have called managing the therapeutic relationship. For this to take place, a range of knowledge, attitudes and behaviour needs to be present. These include a basic acceptance of the clients and appreciation of their potential, as well as an awareness of cultural differences. This informs a set of useful attitudes to working with clients with problematic substance use. Defining how to establish a good therapeutic relationship is not as easy as the other tasks. It is not a concrete thing and reducing it to a set of things to do misses the point. However, if you do not have a therapeutic relationship with your client, it is extremely unlikely that you will be successful in achieving any of the other three tasks.

Engaging clients in treatment

It cannot be overemphasised how crucial it is to engage clients fully in the treatment process. CBT is not done 'to' clients, it is done 'with' them. Engaging clients is about developing a relationship that is understood as supportive, compassionate and useful, but is also goal-directed and has boundaries. Concerted efforts at this stage will provide the basis for the essential collaborative working alliance required in CBT. Effective workers in the field of substance misuse know this and also know the longevity of some counter-therapeutic approaches. The now discredited idea that substance-using clients are particularly 'resistant' or in 'denial' about their behaviour has given rise to approaches that seek to 'break down defences' and confront clients with the reality of their behaviour. Thankfully, these ideas have become less fashionable and the adoption of evidence-based approaches, such as motivational interviewing, has led to more client-centred ways of working.

This is not to say that there are no particular issues to be aware of when seeking to engage clients in treatment. Given the social stigma attached to substance dependence, clients may seek to minimise the extent of their difficulties, particularly if they fear that these may lead to services being withdrawn. Clients may also feel very guilty and be ashamed of their behaviour and may consequently be sensitive to perceptions of others' thoughts and feelings about their substance use. This can become an issue in the therapeutic relationship. Clients are generally likely to have made repeated attempts to change their substance use prior to entering treatment and where this has not succeeded experienced lack of confidence or belief in their self-efficacy.

Neither the rapid changes in brain chemistry and powerful reinforcing potential of many drugs nor their reinforcing effect, whereby clients are quickly distanced from unpleasant emotions and feelings, should be overlooked. Substance use may represent a tried-and-tested coping strategy which some clients may understandably fear giving up. Indeed, substance use for many clients is a rational response to situations in which they are unable to conceptualise alternative responses. This 'self-medication' hypothesis is an important area for discussion and helps you as a therapist to communicate your neutrality regarding the pros and cons of drug or alcohol use with clients.

Taking these issues into account it is likely that the early contacts clients have with a treatment system are crucial to their subsequent engagement, and the approach a worker takes with the client at this stage can make the difference to whether a client is seen again or at least actively participates in the process. For this reason we devote a chapter to the engagement process. In Chapter 4 we advocate strongly for a non-judgemental approach and taking a gentle, inquiring position with respect to the potential complexities outlined above as the most effective way of engaging clients. A CBT therapist would assume that clients have good reasons for persisting in behaviours that are inherently self-limiting and that it is incumbent on them to understand these reasons and in a way that helps the client to consider the alternatives. Just as the avoidant behaviours of a client who experiences panic attacks can be understood as a short-term rational response to autonomic nervous arousal, so substance-using behaviour, with all its associated costs, can be understood as providing a short-term and immediate purpose. Chapter 4 introduces some basic counselling skills that can enable clinicians to explore these issues sensitively, as well as a range of cognitive strategies to enable these conversations to occur in therapeutic work.

Assessment and formulation

If you have glanced at the contents page of this book or have looked ahead at the way we have presented the chapters, you may wonder why Chapter 4, 'Enhancing Motivation to Change', precedes Chapter 5, 'Assessment and Introducing CBT to Clients', as doing an assessment is the usual first stage of treatment. Yet, the crucial point is that the worker's approach will determine how a client experiences this assessment. An assessment done in the right way will engage the client.

Therefore, it makes sense to prioritise enhancing motivation to change. Unfortunately, it is our experience that assessment is often reduced to a tick-box exercise with a harassed therapist feeling pressured to collect various pieces of information on which they are likely to be performance-managed. It is something to get through before the 'real' work can begin. The assessment therefore becomes service-centred as opposed to client-centred and is anything but an engagement tool. It can also make clients feel that it is something done to them, and in many cases, done repeatedly with each new service or worker. Not surprisingly, assessment can become a mutually non-therapeutic experience. Skilled workers will have learnt to integrate the 'must dos' of information collection (e.g. risk assessments) into the process of a useful assessment. By that we mean finding out why clients are taking time to be there – i.e. their hopes, aspirations and understanding of what treatment will entail. Similarly, the process of care planning and outcome monitoring needs to become a part of the clinical review process. It is this robust, key working platform on which assessment relevant to CBT and long-term recovery management should be built.

Chapter 5, therefore, introduces assessment not simply as a way of collecting information, but as a goal-oriented activity for developing a CBT formulation. It outlines the key areas in a client's history and presentation a clinician should consider, presents this within a cognitive and behavioural framework and socialises the client to the treatment approach. The focus of questions begins to shape the way in which the clinician and client can understand the addictive behaviour, which becomes a template for much of the intervention-specific work. For clinicians new to this approach there is another aspect to consider – explaining to clients why they are interested in these areas. Therefore, the clinician is being explicit about why they are asking clients certain questions, providing a rationale for them. This process helps clients understand the process of treatment but also the behaviour itself and serves to engage the clients in treatment.

In CBT, assessment is the vehicle in which a therapeutic relationship should develop, it is the medium in which a client can be socialised to the CBT approach and is the process by which information for the formulation is gathered, synthesised and shared with the client. This is a collaborative process through which the formulation becomes the shared product and the basis for moving on towards an intervention planning and application phase. Formulation is introduced in Chapter 6 and is the synthesis of all the assessment information collected and fitted together within a developmental and cognitive and behavioural framework. The formulation becomes the basis of planning and evaluating the intervention phase of treatment.

Butler (2006) describes how valuable formulation can be. It is the tool that clinicians use to apply theories such as those described in Chapter 2 to actual practice. It also contributes to the process of therapist accountability the 'why did you do that?' which will be discussed with clients themselves as well as in supervision. Formulation can also be used to make predictions about what will help or hinder progress. For clients struggling to make sense of their behaviour it communicates strongly that the behaviour can be understood and places this in a developmental, situational and cultural context. This is an explorative process and can lead to a critical enquiry of these factors. This has the potential to communicate a powerful message of understanding and begin to engender optimism about change. It is recommended that, even at a rudimentary level, an explicit formulation is required before moving on to the intervention phase.

Intervention and treatment goals

There are many substance use-specific treatment goals for which CBT can be helpful. There are debates in the addiction treatment field which include whether abstinence should be the only viable treatment goal, whether controlled use is an option for some, the place for focusing on reducing harm or minimising harm associated with substance use, the provision of substitute medication for drugs of dependency and the relative merits of community treatment vs. residential treatment. Politicians, the media, service commissioners, service providers and drug user advocacy groups may all take strong positions on these issues. We take a pragmatic stance. One of the strengths of CBT is that it can be used to help clients achieve the goals they aspire to. It is theoretically neutral as to whether clients should abstain or seek controlled use. This is not to say it is ignored; it will become part of the focus of the work undertaken between the clinician and client. However, we believe it is unhelpful for a clinician to approach a client with a preconceived idea of what the client's treatment goal should be unless there are clear medical reasons to do so. Our experience shows that clients may wish to try controlled use in the first instance and later, depending on experience, go for abstinence. The goal of controlled use may or may not be an expression of clients' ambivalence about change, but this will become apparent with a sensitive discussion of past experiences of change and their future hopes and aspirations. Again, the clinician's ideas about what should happen could be an impediment to developing a good relationship and working together.

CBT as an approach that enables clients to develop insight and awareness of addictive behaviour shares a common purpose with other therapeutic approaches such as 12-step programmes. CBT is also useful for addressing a host of problems associated with substance use, including the practice of substance use itself. Thus, it can be integrated into a harm reduction approach. This would include focusing on changing routes of drug use to less risky methods of use (e.g. from injecting to smoking) or for a specific aspect of drug use practice (e.g. no longer sharing injecting equipment).

CBT is relevant to all substances as well as poly-substance use, and the approach and methods used are often the same. The key question though is whether and at what point one addresses more than one substance. While this depends on the client's goals, it is important not to overestimate the difficulties that most people have in initiating and sustaining behaviour change. Therapist and client optimism regarding change must therefore always be grounded in the realities of the change process.

Another important point to make is that whilst this book has been written for individual client work, much of what we describe can be adapted for small group work. An example of a structured group looking at cognitive distortions including a client handout is given in Appendices 3.1 and 3.2. For a range of further structured CBT groups, the reader is advised to look at the National Treatment Agency's (NTA) Psychosocial Interventions Resource Library at www.nta.nhs.uk.

Chapters 6–12 introduce a range of cognitive and behavioural interventions that can be used to address these goals. Many are standard CBT interventions, others are our adaptations of these for a substance-using population. Each of these interventions has been used and refined from our collective experience and as such does not claim to be the definitive CBT approach to addictions treatment. We hope that readers will be inspired to develop their own practice and take these ideas forward. The chapters focus on different areas: addiction cognitions; cognitive interventions; behavioural experiments; behavioural interventions; and working with emotions. Whilst these chapters have been written sequentially, they can be used in a number of different ways. You may want to work through each area as we have presented it; however, it is more likely and our hope that your choice of intervention will be based on your formulation and with a specific aim in mind. Introducing an intervention into treatment will also be a decision for each clinician/client to arrive at, based on the evolving experience of treatment. The knowledge of when to apply a specific intervention, as well as when not to, is something that would also be discussed in supervision. This knowledge has been referred to as a meta-competency and is discussed further in Chapter 13 in relation to developing your practice (Pilling *et al.*, 2009).

Therapeutic relationship

To develop an effective working relationship with a client requires more than an understanding of psychological theory and specific therapeutic interventions. We think it is helpful to focus attention on two distinct areas: (i) therapist attitudes; and (ii) therapy structure. The first refers to things that you as a therapist bring to your clinical work. In this area of working it includes your beliefs and ideas about substance use, about the people who develop problems and why and how this might happen. Your beliefs about the change process are also important as well as what you consider to be your role in the change process. Much of this might be highly personal and influenced by your own experience of substance use or of people close to you who may or may not have developed problems related to their substance use. The second area refers to more practical matters and includes issues such as goal-setting and how to structure sessions to make efficient use of time. These directive elements to the approach of therapy are a defining feature of CBT. We recommend *Cognitive Therapy: Basics and Beyond* (Beck, 1995) as a resource to develop these fundamental aspects of the approach. Therapist attitudes and therapy structure are discussed below and we suggest these two areas are regularly brought to supervision for specific direction and reflective practice.

Therapist attitudes

These may be a general set of attitudes you hold in your work or you may find that a particular client invokes a specific set of feelings and beliefs. Although not always easy to identify, we believe some acknowledgement of our own position and influence on the therapy process is highly important. Without it there is a danger that these may be driving the direction of therapy and interfering with the development of an effective working alliance with clients. It is also important to consider your own values and beliefs regarding the use of drugs and alcohol, including your attitudes to illegal use and your attitude towards why people use substances. Finally, we set out what we consider to be a useful set of attitudes and within this an appreciation of the individuality of each client and recognition of their specific social and cultural development.

In the field of substance use treatment there is a range of positions on the nature of addiction and it is not unusual for people who work in services to have personal experience of substance use and/or experience of problematic substance use. Outside the field illegal substance use may generate considerable fear and anxiety or outright moral objection. This may coexist with a relaxed attitude to alcohol use for oneself and one's friends even when this has been hazardous and led to specific problems when drunk. It is rare for a week to go by without a story in the media about drugs and alcohol and what the government, parents, schools or users themselves should or should not be doing. It is clear, however, that societal attitudes and counter-cultural attitudes have changed over time and in response to use of particular substances and to particular users. These have influenced and continue to influence government policy and the way treatment services are oriented. There is not the space here to explore the rights or wrongs or contradictions in these beliefs about drug and alcohol use. However, we suggest that individuals working in the field need some understanding of their own beliefs. Whilst you may be able to keep these beliefs private it is important to be mindful of whether they are subtly influencing your approach to treatment. Might you minimise the problems the clients bring? Or might you see it as a sign of weakness in the clients that they have failed to be controlled and responsible users of psychoactive drugs like yourself?

Similarly, how we understand the nature of addiction can impact on our therapeutic work. Although we have used the term addiction in the title of this book it is not without complications. You may have noted that we have tried to describe a behaviour, 'substance use', which we hope is less ambiguous. This reveals some of our beliefs. We find terms like addiction and dependence to be far from clearly defined constructs. We have also tried to avoid the term 'misuse' as we believe it implies a moral judgement about the behaviour. It is our experience that one person's idea of misuse is another person's use and that these ideas may coexist within relationships between people, families, peers and society as a whole. We have introduced the notion of 'substance use problems' because we believe this is a more neutral and descriptive way of understanding the issue and implies that substance use can be non-problematic. By defining the issue in this way we have attempted to avoid taking a moral stance, but also not to minimise the fact that substance use can lead to problems for individuals and those around them. We also think this helps to set an appropriate attitude to work with people with substance use problems, one that requires sensitivity to their individual experience and how their problems with substances have emerged over time.

Another issue we wish you to consider as a therapist is your attitude to the change process. This is likely to be influenced by those ideas discussed above. We are referring to those ideas about what works in treatment but also what role the client should or should not have in the process. The 'what works in treatment' debate is another area we cannot do justice to in this book. Suffice it to say we can make an assumption that you at least have some interest at this stage in exploring the value of a CBT approach. Your education and professional training are likely to influence what works. Similarly, if you have had personal experience of going through treatment, then this is likely to influence your thinking. We are raising this as an area to consider because we believe that implicit in our own understanding is the risk of assuming an expert position on how change should happen and this overly influencing the way you interact with clients. This may include discounting their experience or blindly pursuing your own change agenda without reflecting on whether this is appropriate or relevant to the individual you are working with.

Once you are aware of your own attitude to substance use and are able to keep an eye on how this may influence the therapeutic relationship there remains your therapeutic stance. This is the way you approach therapy with clients, the way you think about clients in the process of therapy and what they bring to the process. Central to this is how you can be open to clients' cultural values and beliefs.

In our experience of working with people with substance use problems, the need to develop an appropriate therapeutic stance and weave this into a useful set of attitudes to drugs and alcohol is an essential aspect of working effectively with this client group. This therapeutic stance is essentially a client-centred therapy approach, a term developed in relation to humanistic psychotherapy (Rogers, 1951). What we mean by this is an approach that seeks to understand and is oriented towards each client's needs, goals, values and aspirations. Part of this will be an appreciation of specific cultural beliefs (discussed below). Another aspect of this stance is a recognition that these needs and goals will vary over time. The focus of therapy therefore will need to be able to respond to these whilst keeping the bigger picture – what the desired long-term outcome could be – in view. Clients may be focused on immediate aspects of their substance use – for example, being concerned about withdrawal and that they have enough medication – in which case this needs to become the focus of the therapeutic work. If your therapeutic endeavours are focused elsewhere, it is unlikely that the clients will respond favourably. Over time it is possible to broaden the horizon of the therapeutic work, and to facilitate recovery it will be appropriate to help the clients to look beyond the immediate aspects of their addiction. However, in the first instance you need to focus on the clients' current position and attend to the immediate issues and concerns.

Central to this therapeutic stance is being non-judgemental about substance use (and hence being aware of your own beliefs) and recognising clients have autonomy in making decisions about changing or managing their substance use. Your role as a therapist is to work with what the client wants and feels able to do, whilst also helping the client to see what is and could possibly be different. To do this we find it helpful to think about the strengths clients may have and then use them in therapy. First, it is useful to acknowledge these strengths. Given the life experiences that many clients with substance use problems may have had, these strengths may be those associated with survival in the face of traumatic events and resilience in coping with seemingly intractable social problems. Acknowledging these strengths helps to build the therapeutic relationship. Second, find out about and show an interest in resources clients may have developed through their life experiences; things they enjoy or used to enjoy; things achieved or done well; relationships sustained. You will be able to use these experiences as reference points in therapy in assessing the clients' movement towards recovery for life more generally. This can be helpful when things may feel stuck, but they also serve as a bank of ideas to draw on when working together on specific issues.

The final part of the therapeutic relationship we wish to emphasise is the need to appreciate cultural difference and diversity. This is important because culture is central to your clients' identities. It can be thought of as a framework that people use for understanding their experiences. It encompasses values, beliefs and behaviours shared among people with similar ethnic or geographical origins, languages, religions or life views. This includes gender, class or any other aspect of identity including sexual identity. We suggest it is important to be aware and sensitive to issues of cultural difference and distinguish this from ideas of expertise and competence. The onus here is on understanding each individual in his specific cultural, environmental and developmental context. This requires you to suspend your own assumptions about what is and should be important and to be open to asking and hearing what the client has to say. As with attitudes to substance use, your own knowledge may be an impediment to understanding the client you are working with.

We believe CBT, with its implicit focus on each client's beliefs, is well suited to this way of working. However, the majority of research establishing CBT as an effective treatment for a range of psychological problems has been conducted among white Western populations. A review by Miranda and colleagues (2005) suggests that overall research shows that CBT is also effective for Latino and African-American participants, with results equal to or greater than white Americans. A particularly important question is the extent to which CBT interventions need to be culturally adapted to be effective for black and minority ethnic populations. The research literature provides little insight here. Adaptive interventions have been shown to be helpful, but tests of adapted vs. standard interventions are not yet available to guide care. Nevertheless it is clear that culture and context need to be considered in CBT therapy as in any form of therapy. Culturally sensitive interventions should both facilitate accessibility of services and make use of methods that are acceptable and appropriate given the cultural values of the client population in general.

A good CBT therapist will be interested in individual history, culture and context to understand fully the meaning behind a client's substance use. Listed below are some reminders about culturally competent practice in working with clients' substance use problems, many of which are elaborated in Graham & Wanigaratne (2000).

1. Remember that your CBT intervention should always be tailored to the individual, served within the context of that individual's culture and community and applied in a culturally sensitive way.
2. Assess social, familial, economic and cultural influences on your client and his or her substance use.
3. Make an effort to understand perceptions of substance use from your client's point of view, but also from the perspective of peers and broader social group.
4. Assess any additional stress factors your client may be experiencing – for example, the perception of the client's peers about his or her seeking help for substance use problems.

5. Be willing to enquire about, acknowledge and work with your client's religious and spiritual beliefs.
6. Show an appreciation of your client's dialect and language; arrange for an interpreter to be present if necessary.
7. Have respect for your client's cultural and individual style of communicating.
8. Be aware of stereotypes held about drug users and the client's ethnic/cultural group. Also be aware that the client may hold stereotypes about you.
9. Remember that many ethnic minorities and other minority cultural groups face racism and/or prejudice and discrimination on a regular basis and those experiences can have an extremely negative impact on mental and physical health and substance use. You should acknowledge the reality and traumatic impact of such experiences and provide a safe environment for clients to discuss their thoughts and feelings on the subject.

We have only begun to touch on issues that require you as a therapist to reflect on what you bring to the work you do. This self-awareness will enable you to be more open to clients and their unique perspectives, which will be crucial to building a relationship and working collaboratively through the course of treatment. We acknowledge that this process of self-exploration can raise difficult issues for therapists and we recommend that these are discussed within a safe and supportive supervisory relationship. It may also be important to consider the role and place of individual therapy for you, something which, while not stipulated for CBT therapists or those in training, should not be discounted as irrelevant.

Therapy structure

In this section we look at the framework of a session and how it might be organised to make the most effective use of the time. For CBT therapists this will be routine and core to your practice, but some attention to putting drug and alcohol use on the agenda may be required. Depending on the context in which you see your clients they may, justifiably, be concerned about the repercussions of discussing this with you for fear of losing access to treatment. Alternatively, they may not see the relevance of your interest in their substance use. A basic sensitivity to your client's concerns and being open about your reasons for asking particular questions will be helpful. Chapter 4 provides some ideas for engaging clients in substance use-focused work.

For key workers and care coordinators in a drug and alcohol treatment setting the issues might be slightly different. The setting allows for the assumption that drug and alcohol use will be on the agenda, but the work can be very demanding, with multiple elements to the role, only part of which is the psychosocial aspect of treatment. There is inevitably some crisis management, the practical aspects of being a contact point for prescribed medication such as methadone and also supporting clients with social issues such as housing problems. Maintaining structure and therapeutic input to the issue of problem substance use can be very difficult. It is our experience that an approach that is flexible to the immediate issues which clients may present with, that acknowledges there are some 'must dos' of the meeting (e.g. review compliance with prescribed medication), but that also has a structure which is consistent from week to week is the best way to manage these competing demands.

We suggest that each session is structured in the following way:

1. Agenda-setting and recap of previous session
2. Specific agenda items
3. Planning for the next session
4. Session review

Agenda-setting and recap of previous session

The first thing we do with clients is to check how they are feeling and whether there is anything they wish to be covered in the time you have together. This immediately acknowledges their agenda and invites them to be active in the work you do together. The process of agenda-setting becomes a negotiated exercise, with you as a therapist adding items you wish to or must cover. Part of agenda-setting should include a recap of the previous session and making sure you ask about homework tasks the client may have agreed to try. These then become agenda items and the final task is agreeing what you can cover in the time available. This may involve deferring agenda items or designating another time to deal with a particular issue.

Specific agenda items

The content here will be determined by the agenda-setting exercise. However, we would recommend that even if you have only five minutes, then some focus on the psychological aspects of treatment will be worthwhile. It is often easy to focus on the practicalities of medication management and for this to take up the time available. Your role as a therapist is to be highly active in managing the time and if one agenda item seems to be taking longer than anticipated, you need to review the agenda with a revised time schedule in mind. This active, hands-on approach may seem far removed from a client-centred approach, but is actually modelling active collaborative problem-solving skills and bringing the client into the process.

Planning for the next session

This follows from the items discussed which will often result in a goal and a set of action points for you and the client. When setting goals with clients it is important to be as specific as possible and to help them be realistic in what they set out to achieve. It is important for clients to have a successful experience and in the early stages of therapy to have at least done something between sessions. It is easy for clients to drop into their time with you and to forget about this until their next appointment. CBT actively encourages clients to try things out and to do things differently. Setting achievable goals, however small, is crucial to this.

Session review

The closing part of the session is to check with the clients how the session has gone for them and review what they have found helpful or unhelpful. Again, this emphasises the collaborative aspect of treatment and enables you to get feedback about what and how you are doing things. Clients can be great teachers and it is vital to be open to their feedback. The session review also serves the purpose of repeating core information and checking whether the client has fully understood what was covered. Finally, acknowledging any agenda items not discussed and agreeing how this could be tackled next time is also helpful.

    This broad, four-part structure to therapy combined with the appropriate attitude to the client will provide a sound foundation on which the specific techniques in this book can be built. In Chapter 4 we explore the question of motivation to change and what the therapist can do to enhance this. This may lie at the heart of addiction treatment, for while clients present as wanting to change, they are continually making an assessment as to whether such change is going to be for the better or for the worse.

Appendix 3.1: Thinking choices: 'jumping to conclusions'

Staff instructions

Aims:

- For clients to be introduced to why thinking is important and how our thoughts affect how we feel and how we behave.
- Explore definitions through examples of 'Thinking Errors'.
- Consider how to challenge thinking errors and be offered a strategy for making helpful thinking choices.

This group is in six stages		

Stage	*Form and Content*	*Time*
Pre-group	Staff preparation and allocation of tasks	15 minutes
	Ensure clients aware of start time	
Stage 1	Welcome and introductions	5 minutes
Stage 2	Why is thinking important?	10 minutes
Stage 3	Positive vs. negative thoughts balance	5–10 minutes
Stage 4	Examples –'Jumping to conclusions'	15–25 minutes
Stage 5	Thinking choices – Dealing with hot thoughts	5 minutes
Stage 6	Group summary and evaluation	5 minutes
Post-group	Staff evaluation	15 minutes
	Session Length	**45–60 minutes**
	Staff Preparation and Evaluation Time	**30 minutes**

Objectives

Session Structure

Pre-Group 15 Minutes

Staff Preparation

1. Take time to become familiar with the topic and structure of the group
2. Allocate roles/specific sections of the group for all facilitators

Materials and Resources

1. Flip chart sheets (prepared before session) or whiteboard
2. Marker pens in assorted colours

Reproduced with permission from the National Treatment Agency's Psychosocial Interventions Resource Library, www.nta.nhs.uk

3.   Pens/pencils for participants

Sheet 1
Thoughts, Feelings and Behaviour

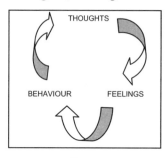

Sheet 2
Positive vs. Negative
Thoughts Balance

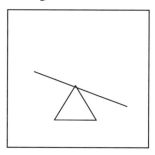

Sheet 3 (One sheet per group)
'Jumping To Conclusions'

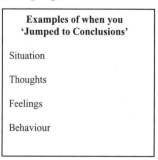

Sheet 4
Dealing with Hot Thoughts:
Traffic Light Diagram

4.   Copies of group handouts: (i)   'Jumping to Conclusions' Handout
                                 (ii) Session Evaluation Questionnaire

Stage 1
5 Minutes

Welcome and Introductions

Welcome all participants as they arrive. Once all are seated, welcome and thank for attending. All facilitators introduce themselves and ask participants to give their names in turn. Review the group rules where relevant.

Introduction to the group:

1.   Today's group is all about why thinking is important, how our thoughts affect how we feel, and how we behave. Sometimes our thinking can be a distortion of the truth, there are certain thinking biases or patterns that we all use. These are best understood as thinking habits (also known as thinking errors).

2. Today we will focus on **'Jumping to Conclusions'** by exploring this defini-
    tion and looking at some examples of this thinking error. We will finally
    consider some ways of dealing with these thoughts and offer a strategy for
    making thinking choices.

Stage 2
10 Minutes

Why Is Thinking Important?

Resources

*   Sheet 1 – Thoughts, Feelings, Behaviour

Brainstorm Exercise Pose the question: Why is thinking important? Write
clients' responses on the whiteboard/flipchart. Spend a couple of minutes on this.

Discuss the links between thoughts/feelings/behaviours (Show Flipchart Sheet
1 to show link visually). It is prudent to avoid discussion situations that elicit very
strong feelings within the group as this can become a distraction from the topic.
A suggested example is shown below:

Situation
Attending AA or NA meeting for the first time and no one speaks to me

Thought
No one wants to speak with me

Feeling
Fed up and cross

Behaviour
Withdrawn body language
Avoid eye contact
Leave early, don't go back

Stage 3
5 Minutes

Positive vs. Negative Thinking

– Thoughts Balance

Resources

*   Sheet 2 – Positive vs. Negative Thoughts balance

Explain: Thinking is important because our thoughts determine how we feel, and how we behave as we discussed in why thinking is important.

Show Sheet 2 – Positive vs. Negative Thoughts Balance The easiest way to change our behaviour and feel better about ourselves is to challenge our thoughts.

This does not just mean thinking positively.

We can just as easily fall prisoner to so-called positive thinking as we can of negative thinking. While positive thinking has its place it can also be illusionary, self serving and unhelpful.

In order to make this scale balance you could add lots of positive thoughts to try to tip the scales, however we think that the most effective thing to do is to try and get rid of some of the negatives. Then any positive thinking you do is more likely to be effective.

	Stage 4
	15 Minutes

'Jumping to Conclusions'

Resources

- Flip chart paper and pens for groups (Sheet 3)

Explain: You can make a negative interpretation even though there are no facts to support it. There are two main ways of doing this:

(1) Mind Reading –You decide that someone is reacting negatively to you or you know what someone is thinking without checking this out.
(2) Fortune-telling – You anticipate that things will turn out badly and you feel convinced that your prediction is an established fact.

- **Group Exercise:** In your groups please think of an example of when you may have **'jumped to conclusions'.**
  Hand out Flipchart Sheet 3 (one sheet per group) and pens.
  If you could spend a few minutes discussing a couple of examples in your group, and for one person to be prepared to feedback to the group as a whole.
- **Discussion:** Facilitate the clients feeding back to the group, develop an enquiring manner and ask the clients if there are any other ways of seeing the situation. Seek out their alternative thoughts.
- **Explain:** Advise group that we are more likely to use or believe this type of thinking when we are feeling depressed, anxious, angry or frustrated. This type of thinking then fuels our feelings and behaviour.

Thinking Choices – Dealing with Hot Thoughts

Resources

- Sheet 4 – Traffic Light Poster

- **Explain:** As we discussed and started doing in relation to your examples from the exercise, there is often little or no evidence for the thinking errors that we may have made, there may well be an alternative way of looking at the situation.

What to Ask Yourself When You 'Jump to Conclusions'

1. What evidence do I have?
2. Am I assuming that I know what the other person is thinking? If so how?
3. Am I overestimating the likelihood of an event occurring?

Show flip-chart – Traffic light diagram

- **Explain:**

"STOP – THINK – CHOOSE!"

"Red = STOP when you have strong feelings, thoughts or automatic behaviour

Amber= THINK, ask yourself: "What am I thinking?
Are there any other ways of seeing this situation?
Can I think of alternative thoughts?"

Green = CHOOSE which thought seems best? Which behaviour seems best?"
If time permits question the group on their understanding.

Stage 6
5 Minutes

Group Summary and Evaluation

Resources

- Evaluation forms
- Pencils
- Handouts ('Jumping to Conclusions')

- **Summarise the group:** Let's summarise what we've discussed today.
- Ask group members to summarise the key points of today's group. Say: 'What do you think are the important things that have come up during our discussions today?' 'What ideas do you think you might use in the future?' You could write responses on the flipchart/whiteboard. Reflect back participants' responses. Open up the discussion by asking whether others have the same opinion, or whether they think differently.
- **Group members identify personal learning:** Go round the room quickly and ask participants to share the most important thing they learned from today's group. Say: 'Take a few moments to think about what you have personally taken from today's group. Then we'd like each person to share with the group at least one thing you've learned from today that you can use in the week ahead. Who would like to start?' Make a point of listening to each person as they share, make eye contact, encourage with smiling/nodding, clarify if necessary and thank them.
- If people are interested in focusing more on their thoughts, they could be encouraged to keep a thought diary over the next week. This could be for their personal use or to discuss in one-to-one sessions.
- **Close the group:** Close by affirming members for coming, working hard in the group and expressing hope that they will find the group useful.

Post-Group
15 Minutes

Staff Evaluation

Facilitators meet and discuss the group dynamics and reflect on their own practice.

Appendix 3.2: Client handout
STOP – THINK – CHOOSE!

RED: STOP when you have strong thoughts, feelings or automatic behaviour.

AMBER: THINK, ask yourself: what am I thinking? Are there any other ways of seeing this situation. Can I think of alternative thoughts?

GREEN: CHOOSE, which thought seems best? Which behaviour seems best?

Thinking Choices

'Jumping to Conclusions'

Why Is Thinking Important?

- We spend a lot of our time trying to change our behaviour and understanding our feelings but less time focusing on our thoughts. Often our thoughts are automatic.
- However thinking is important because our thoughts determine how we feel and how we behave.

Thoughts
↓
Feelings
↓
Behaviour

- One way to change our behaviour and feel better about ourselves is to challenge our thoughts.
- This does not just mean thinking positively, it means being aware that our thinking can be biased.
- Interestingly we are more likely to experience thinking biases when we are depressed, anxious, angry or stressed.

We all use certain types of thinking biases – these can be best understood as habits. Thinking habits fall into these six main groups:

1. 'The Inner Bully'
2. 'Thinking In Extremes'
3. 'Blowing Things out of Proportion'
4. 'Negative Glasses'
5. 'Jumping to Conclusions'
6. 'Over-generalising'

Are You 'Jumping to Conclusions'?

When you 'jump to conclusions' you make a negative interpretation even though there are no facts to support this. There are two main ways of doing this:

1. MIND READING: You decide that someone is reacting negatively to you or you know what someone is thinking without checking this out.
2. FORTUNE-TELLING: You anticipate that things will turn out badly and you feel convinced that your prediction is an established fact.

What to Ask Yourself When You 'Jump to Conclusions'

1. 'What evidence do I have?'
2. 'Am I assuming that I know what the other person is thinking? If so how?'
3. 'Am I overestimating the likelihood of an event occurring?'

Reproduced with permission from the National Treatment Agency's Psychosocial Interventions Resource Library, www.nta.nhs.uk

Chapter 4

Enhancing Motivation to Change

The treatment settings we work in usually require us to acquire lots of information from new clients. However, the question arises when this should be undertaken. Clients will generally have given an account of their history numerous times to many different professionals. You should be clear about what new information is now required and explain this to the client. Facing a barrage of questions early on can be disconcerting for clients, leaving them feeling misunderstood and perhaps leading them to decide not to return. Therefore, it is important to balance the need to gather information against making the client feel heard and understood whilst building components for change. Chapter 5 outlines a framework for gathering assessment information, whilst this chapter outlines a motivational communication style that can be used not only in the assessment session, but also in subsequent sessions.

Our primary concern in this chapter is how to create a positive therapeutic environment, whereby motivation can be enhanced and conditions for engaging in CBT are maximised. We show how this can be done by drawing on the stance and some of the techniques of motivational interviewing (MI) (Miller & Rollnick, 2002) when working within a CBT framework. MI is a counselling style that offers some extremely useful therapist skills that will help build the therapeutic relationship and enhance motivation for change. Note that this chapter does not aim to give an overview of MI, nor does it suggest that MI is CBT. Rather, it highlights what we have found useful to draw on from MI when using a CBT approach for substance use problems. For a comprehensive understanding of MI, readers are

Applied Cognitive and Behavioural Approaches to the Treatment of Addiction: A Practical Treatment Guide By Luke Mitcheson, Jenny Maslin, Tim Meynen, Tamara Morrison, Robert Hill and Shamil Wanigaratne

referred to Miller & Rollnick's *Motivational Interviewing: Preparing People to Change Addictive Behaviour* (2002).

Specifically this chapter looks at:

1. How to establish a rapport with clients using basic counselling skills in order to achieve a therapeutic alliance.
2. How to use ideas from MI and CBT to enhance motivation for change and recovery.

Why spend time enhancing motivation to change?

Motivation is not a fixed concept. It increases or decreases as a function of shifting personal, cognitive, behavioural and environmental determinants (Bandura, 1986). Thus, it is possible that a client's motivation may fluctuate throughout the course of treatment or from one meeting to the next, or even during a single meeting. If this occurs, remember that motivation is not static, consciously owned and controlled by the client, but an evolving interaction between therapist, client and the outside world.

One way of beginning to understand motivation is to understand something about the nature of ambivalence. Ambivalence occurs when one is consciously aware of conflict in one's emotions or thoughts. Ambivalence in the context of important life decisions should not be viewed as pathological; indeed, it is only when ambivalence is the norm or a default response that it may be indicative of difficulties. Rather, ambivalence is often a common precursor to change, including changing substance use, and is normal for all of us. Faced with change people will have conflicting motivations. There may be lots of good reasons *for* change, but equally there may be many good reasons *against* change. So, for example, a client may want to reduce his cocaine use because it is causing problems at work, yet at the same time want to continue using in order to maintain his identity, which is linked to a social life that revolves around drug use in clubs and bars. In this example, it may well be fear of change or lack of confidence in being able to change that lies behind the argument against change.

Miller (1983, 1985) proposed a model of motivation in the early 1980s which has been influential in working with people who have substance use problems. The foundation of Miller's original formulation (1983) of MI is the belief in the 'individual's inherent wisdom and ability to choose the healthful path given sufficient support'. The importance of Miller's work partly lies in the way in which he helped to change the discourse on addiction away from conversations about the client being in denial to one about the client's abilities and desires for change.

Rollnick & Miller (1995) define MI as a 'directive client-centred counselling style for eliciting behaviour change by helping clients to explore and resolve ambivalence'. Three key concepts in MI are that: (i) client motivation is critical for change; (ii) motivation is a dynamic rather than a static trait; and (iii) motivation is influenced by external factors, including the therapist's behaviour. MI is directive in that it facilitates the expression, clarification and resolution of any ambivalence that may prevent the client from making a decision or commitment to change. Confrontation is the implicit goal of MI, but confrontation is not direct because this increases resistance to change. Instead, MI attempts to elicit the reasons for change from the client rather than attempting to persuade him or her that change is necessary (Miller & Rollnick, 2002; Tober & Raistrick, 2007).

Developing a therapeutic alliance to enhance motivation

As outlined in Chapter 3, developing a therapeutic alliance with clients requires establishing both a therapeutic bond and collaborative agreement on the work needed. CBT emphasises collaboration and active participation. Therapy should be viewed as teamwork with joint decision-making about what to work on in each session and what should be done between sessions. Connecting with your clients and gaining their trust is essential. Without it, dropout rates and resistance to change will be high. Whilst building an alliance, you will also be gathering information about your clients, which is an integral part of assessment and formulation.

Beck *et al.* stress the importance of the therapeutic relationship, noting that 'The most brilliantly conceived interventions will be reduced in effectiveness if the patient is not engaged in the process of treatment' (Beck *et al.*, 1993, p. 54). They go on to note a number of reasons why there might be hostility between client and therapist at the beginning of therapy:

1. Clients do not always enter treatment voluntarily.
2. Understandably, anyone would be reticent about opening up to a stranger until feeling more able to trust that person and more confident that this person knows what he or she is doing.
3. Clients may find it difficult to believe that the therapist really cares about their problems, particularly when their life circumstances are markedly different.

It is essential, therefore, to establish rapport quickly in order to start building a therapeutic alliance and maximise client engagement with therapy. Beck (1995) outlines the basic ingredients necessary in any counselling situation: warmth; empathy; caring; genuine regard; and competence. Clarifying the process of CBT and the CBT model (discussed more fully in Chapter 5) is also critical here. This should be done by speaking directly, simply and with minimal jargon. The issue of confidentiality should be discussed from the very start, spelling out its nature and limits according to the requirements of your service. Clients often view the therapeutic space as wholly private and inviolable, and although they may find the limits to confidentiality difficult to hear they will appreciate knowing this.

Using a motivational communication style within CBT

The skill required when talking to clients about the why, how, what and when of behaviour change is about structuring a conversation in a useful way which encourages the client to take as much of the lead as possible in order to start to consider change, which could lead to recovery. Rollnick *et al.* (2008) refer to this as a 'guiding style' as opposed to an exclusively 'directing' (taking charge) or 'following' (going along with) style. This can be achieved by focusing on the four core counselling skills that lie at the heart of MI: (i) asking open questions; (ii) affirming your client's position; (iii) listening reflectively; and (iv) summarising. These skills are also part of the basic principles that underlie CBT (Beck, 1995). Using these skills as a guiding style in your interactions means you are more likely to facilitate motivation to change and foster a therapeutic environment that maximises the success of the treatment intervention.

Asking open questions

Encourage your clients to talk and think aloud in sessions so they can paint a picture while you listen carefully. In doing this you are more likely to have a conversation with the client as opposed to a question-and-answer session and get a clearer picture of the client's 'here and now' problems.

If you are meeting a client who has already been through a formal assessment process for the first time, you should use this meeting to begin developing a therapeutic alliance, rather than just reviewing the assessment. This is particularly important if the client has already been extensively assessed, for example if he is undergoing detoxification as an inpatient. A typical open question is: 'Can you tell me a little more about what brought you here?' Rollnick *et al.* (1999) suggest asking a non-threatening, non-challenging open question about your new client's typical day, such as:

> I realise I don't know a lot about you and the kind of life you lead. Perhaps we can spend a few minutes with you telling me about a typical day in your life from beginning to end. If you like, as you go along, you can tell me where your use of substances fits in.

Alternatively, you could ask about your client's thoughts and feelings about accessing treatment, including asking about expectations, goals, doubts and concerns.

Affirming your client's position

Your therapeutic relationship will be hindered if accusatory or judgemental comments are made. Your tone should reflect curiosity and you should avoid direct confrontation. Few clients start treatment completely ready, willing and able to begin the difficult process of addressing their substance use. In spite of the problems that substance use may be causing in their lives, there will simultaneously be aspects of using that are valued and have either positive or negative reinforcing qualities and are therefore difficult to give up. It is important not to label or judge clients. Instead, empathising with the dilemmas and difficulties your clients tell you about (their ambivalence) with responses such as 'That feels like quite a struggle' will help develop an atmosphere of trust and understanding.

Changing substance use patterns can be hard work and requires courage. This should be acknowledged, along with the realities of the sometimes faltering process of therapeutic change. This may help to counteract any beliefs that the client holds about accepting treatment being a sign of weakness and incompetence. Establishing this notion from the start will help clients get through times of discomfort.

Listening carefully and reflectively

A clear understanding of your clients' experience and not just their drug-using habits is an essential part of CBT. To achieve this you must listen carefully. Listening is an active process which communicates that you are interested in what your clients are saying and want to work with them to achieve change. Not listening carefully can result in your clients feeling misunderstood, rejected, sceptical about treatment, reluctant to talk about what is going on and perhaps disengaging. Reflecting back what your client has said, in a short summary, is a way of demonstrating that you have been listening.

When clients are ambivalent about making change you will usually meet some resistance from them in the form of arguments for things staying as they are. Reflecting this ambivalence communicates empathy, opens up areas of discussion that clients might otherwise conceal and stops you falling into the trap of arguing for change while your client argues against it. Reflecting back any expression of a commitment to make changes to substance use enhances motivation and also helps to set goals for treatment. CBT is a collaborative process and this cannot be achieved without a clear understanding of your clients' experience.

Summarising

Summarising is a key part of both MI and CBT. It shows that you have been listening, provides an opportunity to check that nothing has been missed, allows you to emphasise key points from the conversation and enables you to move on. In CBT there are three types of summary:

1. A *brief* summary when a section of a session has been completed so there is a clear understanding of what you have just done and what you will do next, e.g. 'So, we've just identified some short-term treatment goals. Is it OK if we talk now about something you can do before the next session to start working towards one of these goals?'
2. A *concise* summary of the content of what the client has talked about, in his own words, to clarify that you have been listening and understood. This also provides an opportunity to demonstrate the CBT model.
3. A *final* summary at the end of the session to clarify the major points covered and as an opportunity to instil hope for change and recovery.

Techniques to Enhance Commitment to Treatment

There are several established techniques common to MI and CBT that will enhance therapeutic alliance and commitment to treatment.

Agenda-setting

In CBT it is common to set an agenda at the start of each session (see Chapter 3). The agenda should be explicitly set in collaboration with the client. You might start by saying: 'Now, let's set an agenda. What do you want to put on the agenda to get help with today?' You will also have items carried forward from the previous session and/or a review of the client's homework. The reason for this is to focus the session clearly on the client's needs within the context of CBT treatment. Once the agenda is set you should ask clients what they want to start with. If there are too many agenda items, you can prioritise them in collaboration with the client, agreeing how much time to spend on each one or agreeing what to carry forward to the next week. There may be times when it is necessary to deviate from the agenda, for example if it is clear that more time needs to be spent discussing a particular item. In this case, you should seek your client's agreement.

Monitoring readiness to change

It is important to understand how ready, willing and able your clients feel to change their substance use. Change begins with motivation. Without it 'how to' interventions are unlikely to succeed. If you focus prematurely on the nuts and bolts of what clients need to do to change their substance use, you will more than likely meet resistance. Monitoring clients' readiness to change is thus essential.

Readiness to change is a product of how *important* change is perceived to be and how *confident* someone feels about making change. This can be assessed directly using the 'Importance/Confidence Ruler' (see Appendix 4.1). Often clients have mixed feelings about the value of change (importance), but say they could achieve this fairly easily (confidence). Other clients may feel that change is very important, but lack confidence about achieving this because of failed attempts in the past. It is best to ask your client directly about these. This can be done by asking something like: 'I'm not really sure exactly how you feel about cutting down your drinking or using. Can you help me by answering two simple questions and then we can see where to go from here?'

Use the Importance/Confidence Ruler to locate your client along these two dimensions, asking: 'On a scale of 0 to 10, with 0 being "not important" and 10 being "very important", how important is it right now for you to change your use of heroin? On the same scale of 0 to 10 with 0 being "not confident" and 10 being "completely confident" how confident are you that if you did decide to change your use of heroin, you would succeed?'

If the client is using more than one drug problematically, you should repeat this for each drug. You should also explain the reason for wanting to know about these things. For example, helping clients with strategies for change even when they feel it is important will not lead to change if they have no confidence in their ability to implement these strategies.

Once you have established where your client is on the scale, there are other questions you can ask that help to elicit further self-motivational statements to change (see below). For example: 'You gave yourself a score of 6. So it's fairly important for you to change your drinking. How could you move up from 6 to 8'? Or 'You've rated your confidence to change at 5, how have you managed to get to 5 and not 1?' Remember that 'how' questions are always more useful than 'why' questions because they recognise the client's own work.

If importance is rated as low, you might spend some time looking at the advantages and disadvantages of change (see below). If confidence is rated as low, you might spend time reviewing your client's past efforts to change and building his or her self-efficacy (see below).

Examining the advantages and disadvantages of using substances

Examining the advantages and disadvantages (the pros and cons) of using is a useful technique if your client is ambivalent about change. Motivation for change is partly dependent on the client's perception of the balance of positive and negative outcomes of using. The following exercise can be a helpful means of drawing out this discrepancy.

Begin with a blank 'Advantages/Disadvantages Analysis' worksheet (see Appendix 4.2). You could introduce this exercise in the following way: 'We've talked about what's good and not so good about your current substance use. Could we summarise that discussion by writing down what you've said?' Start by asking about the advantages or 'good things' about using/drinking in the short term and list the pros and cons of using in the appropriate cells of the matrix. Note that if your client has recently stopped using/drinking and intends remaining abstinent, then you should spend less time focusing on the advantages of using as this may be a counterproductive. At a later stage in CBT it may be important for clients to articulate what the positive qualities of using are or have been, so that they are not caught unawares, particularly if they experience strong periods of craving.

The value of completing the 'Advantages/Disadvantages Analysis' is that it:

- Provides an objective and accurate view of the client's substance use that can be examined in an objective and rational fashion by both client and therapist.
- Helps identify the advantages of use in order to find other strategies for achieving the same advantages.
- Allows you to draw out both sides of the ambivalence, which can be reflected back to the client to build motivation.
- Helps identify situations in which substance use is likely to occur.
- Helps identify beliefs about the advantages of substance use that may need to be modified before change can take place. For example, your client might strongly believe that having a drink is the only way to relax. If this belief is rigidly held, then it will be very difficult to stop drinking. Identifying and modifying beliefs is the focus of Chapter 8, which also introduces the Socratic method (Beck *et al.*, 1979), a technique commonly used in CBT to think through the advantages and disadvantages of a particular belief or behaviour.

Examining the disadvantages and advantages of changing substance use

Examining the disadvantages and advantages of substance use, using the 'Decisional Balance' worksheet (see Appendix 4.3) is another useful technique when clients are ambivalent about change. Motivation for change is partly dependent on any perceived discrepancy between present behaviour and important goals or values. One way of introducing the exercise is as a continuation of the ongoing discussion about change, e.g. 'We've looked at what's good and not so good about your current substance use. What do you think about looking at what you might lose or gain in changing your use?' Start by asking the client about the short-term disadvantages of change and then list the pros and cons of change in the appropriate cells of the matrix.

The value of completing the 'Decisional Balance' worksheet is that it:

- Builds on motivation to change because it starts to highlight the perceived discrepancy between current behaviour and client's goals, over both the short and long term.
- Brings out possible self-motivational statements that will be helpful in making change, which is why the discussion should start with the disadvantages of change and end with the advantages.
- Helps start to clarify goals for treatment.
- Helps identify beliefs about substance use and the possibility for change that may need to be modified to facilitate change. For example, clients might believe that if they stop drinking, they will have no friends to spend time with. If this belief is rigidly held, it will be very difficult to stop drinking. Identifying and modifying beliefs is the focus of Chapter 8.

Reviewing clients' past efforts to change

It may be that your clients lack confidence in their ability to change because past attempts were not maintained. Sometimes clients may have had a significant period of positive change and then relapsed. This can result in a biased view of the experience as a complete failure. Open conversations with your clients about previous changes or periods of abstinence will remind them of perhaps forgotten or dismissed strengths and resources. This will also help to identify any thinking errors or cognitive distortions your clients have about their ability to change or maintain this. The utility and accuracy of these distortions can be determined by carefully reviewing the evidence using the CBT techniques described in Chapter 9.

Building self-efficacy

Self-efficacy can be understood as an individual's capacity to cope with a given task or situation. Often clients with substance use problems come into treatment with low self-efficacy and this will be noticeable if they score low on the 'confidence to change' scale. If self-efficacy is low, then there are a number of techniques that can be used to help enhance it:

1. Through conversations. Remind clients of their strengths and competence whenever you get the opportunity. This shows you have respect for their individual talents and assets and increases their sense of self-efficacy. A person's belief in the possibility of change is an important motivator. Your client is responsible for choosing to carry out change, not you. However, the therapist's belief in the person's ability to change can become a self-fulfilling prophecy. You should start supporting your client's self-efficacy from your first meeting by being clear about the purpose and goals of treatment. A long-term goal of CBT is to empower clients by increasing their sense of self-efficacy and teaching them to become their own best therapist. Conversations to build

self-efficacy can also focus on reviewing previous efforts to change and high-lighting successes/challenging unhelpful beliefs about ability to change. It is also valuable to look forward to a time when change has been successful, highlighting the resources the client has to make this change and challenging unhelpful beliefs about his ability to achieve it.

2. By the use of 'behavioural experiments' (see Chapter 10). Basically, behavioural experiments are used to test the validity of clients' beliefs. These beliefs might be about what drugs or alcohol do for them, but could also be about your clients' ability to make and sustain changes to their substance use. Testing one's ability to make a behavioural change leads to cognitive change and an increase in new skills, which leads to an increase in self-efficacy.

Positive self-statements

During conversations with your client you should listen for any positive self-statements your client makes. These could be about things that are going well, things that have been achieved or your client's commitment to change. Whenever you hear a positive self-statement you should reflect this back, affirming and reinforcing what you have just heard. In addition to using the techniques described above to elicit positive self-statements, you could ask the client to complete a positive self-statement log. This is a list of positive things that the client is doing or deserves credit for. This helps balance out any negative cognitive bias and builds self-efficacy for change.

Asking for feedback at the end of the session

The final part of any CBT session should focus on eliciting feedback from the client and should be done from the first session. You should introduce this by saying: 'At the end of each session, I'm going to ask for feedback about how you felt the session went' and then explaining why you are doing this. Asking for feedback reinforces the collaborative nature of CBT, ensures there is an opportunity to clear up any misunderstandings that may have arisen and highlights key messages to take home. It also enhances rapport and ensures the client feels listened to and positive about the session. At the end of the session you should ask your client two things to elicit feedback: (i) 'Was there anything about the session that bothered you?' and (ii) 'Was there was anything important in the session that stood out for you?' It is important not to become defensive if the client gives you negative feedback. Instead, take this as an opportunity to reflect on your practice.

Summary

This chapter has described a number of therapeutic skills that can help to enhance a therapeutic alliance and motivation for change. You should expect your client's motivation to fluctuate throughout the course of treatment. If it does, it will be useful to refer to the skills described in this chapter. If your client appears to be resisting the idea of change, then do not directly oppose this resistance. Avoid arguing for change as this has the effect of entrenching the client more deeply in his position. Instead, invite new perspectives rather than propose them. In fact, if your client does become resistant, this is a sign for you to respond differently. Do not forget that your client is the primary source for finding answers and solutions.

Chapter 5 looks at the process of assessment and introducing your client to the CBT model.

Appendix 4.1: Importance/Confidence Ruler (adapted from Rollnick, Butler & Stott, 1997)

Importance/confidence ruler

On a scale of 0–10, 0 being not at all important and 10 being very important, how important is it right now for you to change your use of _____?

Importance: 0   1   2   3   4   5   6   7   8   9   10

On a scale of 0–10, 0 being not at all confident and 10 being very confident, if you did decide to change, how confident are you that you would succeed?

Confidence: 0   1   2   3   4   5   6   7   8   9   10

Appendix 4.2: Advantages/disadvantages analysis worksheet

	Advantages of using/ drinking	*Disadvantages of using/ drinking*
Short-term		
Long term		

Appendix 4.3: Decisional balance worksheet

	Disadvantages of Change	*Advantages of Change*
Short-term		
Long-term		

Chapter 5

Assessment and Introducing CBT to Clients

Assessment is a strategic enterprise. In this chapter we describe how to do an assessment in a way that will enable you to understand drug and alcohol use within a CBT framework by developing a *situation*-level formulation. We explain how the way you ask and make sense of this information introduces your clients to CBT and to the idea of formulation, and begins to involve them in this process.

Why do an assessment?

The main aims of a CBT assessment for substance use problems are:

1. To develop a specific cognitive/behavioural situation-level formulation of your client's current substance use problems and how these problems are maintained.
2. To begin to socialise the client to the structure of CBT.
3. To elicit information to help understand past vulnerabilities and historical development of the substance use.
4. To develop a shared understanding of goals for treatment.
5. To continue the process of developing a therapeutic alliance with your client.
6. To continue to enhance motivation for change and recovery.

Applied Cognitive and Behavioural Approaches to the Treatment of Addiction: A Practical Treatment Guide By Luke Mitcheson, Jenny Maslin, Tim Meynen, Tamara Morrison, Robert Hill and Shamil Wanigaratne
Copyright © 2010 John Wiley & Sons, Ltd.

Although at this stage you are specifically trying to gather information that will help you formulate your client's problems, assessment should not be thought of as a discrete stage, separate from building motivation to change or from formulation. As you may have discovered, adopting an empathic, non-confrontational, reflective listening style is more likely to foster good therapeutic interactions resulting in the installation of hope and self-efficacy in clients (see Chapter 4). The assessment stage also provides an opportunity to give some simple, structured advice (e.g. harm reduction education and advice about safer drug and alcohol use). Finally, as noted in Chapter 3, assessment is not simply a way of gathering information, but a goal-oriented activity for developing a CBT formulation.

General comprehensive assessment

If you work in a drug or alcohol treatment setting, you will probably have a general, comprehensive assessment tool for any new clients requiring treatment. Alternatively, some assessment information may be available to you, but may not be specific to substance use. Generally, a comprehensive assessment should capture the following information:

1. The client's developmental history (e.g. childhood/adolescent experiences, family atmosphere and cultural influences).
2. Family history (e.g. family relationships with client and family experience of substance use problems).
3. Educational and occupational history.
4. Relationship history (e.g. key relationships in life, past and present).
5. Current life circumstances (e.g. social situation, socialising, hobbies/ interests).
6. Forensic history, particularly its relationship to substance use.
7. Drinking and drug use career, including age first started, times of increase/ decrease and periods of stable or problematic use and abstinence.
8. Treatment episodes for drug and alcohol problems.
9. Mental health problems, including historical review of onset, pattern and how these might relate to substance use.
10. Physical health problems, including how these relate to substance use.
11. Current substance use pattern, including what substances the client is using, when he uses (how many days a week, how using is spaced throughout the day), when he does not use and why, how much he uses, how much he spends on using, routes of use (oral, injection, smoking, etc.), any recent changes in use pattern, what the triggers are for using (e.g. people, places or things), whether he uses alone or with others, and if so with whom, and his usual source of supply. If your client is a poly-drug user, then this information should be sought for each drug as the pattern and reasons for use of each substance may vary.
12. Problems associated with current substance use (e.g. mental health issues, financial problems, relationships, physical health, legal/forensic issues, social problems, work, behaviour).

13. Your assessment should include a risk assessment to determine any risk to your client or others around him. There should be a specific screening tool for assessing risk to children. If risk assessment is to be really helpful for everyone involved, it needs to be integrated into care planning procedures. Risk assessment is therefore no different from treatment planning in that it is an evolving process, with new information being added or qualified the more you get to know your client.
14. Client's goals.
15. Client's reason for seeking treatment at this time, insight into the difficulties substance use is causing and motivation to make changes.

Eliciting information to enable a cognitive and behavioural understanding of substance use

If your client has already been seen by someone for a general assessment, you should acknowledge this and explain that you need to understand this information within a CBT framework. You should review information already gathered to inform your CBT assessment and avoid repeating unnecessary questions.

From a CBT perspective you are aiming to understand three key things:

1. What is the current substance use problem?
2. How is the substance use problem maintained?
3. How did the problem develop?

The information you collect at assessment forms the basis for your unique formulation or understanding of the client's substance use. Formulation will help you develop a treatment plan tailored to your client's use. This can be undertaken at two levels:

1. *Case*-level formulation (also known as developmental or longitudinal formulation). This is a framework for understanding your client's difficulties from a developmental perspective and is discussed in detail in Chapter 6.
2. *Situation*-level formulation (also called maintenance or cross-sectional formulation). This level of formulation examines a current problem situation (e.g. substance use) and develops hypotheses about the cognitive, emotional, physical sensations and behavioural mechanisms underpinning and explaining the situation. This type of formulation can be developed in your first meetings with your client and is described below.

Socialising your client to CBT

During your initial meetings with the client you will be gathering assessment information, but you will also need to introduce (socialise) your client to the CBT model. It is always useful to ask clients what they understand about CBT and use what they tell you as a way of starting a conversation about what CBT is, its utility for substance use problems and why it focuses on thoughts, feelings and behaviours.

A commonly used way of explaining the CBT model is to use the 'Coffee Shop Scenario'. To explain it, draw three columns on a sheet of paper headed 'Thoughts', 'Feelings' and 'Behaviour'. Write these down as you talk your client through the scenario, which goes as follows:

Therapist: Imagine that you are in a coffee shop waiting for a friend to arrive. She is 15 minutes late and a thought goes through your mind, 'Oh no, she's late because she's been in an accident'. How would that make you feel?

Client: I'd feel really worried, panicky.

Therapist: And if that thought went through your mind that she'd had an accident and you felt worried, what would you do?

Client: I'd ring her mobile and try to get in touch with her.

Therapist: Imagine the same scenario. You are in a coffee shop waiting for a friend to arrive. She is 15 minutes late and a different thought goes through your mind: 'Oh no, she's not coming because she hates me'. How would that make you feel?

Client: I'd feel upset, hurt.

Therapist: And if that thought went through your mind that she hated you and you felt upset and hurt, what would you do?

Client: I'd leave the coffee shop and go home.

Therapist: Imagine the same scenario one more time. You are in a coffee shop waiting for a friend to arrive. She is 15 minutes late and a different thought goes through your mind: 'What's she like, she's never on time, in fact she's usually always half an hour late, so I've got a little longer to wait'. How would that make you feel?

Client: Perhaps a bit irritated, but amused.

Therapist: And if that thought went through your mind that she's always late and you felt like that, what would you do?

Client: I'd order another coffee and maybe look around for something to read.

The point of going through this scenario is to show your client that it is 'the thought that counts'. In any one situation there are always many different ways to react and our reaction will depend on how we perceive the situation. That is why it is critical to identify our thoughts if we want to make sense of our behaviour. This is the core of a cognitive behavioural model. It is important to introduce at the same time another component: our physical sensations. So, for example, if we feel anxious, we may notice that our heart is racing, our stomach churning, our muscles tensing, etc. The interaction between thoughts and bodily sensations is particularly important when dealing with clients who have concomitant substance use problems and anxiety or panic-related symptoms.

Assessing current substance use problems

You will want to understand not only your clients' current substance use patterns but also what other current difficulties they are experiencing (mental health, financial, relationships, physical health, forensic, social, occupational or behavioural) and how these problems are related to substance use. It is recommended that the more structured question-and-answer assessment should be preceded and followed by open discussions using a motivational communication style. This format is termed a 'Motivational Assessment Sandwich' (Martino *et al.*, 2006).

Thus, an assessment session starts with broad, open questions to help build the therapeutic alliance and understand the problems from the client's perspective. Questions such as 'Can you tell me about what brought you here?' 'Can you tell me about what difficulties you are facing at the moment?' can be helpful. A more structured assessment then follows. The session should end with open questions to understand your client's readiness to make change in terms of its perceived importance to him. Chapter 4 highlighted one way of doing this through the use of the Importance/Confidence Ruler.

Assessing how substance use problems are maintained

Given the aim of understanding your clients' substance use from a CBT perspective, it is important to have a specific cognitive/behavioural profile to help you understand your clients' thoughts, emotions, physical sensations and behaviours around use. The easiest way to build a cognitive/behavioural profile of your clients' use is to ask specifically about the last time they used substances. One way of doing this is to use Padesky & Mooney's (1990) five-part generic cognitive model (see Figure 1.1 and Appendix 5.1). This provides a useful framework for recording the information in a situation-level formulation. This formulation can then be shared with the client to explain the CBT model in more detail, specifically in relation to his or her own situation. The five-part generic cognitive model focuses on five aspects of current life experience: context or situation, thoughts, moods, physical sensations and behaviour.

You can use the following stages in order to use this model most effectively:

Stage 1:   Show your client a blank Padesky & Mooney five-part diagram (see Appendix 5.1) and explain the model in a general way. For example, you could say: 'We are all affected by our current environment (e.g. family, stress, money worries, friendships) and our past environment (e.g. traumatic events, losses). In addition we all have four aspects of ourselves that make up who we are – our thoughts, moods, physical or biological self and behaviours. There are lines between these four aspects as each of these parts is connected to and impact on the others. They all sit inside the environment and react with it as well'.

Stage 2:   Use an everyday example to explain further how all aspects of the model are linked. You could use the 'Coffee Shop Scenario' to do this. Another way of explaining the CBT model is to ask your client: 'Imagine you are in bed in the middle of the night and you are alone. You are woken by a crash. How could you interpret the situation? If you decide "it's a burglar", how would you feel? What would you do? If you decide "the cat has knocked something over", how would you feel? What would you do?'

Stage 3:   Once the client is clear about the model, say that you are now going to use a situation from his own experience to demonstrate how the model can be used to construct an individual formulation. Ask your client specifically about the last time he used substances. Write down his experiences in each area using your client's own words.

Typical questions to ask are:

- 'Tell me about the last time you used drugs/alcohol?'
- Context or situation questions: 'Where were you? Who were you with? When was this?'
- Thoughts questions: 'What was going through your mind in this situation? What thoughts about drinking/using were going through your mind?'
- Mood questions: 'When you were thinking this way, how were you feeling?'
- Physical sensations questions: 'Did you experience any physical sensations in your body while thinking and feeling this way?'
- Behaviour questions 'When you were thinking and feeling this way, what did you do then?'

You should also ask your client about his or her thoughts and feelings after using drugs or drinking. Often clients think and feel very negatively about themselves and it is important to record how these negative thoughts and feelings can reinforce future use. This will help clarify the exact function substance use serves in your client's life. For example, problem users may use substances to cope with certain difficulties in their lives. Through the repeated experience of short-term benefit, using can become the preferred way of coping, especially in the absence of other skills. Consequently, even negative coping strategies are likely to be reinstated if other more positive coping strategies have not been put in their place.

Stage 4:   Share this situation formulation with the client, highlighting how the different aspects of the model link up. Explain that a small positive change in one area can lead to positive changes in other areas.

Now we want to introduce you to a second character – Sally – and show you how her experience might be formulated in the way we have described above.

Sally

Sally is 33 years old and has an 18-year history of drinking. She drank heavily throughout her teenage years, particularly when socialising with friends. This pattern of behaviour continued in her adult years and she noticed that she drank more than her friends and sometimes embarrassed herself because of things she said and did. She started to drink much more heavily and on a daily basis over the past year. She presented to your clinic saying she drinks four or five cans of strong lager on most days. She says she feels depressed most of the time and finds it difficult to leave the house without drinking first because she feels so anxious about going out. At her last appointment with you she described an incident in the week when she drank in order to help herself leave the house to visit her sister.

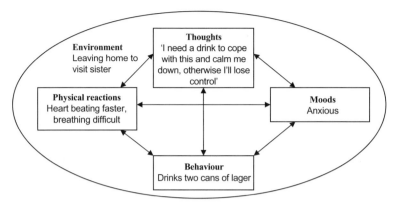

Figure 5.1   Situation-level Formulation for Sally

Thinking about Sally's situation (Figure 5.1) in relation to the five-part model (see Figure 1.1) the questioning above would have revealed that recently she had to leave home to visit her sister (context) when she began to feel anxious (mood) and her heart started beating faster and her breathing became more difficult (physical sensations). Going through her mind was the thought 'I need a drink to cope with this and calm me down otherwise I'll lose control' (thoughts). So she had two cans of lager (behaviour). The consequences of Sally's action reinforced her initial belief that she really was unable to leave the house without first having a drink. The process of mapping out Sally's experience within a CBT framework demonstrates that assessment and formulation are not distinct processes. The situation-level formulation using the five-part diagram is used to guide assessment and should be developed at the same time as assessment.

Internal/external triggers that maintain substance use

You can use the information elicited from this conversation about your client's situation-level formulation to start to compile a list of all the internal or external events that can trigger using. These are often referred to as high-risk situations. Internal triggers include particular moods, whether negative (e.g. feeling rejected, worried, etc.) or positive (feeling happy, feeling confident). You may find that your client confuses moods (emotions or feelings) with thoughts. Moods can usually be described in one word (e.g. depressed, guilty, embarrassed, irritated, happy, anxious, proud, humiliated, etc.). It is important to help your client identify the difference. Learning to distinguish moods will help your client choose actions other than substance use, designed to cope with or alleviate those moods. Greenberger & Padesky (1995) in Chapter 4 of their book *Mind over Mood* provide a useful exercise to help make the distinction between moods, situations and thoughts. It may therefore be helpful to refer your clients to this book as part of their socialisation to the CBT model. Once clients are familiar with the distinction between thoughts and feelings, you can help them identify their internal triggers by using the worksheet in Appendix 5.2 (Center for Substance Abuse Treatment, 1999).

External triggers to substance use could include people, places, objects, times and occasions, i.e. factors external to the individual. You can help your clients identify what their external triggers are by using the worksheet in Appendix 5.3 (Center for Substance Abuse Treatment, 1999).

Cognitions that maintain substance use

Throughout assessment and treatment, you will be aiming to identify the thoughts (or beliefs) that your client has about his or her substance use. Within the CBT model these substance-related thoughts (e.g. Sally's thought 'I need a drink in order to cope and calm down, otherwise I'll lose control') play a major role in maintaining problematic use. In their cognitive model of addiction, Beck *et al.* (1993) describe four types of drug-related belief:

1. *Anticipatory beliefs* involving an expectation of reward from using, e.g. 'I'll feel all right once I have a drink'; 'The buzz of crack is great'.
2. *Relief-oriented beliefs*, where the assumption is that use will relieve uncomfortable states, e.g. 'I only get a proper night's sleep if I smoke a joint before going to bed'; 'Heroin eases the crash of crack'.
3. *Facilitative/permission-giving beliefs*, whereby substance use is rationalised as being acceptable, e.g. 'I've tried and I really can't stop'; 'Since I'm feeling so low, it's OK to use'.

Often these beliefs are fairly rigid and generally accepted as true, sometimes without proper reflection or evaluation. These beliefs tend to promote substance use, but the fourth type of belief can help to constrain use and needs to be dealt with slightly differently.

4. *Control beliefs* help to limit substance use by constructing reasons for not using or limiting substance use, e.g. 'I will not use in front of my children'; 'I will only drink after 6 pm'.

At this stage it is important to look out for these thoughts/beliefs about substance use and keep a record of them. They are central to formulating your client's specific problems from within the CBT model. For some clients images of substance use are key in maintaining their use and these should be elicited too. Images can consist of a visual picture of themselves using or of the substance itself, e.g. Sally might see herself looking calmer as she takes the first sip from a can of lager. Good questions to ask to help elicit thoughts/images about substance use include:

*   What was going through your mind just before you used?
*   What were you saying to yourself just before you used?
*   What else?
*   What do you think were the reasons you wanted to use?
*   What images/memories did you have when using came into your mind?
*   Do you ever have pictures in your mind of using? What is happening?

Chapter 7 looks in more detail at the different types of substance-related belief, including control beliefs. Chapters 8 and 9 outline a step-by-step approach to identifying beliefs and images and the basic interventions to evaluate and analyse them in a structured way.

Structured tools to elicit information

As well as the 'Internal and External Triggers' worksheets, there are three tools that can be helpful in gathering information to understand your client's use. The 'Advantages/Disadvantages' worksheet and the 'Decisional Balance' worksheet are discussed in Chapter 4, the third, the 'Drug/Alcohol Cravings Diary', is a simple but powerful tool that clients can learn to use in order to self-monitor more effectively.

Drug/alcohol and cravings diary

If it is difficult for your clients to reflect on the cognitive behavioural aspects of their substance use, you could ask them to keep a diary of drinking, drug use and/or cravings (see Appendix 5.4). Any time clients drink/use or get the urge to, they record the situation (day, time and place), their specific thoughts, their mood, the intensity of any cravings on a scale of 0–100 and their behaviour. These diaries are particularly helpful in generating cognitions related to activating events and substance use. Information from diaries can be transferred to a five-part diagram (Figure 1.1), which can then be shared with your clients to explain further the CBT model, specifically in relation to their own situation.

Ideally, you should ask your clients to complete the diary over at least a week, perhaps between sessions. Even one recorded instance can yield useful information. Sometimes clients do not complete the diaries in spite of agreeing to and it is important to try to find out why. For instance, there might be practical difficulties such as forgetting the rationale for doing it. In this case you could review the rationale (i.e. to help understand their substance use within a CBT framework) and, if necessary, write it down for them. Alternatively, clients may be waiting too long after the event to complete the diary and are then unable to recall exactly what happened. A discussion around memory attrition would be useful here as well as the importance of ensuring that the diary is easily available when needed. Obviously, if you ask your client to complete a diary, you should always remember to allocate some time to reviewing it in your next session.

The development of substance use problems

Once you have a clear picture of your client's current substance use problems you might explore in more depth how these problems developed, particularly if you want to develop a case-level formulation (see Chapter 6). Showing interest in your client's story is helpful in sustaining rapport and engendering a good therapeutic alliance. Questions around the age and circumstances of first use and how use progressed are helpful, such as:

- When did you first start using drugs/drinking?
- What was going on in your life when you first started?
- What did you like about using then?
- How did your using progress?
- How did your thoughts about drinking/using change over time?
- When did you first think that your use might be a problem?
- What happened when you tried to cut down or stop?

This information may have been gathered in previous assessments, but such questions can take on a new power and meaning once a client has been exposed to the CBT way of working.

Goals

Even at this initial stage of assessment you should collaboratively be identifying and clarifying what the client's goals are as a result of treatment. To do this you could ask a question such as 'If treatment is successful and you are looking back, what would be different in your life?' Clients often express goals in emotional terms such as 'I'd like to feel happier/better'. It is important to specify in behavioural terms what they mean by asking, 'If you were happier, what would you be doing?' There may be goals other than cutting down or stopping substance use but still related to it. For example, Paul might say that one of his goals in treatment is to have more money at the end of the week or to be engaging in more activities so he feels less bored. Sally's goal may be to visit her sister once a week without the need to drink before she leaves home.

There are a number of reasons why it is important to set clear goals:

1. To make sure you and your client are both working to the same agenda.
2. To help structure the intervention.
3. To emphasise the possibility of change and recovery.

Whatever goals are set they should be Specific, Measurable, Achievable, Realistic and Time-based (SMART). It is also good practice to review goals throughout therapy as these can change.

Summary

This chapter has focused specifically on assessment and the situation-level formulation. Remember, however, that the process of assessment is multifaceted and includes socialising your client to the CBT model and formulation while continuing to build the therapeutic alliance and your client's motivation for change.

Appendix 5.1: Padesky & Mooney's (1990) Five-part generic cognitive model for situation-level formulation (© 1986 Center for Cognitive Therapy, www.padesky.com)

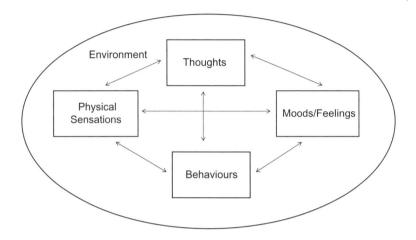

Appendix 5.2: Identifying internal triggers worksheet

Certain moods or emotions can trigger a desire to use substances. Below are lists of common moods/emotions that are associated with substance use. Tick the boxes that apply to you and circle the internal trigger with which you struggle the most.

'Negative Emotions'

☐ Feeling afraid
☐ Feeling ashamed
☐ Feeling criticised
☐ Feeling guilty
☐ Feeling inadequate
☐ Feeling jealous
☐ Feeling overconfident
☐ Feeling _____

☐ Feeling angry
☐ Feeling anxious
☐ Feeling depressed
☐ Feeling hateful
☐ Feeling irritated
☐ Feeling left out
☐ Feeling overwhelmed

'Normal Emotions'

☐ Feeling bored
☐ Feeling frustrated
☐ Feeling lonely
☐ Feeling nervous
☐ Feeling relaxed
☐ Feeling tired

☐ Feeling embarrassed
☐ Feeling insecure
☐ Feeling neglected
☐ Feeling pressured
☐ Feeling sad
☐ Feeling _____

'Positive Emotions'

☐ Feeling celebratory
☐ Feeling excited
☐ Feeling happy
☐ Feeling passionate
☐ Feeling strong

☐ Feeling confident
☐ Feeling exhausted
☐ Feeling 'normal'
☐ Feeling sexually aroused
☐ Feeling _____

Center for Substance Abuse Treatment. Treatment for Stimulant Use Disorders (1999). Treatment Improvement Protocol (TIP) Series 33. DHHS Publication No. (SMA) 99-3296. Rockville, MD: Substance Abuse and Mental Health Services Administration

Appendix 5.3: Identifying external triggers worksheet

There are many external things that can trigger a desire to use substances. Below are lists of people, places, events, objects and activities that can be associated with substance use. Tick the boxes that apply for you and circle the external trigger in each section with which you struggle the most.

People
- ☐ Dealers
- ☐ Co-workers
- ☐ Family members
- ☐ Dates
- ☐ _____
- ☐ Friends
- ☐ Employer
- ☐ Spouse/partner
- ☐ Neighbours

Places
- ☐ Neighbourhoods
- ☐ Pubs/clubs
- ☐ Work place
- ☐ Certain roads
- ☐ Drug storage place
- ☐ High street
- ☐ Friend's home
- ☐ Hotels
- ☐ Concerts
- ☐ Toilets
- ☐ School
- ☐ _____

Events
- ☐ Meeting new people
- ☐ Parties
- ☐ Calls from creditors
- ☐ During work
- ☐ Going out
- ☐ During sex
- ☐ Anniversaries
- ☐ _____
- ☐ Group meetings
- ☐ Pay-day
- ☐ Before work
- ☐ After work
- ☐ Before sex
- ☐ After sex
- ☐ Holidays

Objects
- ☐ Paraphernalia
- ☐ Pornography
- ☐ Television
- ☐ Credit cards
- ☐ _____
- ☐ Magazines
- ☐ Films/DVDs
- ☐ Cash
- ☐ Cash machines

Behaviours and Activities
- ☐ Listening to music
- ☐ Going out to dance/eat
- ☐ Hanging out with friends
- ☐ Driving
- ☐ After paying bills
- ☐ Before/during a date
- ☐ When home alone
- ☐ Dancing
- ☐ After an argument
- ☐ _____

Center for Substance Abuse Treatment. Treatment for Stimulant Use Disorders (1999). Treatment Improvement Protocol (TIP) Series 33. DHHS Publication No. (SMA) 99-3296. Rockville, MD: Substance Abuse and Mental Health Services Administration

Appendix 5.4: Drug/alcohol and cravings diary

Situation Day, time, place	Thoughts What is going through my mind? What am I saying to myself?	Mood How am I feeling?	Intensity of craving 0–100	Behaviour What did I do? Did I use? If I used, what and how much?

Chapter 6

Formulation

In Chapter 5 we looked at the process of assessment, socialisation to the cognitive-behavioural way of working and developing a situation-level formulation. In this chapter we examine the role of formulation within CBT further, integrating all the information gathered in the initial stages of assessment and developing a case-level formulation. Remember that assessment and formulation are not distinct processes, as formulation can be used to guide assessment and should begin to be developed at the same time as assessment, although it may evolve as your client progresses through treatment.

Why undertake a formulation?

There are two main reasons for undertaking a formulation. The first is to understand your clients' difficulties by describing their current substance use problem, exploring how the substance use problem is being maintained (functions of use) and explaining how the substance use problem came about (cause). The second reason is to develop and implement appropriate treatment strategies to help alleviate or solve the client's problems and symptoms as he or she works towards recovery.

Integrating assessment information

Every formulation, developing and evolving from information gathered from the client, is unique, rather like a single case study. Formulations focus on experiences,

Applied Cognitive and Behavioural Approaches to the Treatment of Addiction: A Practical Treatment Guide By Luke Mitcheson, Jenny Maslin, Tim Meynen, Tamara Morrison, Robert Hill and Shamil Wanigaratne
Copyright © 2010 John Wiley & Sons, Ltd.

cognitions, emotions, physical sensations and behaviours specific to each client, which underpins his substance use. The outcome of treatment based on this formulation serves as a test of treatment utility. In other words, if the outcome is poor, then it is possible that the formulation and treatment plan based on the formulation needs to be revised.

As highlighted in Chapter 5, there are two levels of formulation:

1. Formulation at a case level (also known as developmental or longitudinal formulation). This is a framework for understanding your client's difficulties from a developmental perspective and is discussed fully below (adapted from Dudley & Kuyken, 2006).
2. Formulation at a situation level (also called maintenance or cross-sectional formulation). This type of formulation was introduced in Chapter 5 and sits within overall case formulation. Situation formulation examines a current problem situation (e.g. substance use) and develops hypotheses about the thoughts, feelings, physical sensations and behaviours underpinning and explaining that situation by using the Padesky & Mooney (1990) five-part generic cognitive model as a framework for doing so. Used in this way CBT allows you to maintain the focus on current problems without having to understand the whole client or his life.

Working collaboratively to develop formulations

The formulations you construct with clients are your working hypothesis based on the information you have collected. They help you understand the way thoughts, feelings, physical sensations and behaviours underpin and maintain problematic substance use behaviour. They are not static but ever-evolving over the process of treatment as new information is available or becomes clearer – akin to 'fine-tuning'. As formulation is a collaborative process, it is important to stress to clients that they are the experts on their own experiences and that you as the therapist bring to the table training and experience in understanding substance use from a cognitive-behavioural perspective. You should ask regularly for feedback from your clients as to whether they understand the formulation and whether it makes sense to them. If at any time the client either does not accept or understand the formulation, then pause to address this together before continuing. Two useful ways to ensure that you are effectively collaborating are to:

1. Use summaries at the end of your session and, as described in Chapter 3, elicit feedback. In early sessions you should summarise the main points covered during the session and ask for feedback. As the therapeutic alliance develops and clients understand more about CBT, you should ask them to summarise what you have discussed at the end of a session. This rehearsal of session material not only helps you as the therapist to monitor clients' understanding, but also helps them to remember the material later.
2. Make a bridge from the current session to the previous session. You should briefly check your clients' perception and understanding of the previous

session at the start of the current session. Ask clients what was useful about the last session, what was not useful and whether they had any subsequent thoughts since last meeting.

Case formulation – building a developmental perspective

Case-level formulations help clients understand what led to their substance use problems developing. A case-level formulation will also help you as the therapist to understand whether there are any underlying psychological issues that contribute to maintaining substance use problems. It can also help you discover strengths in your clients that will be helpful to draw on when they are making changes to their substance patterns. Beck and colleagues (e.g. Beck *et al.*, 1993; Liese & Franz, 1996) present a comprehensive cognitive model to understand how substance use problems develop and are maintained (see Figure 2.11). As outlined in Chapter 2, their model suggests that early life experiences make lasting impressions on individuals and result in the development of beliefs and dysfunctional assumptions, which become fused with drug-related beliefs and are influential in driving substance use behaviour. This model will be familiar to anyone who knows Beck *et al.*'s (1979) work on depression and is particularly useful for clients who are aware of negative or abusive childhood experiences.

An alternative way of approaching formulation is the longitudinal method proposed by Dudley & Kuyken (2006). Their approach describes the levels and processes of formulation in terms of five Ps: (i) predisposing factors; (ii) precipitating factors; (iii) perpetuating factors; (iv) presenting issues; and (v) protective factors. These factors as applied to Paul (see Chapter 1) are shown in Figure 6.1.

As you can see from Figure 6.1, a good case-level formulation tells a logical story about particular events and/or mood states. Clients will often say that they have no idea or awareness of how they ended up in a particular situation or doing a particular activity. Case-level formulations help to demystify this and so allow clients to identify patterns and commonalities in their behaviour and emotions. This is not always a negative experience. As you can see, Paul has some strengths and resilience and these should always be highlighted and where possible strengthened. In Chapter 13, we talk a little more about these positive qualities, in particular resilience.

Predisposing factors

At this stage of the formulation we are looking at what early family, social, cultural and/or economic life experiences might have contributed to your client's vulnerability to developing substance use problems. Negative experiences in these areas can lead people to develop certain dysfunctional core beliefs about themselves, other people and the world. Beck *et al.* (1993) state that beliefs about the self tend to fall into two categories: (i) 'I am unlovable' (which may be expressed as 'I am unwanted', 'I am rejected', 'I am bad', 'I am uncared for', etc.); and (ii) 'I am helpless' (which may be expressed as 'I am inadequate', 'I am powerless', 'I am inferior', 'I am incompetent', 'I am weak', etc.). So, for example, someone might develop a belief about themselves such as 'I am powerless' as a consequence

Developmental experiences   PREDISPOSING FACTORS
Physical and emotional abuse by family
Withdrawn and socially isolated

Core beliefs
I am unlovable. People will hurt me.

Rules and assumptions or conditional beliefs
If I use drugs then I have friends

Compensatory strategies
Never refuse my drug-using friends

Triggering events   PRECIPITATING FACTORS
Being with drug-using friends
Feeling bored

Maintenance cycles   PERPETUATING FACTORS

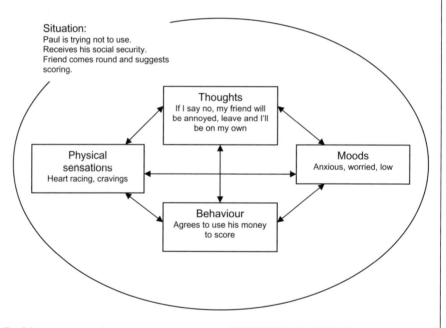

Problems   PRESENTING ISSUES
Financial, boredom
Unable to reduce drug use any further

Resilience and strengths   PROTECTIVE FACTORS
A sister he has always been close to
has already cut down use
Interest in art

Figure 6.1   Illustration of a Case-level Formulation for Paul

of growing up in a hostile, abusive environment. In an attempt not to be overwhelmed by these core beliefs the individual might develop rules, assumptions or conditional beliefs in order to cope. These are often phrased in the style of 'If … then', or start with 'I must' or 'I should'. For example, someone who believes he is helpless may cope by developing a belief such as: 'If I always have people around me, then they can help me'. Unfortunately, such compensatory strategies may keep people trapped in their beliefs (e.g. never attempting anything on their own will reinforce their sense of personal helplessness when faced with future challenges).

In addition to beliefs about the self, someone who grew up watching his parents cope with difficulties by using substances might develop a belief that 'drugs help people cope'. Holding such a belief may make it more likely that this person will turn to substances in later life when faced with his own difficulties. At this point there will be some fit between the beliefs that person holds about him- or herself, other people and the world and the way that substances make him feel. So, for example, people who believe they are powerless may use crack cocaine and develop the conditional belief: 'If I use crack, I can do anything'.

Precipitating factors

Precipitating factors are the immediate external and internal factors that trigger substance use. Central to the cognitive model is the theory that it is not events themselves that we respond to but our view or perception of them. So, for example, your client might say: 'I started drinking heavily because my job was stressful'. Whilst superficially this sounds like a convincing explanation, not everyone responds to a stressful job by drinking heavily and therefore some other factors must be involved. One of these is your appraisal of the situation and it is this that determines what you do. If your appraisal is 'The only way I can cope with this stressful job is to start drinking as soon as I get home', then it becomes understandable how an alcohol problem may develop.

Therefore, the thoughts that occur in response to a situation are not necessarily facts or truths, but points of view or hypotheses. Using the collaborative style of CBT the therapist can ask whether everyone would feel the way the client does in response to an event, whether others would react differently, or whether the client would have thought and reacted differently in the past.

Perpetuating factors

Perpetuating factors are the elements in the five-part generic cognitive model (Padesky & Mooney, 1990) you are using with your client to formulate at a situation level. Within the context of a precipitating factor (internal or external trigger) there is a circular relationship between the aspects of thoughts, feelings, physical sensations and behaviour. The five-part model helps to show the reinforcing and spiralling nature of the problem. Take the example of the person who believes his job to be stressful and that 'the only way I can cope with this stressful job is to start drinking as soon as I get home'. Thus a 'stressful' day at work will trigger thoughts about drinking ('I can't cope, I need a drink') and possible feelings of sadness and anxiety. The thoughts and feelings trigger physical sensations of edginess and cravings and the person decides to go to the pub, drinks a lot and wakes up the next morning with a hangover. Going to work with a hangover may make work appear more stressful than it needs to be and so the cycle is perpetuated. Avoiding difficulties by using alcohol/drugs can lead to a reduced repertoire of coping behaviours and become an automatic response in any precipitating situation.

Presenting issues

All presenting issues should be related to substance use behaviour in a case formulation. However, other difficulties may also be present in areas such as mental health, finances, relationships, physical health, forensic, social, occupational or behavioural problems. Through collaborative discussions and using a motivational communicating style it should become clear how these problems are related to substance use behaviour. Often it is these types of problem that bring clients into treatment and it is not initially clear to them how substance use is playing a part in the problem. We introduce our third hypothetical client, Simon, to illustrate this point. He has come into treatment because he has been missing days at work and is concerned he will be tested for drug use. However, he is ambivalent about changing his substance use and is adamant his use of cannabis causes no problems in his life. Some additional background information for Simon is included below.

Simon

Simon is 26 years old and drinks alcohol and uses up to 4 g cocaine every weekend and smokes herbal cannabis (skunk) every day. He has a well-paid job, but in the last six months has had a number of days off sick, so his manager has arranged an appointment for him with occupational health. He is concerned that he might be tested for substance use and has approached your clinic as a pre-emptive and possibly useful measure. He has smoked cannabis and used a variety of stimulant drugs from his early teenage years.

Simon has made a short-term treatment contract of four sessions to look further at his substance use. He has avoided any disclosure of his substance use at work but has been given a written warning about his poor attendance record. He is ambivalent about making any changes in his substance use. On the one hand, he recognises that his boss has a reason to be concerned. He also reveals that his girlfriend is no longer as interested in partying every weekend and has commented about how much Simon spends on cocaine and the amount of alcohol he drinks. On the other hand, he is reluctant to compromise his social life and feels attached to a wide circle of friends and a scene that revolves around clubs and bars. He does not consider himself to be addicted to cocaine as he only uses it in these settings and says he would never use at work. Regarding his cannabis use, Simon was initially adamant that it was not of any concern whatsoever. However, he has begun to consider that it might be impacting negatively on his mood and contributing to his feeling stuck in his current lifestyle. He says that he is disinterested in his work and would prefer to be working on his own business project.

Protective factors

A good CBT formulation will include a description of protective factors that have stopped your clients' substance use escalating, along with resources for helping gain control over their use. Clients usually experience some variation in their substance use and are not drinking or using constantly. Protective factors include your clients' personal resources (e.g. determination) and social resources (e.g. a supportive friend) and their control beliefs (discussed in Chapter 5) about substance use that decrease the likelihood of use at certain times or in certain situations. At the assessment and formulation stage it is useful to talk with your clients about the times when they *do not* use substances and why that is. Asking about control beliefs is particularly useful as it provides evidence that contradicts beliefs that maintain substance use and helps with the development of more control beliefs. Chapters 8 and 9 discuss more fully how to do this.

Linking formulation to intervention

As previously stated, it is not necessary to have a comprehensive case formulation with your clients to work with them. It is enough to be able to formulate at a situation level, using the five-part framework. From this you can start to build a case formulation which evolves over time, if you wish.

Formulating at a situation level will help direct your interventions. Later chapters describe different cognitive and behavioural intervention techniques to use with your clients. Cognitive intervention techniques address substance-related beliefs and automatic thoughts that contribute to urges and cravings and maintain substance use. Behavioural techniques help the client test the accuracy of substance-related beliefs that trigger and maintain substance use and are also used for teaching skills to deal with high-risk situations, urges and cravings. Figure 6.2 gives some examples of which interventions relate to each of the components of the five-part model.

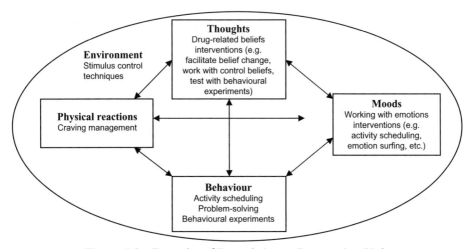

Figure 6.2 Examples of Formulation to Intervention Links

The chapters that follow discuss when it is appropriate to use the different interventions. In reality you will usually be using a mixture of cognitive and behavioural interventions at the same time, as the two cannot really be separated. A good example is in the use of behavioural experiments to test beliefs (see Chapter 10). Generally, it makes sense to use behavioural interventions in the first phase of treatment because they are easily understood and are more likely to give your client immediate skills in controlling his substance use. Early successes will mean that any negative beliefs about coping and self-efficacy start to be challenged and your client's confidence will be boosted. Behavioural interventions are also useful in continuing to socialise your client to the model and increasing engagement in the therapeutic process.

There are no fixed rules about where to start intervening in response to your formulation. Ultimately, this will be decided from the client's own presentation and needs, your own experience, the strength of the therapeutic alliance and a clear formulation based on a thorough assessment. Discussing your formulation and chosen interventions in supervision will also help you. In our practice, we have found the following principles help us decide where to start:

1. Beck (1995) suggests that the interventions you employ will be determined by what you are trying to achieve in treatment overall and in each individual session. Asking yourself 'What is the specific problem here and what am I trying to accomplish?' will keep therapy focused on agreed goals and moving in the right direction.
2. Having collaboratively developed a formulation with your client, you should also collaboratively agree where to start intervening. In doing this, you can agree with the client what the main issues are and where he might like to start, based on preference and capacity to engage with the intervention. Padesky (2003) suggests a useful question to help with this: 'Looking at your formulation, at the issues you face, what small change can we make that would make the biggest difference to you and your life?'
3. Once the issues have been identified, you might ask yourself: 'What interventions might help address this issue? If this intervention was successful, what impact might it have on the other issues and the formulation?' So, for example, you might initially focus on:
    a) Environment: Is there something about the client's current situation that needs addressing that will help the client and also help engagement with therapy, e.g. a housing or welfare problem?
    b) Substance use: If use is very frequent, a logical first place to start might be with stimulus control and craving management (see Chapter 11).
    c) Mood: If, for example, your client's mood is low and he has stopped doing things previously enjoyed, then activity scheduling might be a useful place to start (see Chapter 11). Alternatively, if anxiety is contributing to the use of substances, some anxiety management strategies might be helpful, so the client has alternatives to manage his mood when he is reducing use (see Chapter 12).
    d) Beliefs: What beliefs does the client have about his substance use? Are they central to the formulation and do they have a major influence in

maintaining the main problems? Is there a need to focus on facilitating some belief change? Chapter 8 will help you explore this.

4. If the chosen intervention is not successful or the client does not find it helpful, it is also worth asking yourself: 'What would I do next and how would I do it?' So, for example, if you are struggling to facilitate belief change through discussion, a behavioural experiment may be a more helpful way of demonstrating alternatives.

5. Remember that discussing your formulation in supervision will help you in deciding where and how to intervene.

Your case-level formulation will also help you identify whether there are any underlying psychological issues that need to be addressed before your clients can confidently make sustained changes to their substance use behaviour. For example, some clients have extremely negative developmental experiences (e.g. emotional, physical or sexual abuse) that have led to entrenched and rigid negative core beliefs about themselves, others and the world. It may be that additional specialist input is needed in order to deal with the legacy of these experiences. If you do decide to refer your client to a clinical psychologist within your service, for example, then this will not preclude you from continuing to work with your client around his substance use behaviour using CBT techniques.

Summary

Formulation, at either a situation or case level, is central to CBT. It is like the master plan for a building project, incorporating all the relevant information so everyone knows what and when things need to be done. When things do not go as planned with your client, the formulation is the first place to look to and review in light of any new information. Formulation is your organising template for understanding your client and delivering CBT interventions. When shared effectively with your clients it can offer an enhanced understanding of often entrenched and difficult behaviours, as well as developing optimism for how things could be different.

Chapter 7

Introduction to Substance-related Cognitions and Interventions

Overview

As we have seen in previous chapters, our clients begin, continue and stop taking substances for a variety of reasons. In our case studies Paul (Chapter 1) used heroin because it relaxed him, while Sally (Chapter 5) continued to use alcohol because she felt less anxious and unhappy after drinking. People also impose limits on their drug-taking and alcohol use, and may hold strong convictions about why, when and where they should not use substances. For example, Simon (Chapter 6) tried not to take cocaine outside of his clubbing hours since he believed that it could be addictive and did not want it to interfere with his work. Cognitive therapy for substance use problems is therefore based on the assumption that a person's choice for using/not using drugs and alcohol lies in the *beliefs* held about the substance.

How to use this chapter

The aim of this chapter is to highlight the different types of substance-related cognitions we have come across in our clinical work and in the literature. These cognitions should then be the target of the cognitive and behavioural interventions described in Chapters 8–11. In this chapter we describe a number of common substance-related cognitions, why it is important to tackle these in therapy, and

Applied Cognitive and Behavioural Approaches to the Treatment of Addiction: A Practical Treatment Guide By Luke Mitcheson, Jenny Maslin, Tim Meynen, Tamara Morrison, Robert Hill and Shamil Wanigaratne
Copyright © 2010 John Wiley & Sons, Ltd.

suggest some interventions that may be used to work with them. These interventions will then be described in more detail in Chapters 8–11.

As previously discussed, the first step is always to identify your client's drug and alcohol-related beliefs and to integrate these into the individual formulation, highlighting the maintaining role of cognitions on substance-using behaviour (see Chapter 5). Identifying substance-related cognitions should be an ongoing process. You will find that as your work with your client progresses, more cognitions will emerge as you both seek to gain more insight into the function of the substance use and what is maintaining it. Once you have identified your client's substance-related cognitions, you may want to use this chapter to gather further information about which type of cognition you have identified and chosen to work on (see Chapter 8) and what interventions you could use.

Nine key cognitions that maintain substance use

While no list of substance-related cognitions and beliefs can be complete or universal for all clients, a review of the literature, along with our own clinical experience, has resulted in what we consider to be nine key cognitions to target in clinical work. These are highlighted in Table 7.1.

Beliefs about coping and self-efficacy

In Chapter 2 we described the work of Bandura (1977b) on self-efficacy and how this had been taken up and developed further by Annis and her colleagues in relation to high-risk situations. Self-efficacy as defined by Beck and his colleagues 'refers to one's judgement about one's ability to deal competently with challenging or high-risk situations' (Beck *et al.*, 1993, p. 13).

Why are these beliefs important to tackle in therapy? We have identified three key reasons:

1. In relation to the maintenance and treatment of substance use, clients need to believe that their actions (e.g. coping skills) will result in a desired goal (e.g. abstinence), otherwise there would be very little incentive to work

Table 7.1 Key Substance Use-Related Cognitions and Beliefs

1. Beliefs about coping and self-efficacy
2. Beliefs about positive outcome expectancy
3. Beliefs about craving and withdrawal symptoms
4. Beliefs about the pharmacology of substances and methods of use
5. Permission-giving beliefs
6. Control beliefs or negative outcome expectancies
7. Negative beliefs about the self and substance use
8. Images relating to substance use
9. Cognitive biases and drug and alcohol-related beliefs

through the difficulties when challenges present themselves (e.g. craving for drugs whilst feeling bored).

2. Clients with a strong sense of self-efficacy are more likely to treat their problems as challenges to be mastered rather than unachievable tasks to be avoided. They will therefore be more likely to problem-solve, set goals and to be motivated and committed to change. Confidence in being able to make changes to drug or alcohol use will increase clients' sense of responsibility for change. Self-efficacy is undermined when clients see themselves as victims under the influence of the substance or circumstance.

3. Having self-confidence can help clients overcome a setback (e.g. a lapse) and see this as something to learn from, rather than putting it down to personal failure. Conversely, a negative belief about their ability to cope (e.g. with a setback) could result in clients continuing to use after a lapse.

In our case examples, imagine that Sally has a belief that she cannot cope with the simplest daily living tasks without using alcohol. This will clearly undermine her confidence and belief that she can stop drinking. Similarly, we have established that Paul has no confidence in his ability to stop using heroin, based on his observation that many of his friends have been unable to stop.

What interventions can be used to work with beliefs about coping and self-efficacy?   Bandura (1982) states that the most important way to develop a strong sense of our abilities is through the direct experience of mastery. In other words, through our direct involvement in a task we may learn what we can achieve, and the experience may help us understand better what we are good at, what works and what limitations we have that need further development. Therefore, when working with your clients, an important aim is to help them learn and practise different coping strategies, initially role-played and rehearsed in sessions, and then applied out of sessions.

We have found the following behavioural interventions useful as a first step in increasing a client's sense of self-efficacy:

*   Craving management strategies to deal with cravings.
*   Problem-solving to deal effectively with problems as they arise.
*   Activity scheduling to promote a sense of mastery and achievement.

These interventions are described in Chapter 11. The basic cognitive techniques described in Chapter 8 could then be used to work directly on changing unhelpful beliefs about coping and self-efficacy. For example, when working with Paul, you might want to explore the accuracy of his belief that 'I cannot stop using heroin because many of my friends have been unable to stop'. The interventions outlined in Chapter 8 include:

*   Defining and operationalising the belief.
*   Evaluating the accuracy of the belief.
*   Developing an alternative belief.

In addition, when working on beliefs about self-efficacy and coping, you could use imagery to practise ideal coping and mastery over problems (see Chapter 9).

Beliefs about positive outcome expectancy

In essence, positive outcome expectancy in substance use refers to the belief that there will be a positive benefit from consuming the drug. For example, Paul may say, 'I take crack because I like to get high'; Sally may say, 'Drinking a can of beer helps me relax'; and Simon may say, 'Cannabis helps me sleep'.

Positive outcome expectancies regarding drug use often have certain themes. These usually fall into two categories: (i) anticipation of better performance; and (ii) relief from negative states. The list below provides examples of the most common positive outcome expectancy themes we have encountered in our clinical work with clients.

Anticipation of better performance
- Enhancement of social performance (e.g. 'I need a drink to make me more sociable')
- Enhancement of physical pleasure (e.g. 'I love the buzz you get off coke').
- Enhancement of cognitive functioning (e.g. 'Cannabis makes me think more creatively').
- Enhancement of physical functioning (e.g. 'Ecstasy will help me dance all night').
- Increased sexual arousal and competency (e.g. 'Crack will keep me going all night').

Relief from negative states
- Reduction in unwanted emotional states (e.g. 'When I'm feeling low, a good drink will pick me up').
- Reduction in sleep problems (e.g. 'A couple of benzos will knock me out').
- Removal of difficult memories (e.g. 'The past doesn't bother me when I smoke heroin').
- Avoidance of physical pain (e.g. 'After I inject heroin, I can't feel a thing').
- Avoidance of worry (e.g. 'One pipe and I'm in a different world where nothing matters').

Why are these beliefs important to tackle in therapy?   There are three good reasons for tackling outcome expectancies with clients:

1. Positive outcome expectancies influence all aspects of substance use from initiation, through continued use, to lapse and relapse. Positive outcome expectancies increase the risk of relapse even if your client has practical coping skills to deal with triggers and cravings. For example, Simon may be able to identify and manage his high-risk situations, but would still be drawn to using in these circumstances if no work is done on challenging his beliefs about the positive outcomes from using.

2. Positive expectations play an important role in the build-up and anticipation phase leading to actual craving and subsequent drug and alcohol use. Changing these beliefs may reduce the frequency and perhaps the intensity of craving, which in turn makes the craving easier to manage.
3. Positive outcome expectations are often distorted or biased. Typically, a client may have a tendency to overestimate the likelihood of good things happening from using substances and selectively remember only the positive experiences of recent use. Remembering only the more positive aspects of using is sometimes labelled 'euphoric recall' (Gorski, 1990). The idea is clearly expressed by many clients taking stimulant drugs like crack cocaine, where they continue to use in order to relive the sensations of the first, most intense hit.

What interventions may be used to work with beliefs about positive outcome expectancy?   We have found the following cognitive interventions (see further Chapters 8 and 9) helpful in challenging positive outcome expectancies:

- Defining and operationalising the belief.
- Evaluating the accuracy of the belief, with particular consideration of the long-term consequences of substance use.
- Using an advantages/disadvantages analysis to evaluate the utility (helpfulness) of the belief (i.e. what are the advantages and disadvantages of thinking this way? How helpful is it?)
- Developing an alternative belief.

It is important to identify as many positive outcome expectations as possible and ask your client to write the alternative beliefs on a flashcard to carry around with him (see Chapter 11).

Beliefs about craving and withdrawal symptoms

There seems to be little consensus on what constitutes a craving. Drummond (2001, p. 35) defines a craving as 'the *conscious* experience of a desire to take a drug'. Marlatt & Gordon (1985) suggest that the craving experience is driven by the *anticipated* effects of taking the drug. Beck *et al.* (1993) identify three craving-related beliefs: (i) the desire to take away the physical discomfort associated with withdrawal symptoms (e.g. 'I can't stand these body cramps'; (ii) the need to alter negative psychological states (e.g. 'I need a smoke to calm me down'); and (iii) the wish to enhance a positive experience (e.g. 'I'll be able to have sex all night long').

Why are these beliefs important to tackle in therapy?   These definitions highlight a strong cognitive element to the experience of cravings. Both cravings and withdrawal states can play an important role in maintaining substance use problems and can lead to the client quitting treatment. It is therefore an important part of therapy to identify these craving/withdrawal-related cognitions.

What interventions may be used to work with beliefs about craving and withdrawal symptoms?   The following behavioural techniques (described in Chapter

11) can be used to help your clients deal more realistically with cravings and withdrawals, which should also lead to changes in their beliefs about these:

- Normalising the experience of cravings
- Distraction
- Relaxation
- Urge surfing
- Positive self-talk
- Flashcards

The following cognitive techniques can be used to work directly with beliefs about cravings:

- Using imagery to practise ideal coping and mastery over cravings (described in Chapter 9).
- Behavioural experiments (described in Chapter 10) to help your clients examine the accuracy of their beliefs about cravings and to demonstrate that directing their attention away from cravings reduces them and that they can actually do something to control the craving (i.e. use the above behavioural strategies).

Some clients experience cravings in other sensory modalities. For example, people who smoke crack cocaine sometimes hear the 'crack' sound or taste or smell the distinctive odour when crack is burnt. We have found that clients can develop creative ways of dealing with these types of craving. For example, one woman used a spray of her perfume to replace the imagined smell of burning crack with a 'clean' smell of scent whenever she was craving. Another client replaced the metallic taste of crack with the 'fresh and healthy' taste of mints. As a therapist your task is to help the client construct such alternatives.

Beliefs about the pharmacology of substances and methods of use

Beliefs about the pharmacology of substances and methods of use can vary considerably in terms of how unhelpful/helpful these beliefs are, depending on the extent to which they maintain substance use problems or contribute to controlled use or abstinence.

The psychoactive properties of drugs and alcohol produce profound changes in the central nervous system which generate widespread effects on physiological and/or psychological functioning. It is therefore not surprising that your clients' drug of choice and continued use will be influenced by the specific properties of that drug and the experience they are looking for. For example, Simon may drink alcohol because it makes him feel relaxed and take cocaine because it gives him energy. Paul illustrates another common example of taking crack cocaine and heroin together in order to receive the 'rush' of the crack, but to lessen its intensity and subsequent depressant hangover with the longer-acting and relaxing effects of heroin.

Drugs can be taken in different ways and beliefs can develop about the different methods of use. Beliefs about methods of use are often linked to the subsequent physiological and psychological effect of that drug as injecting, smoking, snorting and taking a substance orally can lead to different effects. For example, many clients we have worked with are initially reluctant to smoke heroin instead of injecting it because they report experiencing a stronger hit from injecting and perceive this as a more financially economical method of use (i.e. they get more for their money).

In addition to beliefs associated with the pleasurable effects of taking drugs, clients often develop beliefs about the negative effects of the pharmacology of substances. These beliefs can develop into control beliefs. For example, many people who experiment with a drug for the first time will be deterred from taking it again because they did not like a particular immediate effect (e.g. nausea associated with heroin use or paranoia associated with cannabis use). Longer-term users may limit their use as a result of more helpful beliefs, for example limiting how much crack is used in one go because of subsequent feelings of aggression or financial implications.

With regards to methods of use, your client may only smoke crack in a joint because smoking from a pipe is found to be too intense and anxiety-provoking. Someone else may smoke heroin on foil to avoid any disfigurement of the body from injecting, or believe that injecting drugs is more likely to lead to long-term addiction. Beliefs can also develop about where the drug is taken, for example, your client may believe it is acceptable to drink alcohol in social settings but not alone. Cultural factors can also greatly influence when a particular drug is favoured, such as the more common use of Khat among East African communities and the almost world-wide legality of alcohol.

Why are these beliefs important to tackle in therapy?   Unhelpful beliefs about the pharmacology of drugs and alcohol are important indications as to what the function of the drug and alcohol use may be for your client and what some of the triggers are (e.g. feeling tense or tired in Simon's case). The more helpful beliefs about the pharmacology of drug and alcohol use can be developed into control beliefs (see Chapter 8) and can aid harm-minimisation work.

What interventions may be used to work with beliefs about the pharmacology of substances and methods of use?   After asking your clients their views on the pharmacology of the drug/s they are using and their method of use, the primary goal should be to provide factual information and education about the effects of different drugs and alcohol. Rather than simply informing clients, we recommend taking a collaborative approach to examining the evidence for and against potentially unhelpful or inaccurate beliefs about pharmacology and methods of use and then developing alternative beliefs (see Chapter 8), which may incorporate the information shared. You could also use the advantages/disadvantages analysis described in Chapter 9, incorporating both the short- and long-term consequences of the drug or alcohol use. Such a discussion with Simon may involve your asking him: 'What evidence do you have that alcohol relaxes you in the short term? What evidence suggests this is not always the case? What about its long-term effects?' In addition, you could test the drug-related and alternative beliefs using a behavioural experiment (see Chapter 10).

Permission-giving beliefs

Clients who are trying to control their drug or alcohol intake often report feeling frustrated when they find themselves unable to stop using. They may continue to use at an unwanted level even though they hold very strong convictions as to why they should stop. When asked to explain why this happens, clients often say that they can talk themselves into using. They sometimes describe it as an internal debate or that the drug talks to them. Beck *et al.* (1993) suggest that this phenomenon is caused by the activation of 'facilitating' or 'permission-giving' beliefs. These beliefs essentially give the individual permission or justification for using drugs and resolve any inner conflict they may be having. Examples of these beliefs from our three case studies may be Sally thinking, 'It's been a hard week, therefore I deserve this', Simon thinking, 'Everyone else will be doing it, so it's OK' and Paul thinking, 'I'll have just one hit and then I'll stop'. (For further examples of common permission giving beliefs, see Appendix 9.1.)

Why is it important to tackle these beliefs in therapy? It is important to identify and tackle permission-giving beliefs since their continued activation has unwanted consequences in maintaining substance use, contributing to ambivalence about using and undermining control beliefs.

What interventions may be used to work with permission-giving beliefs? As with previous types of beliefs, we have found the following cognitive techniques (discussed in Chapters 8 and 9) helpful:

- Reviewing the evidence for and against the permission-giving beliefs.
- Using an advantages/disadvantages analysis for permission-giving beliefs that may be unhelpful.
- Developing an alternative belief.

For some clients it can be helpful to frame these permission-giving beliefs as a 'drug-using voice'. Some clients find it liberating to locate this 'voice' as slightly separate from themselves as this enables them to harness the necessary strategies to tackle it.

Control beliefs or negative outcome expectancies

As we have already indicated, most of your clients will have reasons for not using or limiting their substance use under certain circumstances. For example, a parent may not smoke cigarettes in front of his or her young children for health reasons. In Simon's case, he may not like to drink alcohol at work because it negatively impacts on his performance. In our experience, even the most chaotic of drug users do not use drugs continually. For example, they may feel like taking a break after a few days because they feel exhausted or their money has run out. For clients who are alcohol-dependent the situation is complicated by the physiological need for ethanol. However, even here there will be periods when less alcohol is used.

Beck *et al.* (1993) label drug-related cognitions that limit substance use 'control beliefs'. These beliefs are associated with a desire to avoid physical complications, negative social or cultural consequences (e.g. stigma) and psychological problems (e.g. paranoia). Beck and colleagues also believe that these control beliefs are learnt from past experiences. Examples can be seen in our case studies. For example, Simon limited his use of cocaine to weekends because he held the belief that it could be addictive and hinder his vocational and social opportunities. Paul had begun to believe that his heroin use was eroding his standard of living, reducing the time and money he spent on self-care and basic needs.

Why are these beliefs important to tackle in therapy?   Working with control beliefs is an important therapeutic task as their development contributes to a reduction in substance use and maintenance of changes made. The development of control beliefs is therefore central to the process of treatment and is one of the main aims of CBT for substance use.

What interventions may be used to work with control beliefs?   All the cognitive and behavioural interventions described in the following chapters can contribute to the development and strengthening of control beliefs. Specifically, Chapter 8 describes the basic steps involved in developing control (alternative) beliefs with your clients. Conviction in these control beliefs can then be strengthened through behavioural experiments (see Chapter 10).

Negative beliefs about the self and substance use

We often use terms like self-image, self-esteem or self-worth to describe how we see ourselves. Beliefs about the self are often developed and maintained by our activities, relationships and our self-evaluations. It is therefore no surprise that the activity or behaviour of using substances impacts on individuals' beliefs about themselves. For many clients, the first initiation into drug-taking is closely linked with a social group and the need to be noticed, accepted and respected. The perceived reaction from others can positively reinforce the substance-taking behaviour, which is then repeated. Our clients often talk about the lifestyle that goes with substance use initially providing social integration and a sense of purpose, as illustrated by Simon who uses cocaine because it helps him identify with his clubbing friends. However, beliefs about the self can also protect against substance use and these beliefs can be articulated as control beliefs (e.g. 'I feel a stronger person if I don't take crack'; 'I'm a thoughtful and caring person when I'm not drinking').

Why are these beliefs important to tackle in therapy?   Unfortunately, substance use that has become problematic can lead to either the development or maintenance of negative beliefs about the self. For example, individuals may see drug-taking as character weakness, dirty or anti-social. They may not like how they act under the influence of drugs (e.g. 'I treat my family terribly when I'm on drugs') or may not like how others see them (e.g. as untrustworthy or dangerous). Indeed, the social, legal and cultural stigma attached to using drugs can contribute significantly to these negative self-beliefs.

In addition to maintaining the role negative beliefs about the self can have on substance use problems, positive beliefs about the self are fundamental in building confidence in being able to take on new challenges and manage difficulties. Literature on the recovery model (White, 2004, 2005) shows that developing a positive social identity away from a drug-using life and culture can be an important motivator to stop using drugs.

What interventions may be used to work with negative beliefs about the self? Although much of the early work with clients will be centred on developing techniques and strategies to increase control over substance use, it is the development of a drug-free lifestyle which will give your client robust reasons for remaining drug-free in the future. Activity scheduling (see Chapter 11) is the initial key intervention that focuses on helping your clients develop a drug-free lifestyle. The behaviour and lifestyle changes that take place through activity scheduling will help change some of your clients' negative beliefs about themselves, in addition to having a positive impact on their mood. The cognitive techniques outlined in Chapter 8 and the pie chart technique described in Chapter 9 can also be used to work with your clients on challenging their negative beliefs about the self and developing alternative, more helpful beliefs. The changes made through activity scheduling can be explicitly incorporated into the evidence against your clients' negative beliefs.

Images relating to substance use

When working on identifying drug and alcohol-related beliefs, it is important to ask your clients whether they have any images (pictures in their mind), either when craving or when they encounter internal or external triggers to their substance use. There is some indication that mental imagery is central to the experience of drug-related cravings. May *et al.* (2004) suggest that drug-related images are triggered when clients are in high-risk situations.

Why are images important to tackle in therapy? The content and experience of images can be unpleasant for some clients. Others may be less aware that they are experiencing images until you explore this with them. By talking about images with your clients, you may help them identify a powerful trigger and maintenance factor to their substance use that had previously been out of their immediate awareness. Furthermore, images can be very meaningful, often linked to past memories. Identifying the image may give you and your clients further insight into the function of their substance use. Finally, images can be altered through the use of different cognitive techniques, which can reduce their power in maintaining drug or alcohol use.

What interventions may be used to work with images relating to substance use? When working with images, you need to be aware that they can be triggered quite easily, can elicit a strong emotional and physical reaction, and can be difficult to 'turn off'. Therefore, any exploration and intervention should be done with the full consent of your clients and be instigated if confident in their ability to change the image and soften its impact. Chapter 9 describes the assessment of imagery and some techniques that we have found useful when helping clients change their unwanted images. In addition, Chapter 11 describes the use of imagery as a relaxation technique and the use of imagery as a craving management strategy (the 'red box' technique).

Cognitive biases and drug and alcohol-related beliefs

As we shall see in Chapter 8, the key cognitive and behavioural interventions aim at challenging the content of a belief. However, cognitive behavioural models also highlight the importance of identifying and working with persistent biases in thinking (i.e. in the way individuals attend to and interpret information). These cognitive biases influence individuals' interpretation of events (i.e. the content of their thoughts) and are driven by underlying beliefs about themselves, others and the world. They can be seen as an attempt to make the world seem consistent and predictable. Beck (1995) provides a comprehensive list of these biases. Below are some examples of cognitive biases that we have often come across when working with drug and alcohol-related beliefs.

All or nothing thinking.   This is often referred to as dichotomous (black-and-white) thinking because it seems that there are only two choices, with no middle ground or shades of grey. For example, clients may believe that they are either totally in control of their use or totally out of control. Other beliefs expressed in this style may be: 'I've used once so I may as well carry on using', 'I feel sick so my methadone is not going to work' or 'I've used, so I've failed'.

Catastrophising.   This is where your clients predict the very worst thing that could happen. Common examples include: 'I'm never going to be drug-free' or 'People will always think I'm a total failure because I've taken drugs'. This cognitive bias usually contains an element of 'fortune-telling' (predicting the future) or 'mind-reading' (making assumptions about what other people are thinking).

Emotional reasoning.   Here your clients use how they feel emotionally and physically as evidence that their belief is accurate. For example, your clients may say, 'I feel like my cravings are never going to end' or 'I feel terrible, this will never end' whilst they are experiencing cravings.

Overgeneralisations.   This involves drawing sweeping conclusions from one or more selective events. Drug-related examples include: 'Everyone I know enjoys using drugs, so it must be normal'; 'I have not been able to stop using today so I will never have control over my use'; or 'Most people never really stop drinking'.

Magnification and minimisation.   This is where your clients magnify the positive consequences of using drugs (e.g. 'We spent the whole holiday having so much fun totally off our faces') and minimises the more negative consequences of using drugs (e.g. 'I only lost half the day with a hangover'). Alternatively, your clients might magnify the negatives (e.g. 'I've had a lapse') and minimise any positive changes or progress they have made.

Tunnel vision.   This occurs when your clients see only one side of an argument, perhaps only the negative side or only evidence that is consistent with their drug and alcohol-related beliefs. It is very common for clients to attend to information consistent with their substance-related cognitions only, and in a sense filter out any inconsistent information.

Personalisation.   This is where your clients believe that they are responsible for events, or that other people's behaviour is directly in response to them. For example, your client may believe: 'My father died because of all the stress I put him through because of my drug use' or 'My key worker cancelled my appointment today because he/she doesn't like me'.

Why is it important to tackle these biases in therapy?   Cognitive biases filter information in the environment in a distorted way, which can reinforce drug and alcohol-related beliefs. These cognitive biases usually exaggerate and select only the positive reasons for taking drugs, give the client permission to use and minimise any attempts by the client to control the using pattern, which in turn maintains the substance use problems.

What interventions may be used to work with cognitive biases?   Working with cognitive biases should usually be carried out in parallel with working with the content of drug and alcohol-related beliefs using the techniques described in Chapters 8–10. To focus specifically on cognitive biases it can be helpful to provide your client with psycho-education about the maintaining role of these biases and the different examples provided above. We would then recommend encouraging your client to identify the cognitive biases reflected in the drug and alcohol-related belief you are working on. Generally, more than one type of cognitive bias will be reflected in each drug-related belief. Your client could continue this work between sessions by monitoring specific cognitive biases. For example, when having thoughts about using, we often ask clients to look out for and write down examples of tunnel vision or emotional reasoning. If clients have had a lapse, it can be helpful to ask them to look out for 'all or nothing thinking'.

You could then ask your clients to think about whether the cognitive bias/es they are making are helpful or unhelpful. As a general rule, beliefs containing cognitive biases are rigid, inaccurate and unhelpful. Therefore, identifying the presence of one or more cognitive biases can be your clients' clue that they need to work on the content of this belief, so it becomes more accurate and/or helpful. In addition, we have found the cognitive continuum technique described in Chapter 9 useful in helping clients tackle drug and alcohol-related beliefs that contain all or nothing thinking, catastrophisations and overgeneralisations.

Occasionally, a belief containing a cognitive bias may be accurate and/or helpful. For example, some clients find it helpful to think: 'I can never drink alcohol in any situation'. Whilst this could be seen as an overgeneralisation, it is often an accurate and helpful way of thinking for these clients, so you should not challenge this.

Summary

This chapter highlights nine types of substance-related cognitions, explains why they are important to work on and indicates some of the interventions that you can use to tackle them. The following chapters describe in more detail the cognitive and behavioural interventions that we have found useful when working with substance-using cognitions and behaviour.

Chapter 8

A Basic Framework for Working with Substance-related Beliefs

Overview

The aim of CBT for substance use is to break the vicious circle of continued drug and alcohol use and help clients gain more control over their using. This process usually requires a combination of cognitive and behavioural techniques. In general, the cognitive interventions target the substance-related beliefs and images which contribute to use. The behavioural techniques focus on strategies to deal with high-risk situations and cravings, in addition to tackling unhelpful cognitions.

Chapters 9–11 describe the cognitive interventions used to facilitate changes in drug and alcohol-related beliefs. This chapter focuses on the steps that form the basic framework for initiating belief change. Chapter 9 describes other cognitive techniques that can be used alongside the basic steps. Chapter 10 explains the role of behavioural experiments and highlights their importance in the process of consolidating belief change.

In many cases it may be more useful to introduce behavioural strategies (described in Chapter 11) to your client before discussing cognitive interventions, since these practical approaches will provide your client with immediate skills in controlling substance use, which can lead to early successes. Why, then, are we presenting material on cognitive interventions first? There are two main reasons. First, in order to introduce behavioural interventions successfully, you need a thorough understanding of the role of cognitions in supporting behaviour change. Second, although behavioural interventions can be usefully introduced first, this

Applied Cognitive and Behavioural Approaches to the Treatment of Addiction: A Practical Treatment Guide By Luke Mitcheson, Jenny Maslin, Tim Meynen, Tamara Morrison, Robert Hill and Shamil Wanigaratne
Copyright © 2010 John Wiley & Sons, Ltd.

is not always the case and sometimes behavioural interventions cannot be separated from more cognitive work. A good example of this is the use of behavioural experiments to test the accuracy of beliefs (see Chapter 10).

It is worth repeating that the basic idea behind cognitive interventions is to explore with your clients their reasons for taking substances and to examine whether these reasons are feasible and/or helpful in line with the changes they may want to make. At the same time, your clients are asked to identify and work with the beliefs that help limit their use. This work on control beliefs (see Chapter 7) is important as your clients may already be using these beliefs successfully to limit their use in particular circumstances.

How to use this chapter

This chapter outlines a step-by-step approach to identifying and changing drug and alcohol-related beliefs. There are some additional points to consider when working through these steps and these are listed at the end of this chapter. We recommend reading this chapter before you read the following chapters. The interventions described in Chapters 9 and 10 build on the techniques discussed here and can be fitted into the basic framework described below.

The core steps described in this chapter represent the most common conversations we have with our clients when working with them on their substance-related cognitions. The steps are presented in a logical order to help guide you, but over time you may wish to adapt this format. If you are new to CBT, you may feel self-conscious about your skills and knowledge, and at first verbal challenge discussions may feel static and contrived. However, as you become more familiar with the questions, it not only becomes easier, but you will develop your own style. With practice and supervision you will also find that you become more proficient in selecting the most helpful questions to ask.

Basic cognitive techniques for facilitating belief change

Step 1: Defining and operationalising beliefs

Eliciting meaning. The words and phrases clients use to describe their experiences do not always convey *all* the underlying meaning. For example, your clients may say, 'I need to take drugs' or 'I will not be able to cope unless I use alcohol'. Both statements suggest that your clients believe substances are necessary if they are to function, however, they do not say why. In other words, we have no idea what the 'need' is or what 'not coping' means. In the latter case, 'not coping' could mean not being able to deal with the practical issues of a daily event such as collecting the children from school, or not being able to cope with strong emotions such as anger.

In CBT, if we do not elicit the exact meaning of a belief we cannot assess whether that belief is an accurate interpretation of a real situation. Without this knowledge, it is very difficult to challenge a belief effectively. So, if the belief remains vague or undefined, you need to ask your clients to elaborate what they have said until you arrive at a clearly defined meaning. Once the belief and its meaning have been identified, it can be very helpful to write it down as the focus of subsequent work.

As well as utilising basic listening skills, such as summarising and reflecting back what your client has said, the following questions can be asked to develop understanding and elicit meaning:

Questions to elicit meaning
- When you say that you 'can't cope without drugs', what do you mean?
- If you are 'not coping', what is the worst that could happen?
- How would we know that you are 'not coping'?
- What does 'not coping' look like?

The following example illustrates a conversation with Sally aimed at eliciting the meaning behind a belief:

Therapist: You said that you felt unable to cope with things unless you drink alcohol. These are obviously strong feelings, so I would like to try to understand them better. When you say 'not coping' what do you mean?

Sally: I can't seem to do anything without having a drink.

Therapist: So if you did not have a drink, can you give me an idea of what you would not be able to cope with?

Sally: At the moment even leaving the house is hard for me. It seems I need to have a drink just to get the confidence to leave the house.

Therapist: So 'not coping' here is the idea that you don't have the confidence to leave the house unless you have a drink first?

Sally: Yes that's it. Without alcohol I'd be stuck at home all the time.

Therapist: Anything else?

Sally: Well by not leaving my home I wouldn't get things done, such as shopping or going to the post office, and I won't see my friends.

Measuring the strength of belief. Once you have defined the belief it is helpful to measure its strength. A scale of 0 (don't believe it at all) to 100 (totally believe it) allows you to gauge how important the belief is in terms of maintaining the substance use and also helps you assess any belief change as a result of your interventions. For example, Sally initially believed 100 per cent that she 'won't be able to leave the house without drinking alcohol'. After some cognitive work and successful experiences of leaving her home and engaging in social events without alcohol, the strength of this belief had decreased to 10 per cent using the same rating.

At this stage, it can be helpful to show your clients how the substance-related belief and the strength of its conviction fit into their formulation. This will help them gain greater understanding of how the belief is central to maintaining their problems. This is called socialising the client to the model and is explained in more depth in Chapter 5.

Choosing which belief to work on. Most of your clients will have several substance-related beliefs, so you will need to elicit the meaning and strength of each one. The next step is to choose which belief you are going to tackle in the session. The following questions may help you make this decision:

A guide to choosing the right belief to work with
- Will work on this belief help address the therapeutic goals?
- How central is this belief to the ongoing formulation?
- Does the client see how this belief is unhelpful?
- Is the belief an inaccurate perception of the situation?
- Would changing this belief help change other beliefs the client might hold?
- How generalisable will the intervention be?

Step 2: Evaluating substance-related beliefs

Now that you have defined and selected a substance-related belief to work with, the next step is to explore with your client the quality of the evidence that supports it. A common misconception about this is that it involves a direct challenge to your client's beliefs, rather like a debate, and that the aim of therapy is to instil positive thinking. Both misconceptions are at odds with the collaborative nature of CBT and may lead to your client feeling misunderstood.

Remember, it is not that your client is wrong and that you are right. All beliefs usually contain elements of truth and reflect your client's view of the world. Substance-related beliefs have usually developed over a long period and in that time clients will have formed many reasons why drugs or alcohol are helpful to their lives or why they find it difficult to stop. So, don't expect their beliefs to evaporate in the course of a 20-minute discussion. It might be helpful to think of yourself as being on a fact-finding mission, where it is helpful to develop a real sense of curiosity rather than embark on confrontation and challenge. Find out why they believe something as strongly as they do. The purpose of evaluating substance-related beliefs is not to change what clients think, but to help them see that there may be an alternative, perhaps more realistic and helpful way of looking at their drug or alcohol use.

Review evidence for *the substance-related belief.*   In order to begin the process of evaluating a substance-related belief and discovering alternative explanations, you need to start by understanding why the client holds the belief so strongly by looking at your client's evidence that supports that belief. One belief may be supported by many pieces of evidence. It is therefore important to make sure that you elicit and understand *all* your client's evidence.

The following questions are a guide:

Questions to elicit evidence for the belief
- What makes you think this is true?
- What is your evidence for this belief?
- How do you know that will happen?
- What are your reasons for thinking that will happen?
- How do you know that your belief is true?
- What led you to believe this?

- Where did you get this idea from?
- How confident are you of that belief?

The following example illustrates a conversation with Simon aimed at eliciting the evidence that he is using to support the belief 'cocaine makes me enjoy the weekends more':

Therapist: Simon, you said, 'Cocaine makes me enjoy the weekends more'. Can you tell me why you think that?'

Simon: You know, I like to go clubbing at the weekend. I enjoy being part of that party scene.

Therapist: Can you say a little bit more about that?

Simon: The weekend is a time to let go and relax. Coke is a really sociable drug – makes everyone feel good and friendly.

Therapist: How do you know that everyone is feeling good and friendly because they are using coke?

Simon: Everyone I know in the club takes coke and you look around and everyone's dancing and chatting – they seem much more relaxed than when you meet them in the pub or at work.

Therapist: OK. Are there any other reasons why you believe the weekends are more enjoyable when you're taking cocaine?

Simon: I enjoy taking cocaine when I'm clubbing because it gives you energy. It keeps you going for longer.

Therapist: Have there been times recently where this has happened?

Simon: Yeah. It happens all the time. You've had a hard week and are feeling tired on Friday night. Sometimes you don't feel like you've got the energy to party all night but the coke gives you an energy boost. You can also see other people flagging and going home early and they're usually the people who don't use as much coke.

Therapist: OK, Simon, let's tie some things up here. You obviously enjoy clubbing and see it as a great way to relax with your friends after a hard week at work. You also believe that clubbing is more enjoyable when you've taken cocaine since it makes you and others more friendly, especially with regard to chatting with one another and dancing. You also believe that taking cocaine whilst clubbing can combat tiredness and it allows you to stay up longer enjoying the party with your friends.

Review evidence against the substance-related belief. The cognitive model suggests that we tend to select and concentrate on information that fits with our belief system. As we have seen in Chapter 7, this information may be a biased view of the situation. For example, a client may only see the positive aspects of using substances and overlook the more unpleasant aspects of using. Using a style of curious questioning to help encourage clients to adopt a more flexible way of thinking, where they begin to consider all perspectives of their drug/alcohol use, is the most appropriate intervention at this stage. This is commonly known as Socratic questioning, or guided discovery, and aims to draw out contradictions and enable clients to challenge themselves about the accuracy of their thinking.

The following questions are a guide to elicit evidence against a drug or alcohol-related belief:

Questions to elicit evidence against the belief
- Is there any evidence that does not fit your belief?
- What has happened to you that doesn't fit with this? (Look for exceptions.)
- What experiences suggests this is not 100 per cent true or does not always happen?
- Are there times in your past when this was not true?
- Would you view this situation differently if you were not craving or withdrawing/if you were feeling differently?
- Have you always thought this? What did you use to think?
- What would a friend say to you about this belief?
- What would you say to a friend if he held this belief?

The following illustrates a conversation with Simon aimed at reviewing the evidence against his belief:

Therapist: You have said that cocaine makes your weekends more enjoyable. I was wondering whether this was always the case?

Simon: What do you mean?

Therapist: Are there ever times when the weekend is less enjoyable because you have been taking cocaine?

Simon: Well, there have been times when I've taken too much. Sometimes I can get too wired, unable to relax and too paranoid. That's not so good.

Therapist: OK, it sounds like there are also some not so good things that go with taking cocaine at the weekend. How do you cope when that happens?

Simon: If it all gets too much, you have to leave the party early. I'll usually go straight home and try to relax. In this state it can take hours to calm down or get to sleep.

Therapist: So if you take too much cocaine, it can disrupt your sleep pattern but can also put an abrupt end to the partying. This is an important part of taking cocaine for you, the social side that goes with it. Are there any other ways when taking too much cocaine takes away from the enjoyable social side of things?

Simon: I suppose there comes a point when people take too much. When the people are not really having conversations but rather end up talking at each other it becomes a bit meaningless.

Therapist: Are the any other things that make taking cocaine unenjoyable?

Simon: If you get into coke you can quickly run out of cash. You can blow hundreds of pound in a weekend and have nothing to show for it at the end, apart from a large hangover.

Therapist: Anything else?

Simon: It can be difficult to remember stuff in the morning. A lot of things get lost in the haze of the night before.

Therapist: Have there ever been times when you have not taken cocaine but still enjoyed the weekend partying?

Simon: Yeah. I went out clubbing for my sister's birthday recently. She does not do any drugs and does not know that we do. So when we went out, me and my girlfriend did not take anything.

Therapist: How did that go?

Simon: It was a really good venue and the music was great. We all had a good time.

Therapist: What do you make of that?

Simon: I suppose that when you put the spotlight on it there are some negative things about taking coke. I can also have an enjoyable time clubbing without taking drugs.

Step 3: Developing an alternative substance-related belief

Having spent time discussing and perhaps listening to all the evidence for and against the drug or alcohol-related belief, the next step is for you and your client to summarise both lists of evidence. Once you have done this, ask your client whether, in the light of these summaries, he still believes the original belief to the same extent or whether there has been a change in his thinking. You may find that your client now holds a different perspective or that his conviction in the belief is less strong. If this is the case, the next step is to ask your client to use summaries to construct a new, more realistic belief that better fits the evidence. This now becomes the alternative or control belief.

In the case described above, Simon's original belief was 'cocaine makes me enjoy the weekends more.' After reviewing and summarising all the information for and against this belief, he formed a new, alternative belief: 'I enjoy my weekends because I get to see and party with my friends. Cocaine use is only a small part of that and it can sometimes interfere with my enjoyment'. This new belief becomes a reference point from which to discuss behaviour change (i.e. changes to substance-using behaviour), through questions such as 'So what does this new belief mean in terms of the drug/alcohol use?' or 'Given this new point of view, what could you try to do differently?'

Additional points to consider

While carrying out the steps described above with your client, you might want to consider the following points to help with the process:

- It is good practice to list in two columns the evidence *for* and *against* on a single sheet of paper (or white board), inserting a dividing line down the centre. Alternatively, you can use a thought record (see Appendix 8.1). The advantage of a thought record is that it allows both you and your client to visually and systematically work through this process
- Begin the 'evidence against' column by countering the evidence from the 'evidence for' column. In Simon's case, a discussion of the evidence against his belief could begin with your saying: 'You mentioned in your list of evidence for that cocaine is a sociable drug. Is that always the case?' or 'Are there

times when taking cocaine gets in the way of you or others being friendly or sociable?'

- The process described in this chapter should be done as collaboratively as possible, allowing your clients to find their own evidence. You can make suggestions of your own when your client cannot think of anything, but you should avoid imposing your own ideas. For example, you could say to Simon: 'People sometimes report that taking a large amount of cocaine disrupts conversation and how people get along with one another. Has that ever happened with you?'
- Once the alternative belief has been formed, it is helpful to re-rate the original belief to ascertain when there has been any change in its strength and to rate the strength of the new, alternative belief. The techniques described in Chapters 9 and 10 can be used to strengthen the alternative belief.
- Clients should be encouraged to remind themselves regularly of their alternative beliefs. For example, they could write the new belief on a flashcard to carry around with them (see Chapter 11). This can be referred to whenever they feel tempted to use drugs or alcohol.

Summary

Working with beliefs about substance use is central to the treatment approach set out in this book. The steps described in this chapter set a three-stage process which forms the basic framework for identifying and changing drug and alcohol-related beliefs. These steps are: (i) defining and operationalising; (ii) evaluating; and (iii) developing alternative control beliefs. This process can be used to tackle all types of substance-related beliefs. The techniques described in Chapter 9 can be integrated in this framework.

Appendix 8.1: Thought record

Drug Related-Belief	Evidence For	Evidence Against	Alternative Belief (Control)

Chapter 9

Additional Techniques to Facilitate Cognitive Change

Overview

In Chapter 8 we described a basic framework for identifying and working with drug and alcohol-related beliefs. This chapter builds on this framework by detailing nine techniques we have found useful in facilitating cognitive changes and enabling clients to gain control of their substance use. These techniques can be used to facilitate change in the *content* of beliefs and used to tackle *cognitive biases*.

How to use this chapter

We recommend reading through and familiarising yourself with the techniques described in this chapter. This will give you some ideas for other techniques you can integrate into your work. If you are less familiar with these techniques, perhaps select one or two initially. The technique you select should be guided by your client's formulation and the content of the belief you and your client are working on. There are no set rules about which technique to use with each type of cognition. However, as a guide, Chapter 7 provides an introduction to some of the techniques we have found helpful for each type of cognition, and this chapter elaborates further on this as each technique is described.

Applied Cognitive and Behavioural Approaches to the Treatment of Addiction: A Practical Treatment Guide By Luke Mitcheson, Jenny Maslin, Tim Meynen, Tamara Morrison, Robert Hill and Shamil Wanigaratne
Copyright © 2010 John Wiley & Sons, Ltd.

Nine additional techniques to facilitate cognitive change

Distinguishing a belief from a fact

During high-risk situations, when craving or withdrawing, and after a period of using, drug and alcohol-related beliefs can *feel* like facts, particularly if they have been held for many years. It is important to remind clients that thoughts and beliefs are hypotheses, opinions or even just guesses. Beliefs and facts are not necessarily the same thing. Just because we think something it does not necessarily mean that it is absolutely true. It can be useful to discuss this with your client, especially before reviewing the accuracy or evidence against a drug-related belief (see Chapter 8). This can be useful for all types of substance-related cognitions.

Clients may not immediately accept that their beliefs are not facts. However, all that is needed is the slightest doubt or curiosity, perhaps generated through a discussion of the evidence (described in Chapter 8). A behavioural experiment (see Chapter 10) can then be undertaken to collect further evidence that beliefs are not necessarily totally accurate.

Another way to demonstrate that a belief is not a fact is to use an example. We often draw on the story of Christopher Columbus. Before he sailed round the world most people believed that the world was flat. Now that idea is ridiculous because we can prove that the world is not flat. Perhaps follow this up by asking your clients for an example of where they have believed something to be completely true only to find out later that it was not.

It can also be useful to demonstrate the belief vs. fact idea by referring to the cognitive bias of 'emotional reasoning' (see Chapter 7). Ask your clients to think about how often they (and others) believe something to be true because of the mood they are in, or because they are craving, only to believe it less or to believe something different when that mood, or craving, has passed. Can your clients think of an example when emotions clouded their or someone else's perception of what was really happening?

Advantages/disadvantages analysis

We described this technique in Chapter 4 in relation to enhancing motivation to change and in Chapter 5 in relation to assessing the content of drug and alcohol-related beliefs. This technique is also useful in examining the utility or helpfulness of certain drug and alcohol-related beliefs. There is, however, a slight difference here. To enhance motivation and assess the content of drug-related beliefs, the advantages and disadvantages of the *behaviour* of using substances are explored. To work with your clients on examining the helpfulness of their belief, the advantages and disadvantages of holding that *belief* are explored, in addition to the actual behaviour of substance use. Examining the advantages and disadvantages of holding a particular belief should incorporate a discussion about both the short- and long-term consequences.

We have found this a particularly good strategy for working with permission-giving beliefs that may be accurate (e.g. 'I've not used for two weeks so deserve a treat, so am going to use heroin') but not particularly helpful (i.e. it is true that this client has made important changes and deserves to be rewarded, but ideally not with drug use). The advantages/disadvantages analysis can also be used to examine the helpfulness of beliefs about positive outcome expectancy and beliefs about the pharmacology of substances and methods of use.

When developing an advantages/disadvantages analysis with your client you may also like to underline the belief in each section that carries the strongest meaning. In this way, strong drug-related beliefs can be identified and worked on using the reviewing evidence and counterevidence method described in Chapter 8. Paul's advantages/disadvantages analysis is illustrated in Figure 9.1.

Figure 9.1   Paul's Advantages/Disadvantages Analysis

The 'defence barrister' role-play

Another way to evaluate the accuracy of all types of drug and alcohol-related beliefs is to use the 'defence barrister' role-play (Leahy, 2003). This is a great way to help clients challenge their substance-related beliefs and understand that the evidence they use to support those beliefs is questionable. As in a law court, the client takes the role of a defence barrister and is given the task of discrediting the evidence that supports his or her substance-related belief. The client should attempt to cast doubt on where the evidence came from, how reliable the source is, to what extent it stands as an undisputed fact and whether there is any corroborating and contradictory evidence.

To demonstrate: Paul held the belief 'I don't think I'll ever be able to stop using drugs'. The reasons he gave for believing this was that all his drug-using friends still used and he had tried to give up once before but failed. In session this belief was examined in detail using the defence barrister role-play. The following five steps describe how you might do this:

Step 1.   Provide the client with a rationale for the role-play. You could say: 'As we have discussed, sometimes it is important to explore whether our drug-related beliefs are true. I'm going to show you a way of doing this. We are going to pretend that we are in a court of law. The prosecution has been trying to prove that your drug-related belief is true (i.e. you are not ever going to stop using drugs) and have tried to convince the jury that this is true because of the evidence (i.e. all your friends still use and you have failed on one other occasion to stop using).'

Step 2.   Next explain the role that you would like your client to play. You could say: 'You are going to take the role of the defence barrister and challenge the prosecution's evidence. A defence barrister aims to cast doubt on the prosecution's case (i.e. that you are not ever going to stop using drugs because all your friends still use and you have failed on one other occasion). Why should the jury doubt the evidence the prosecution has put before them? Has the prosecution deliberately twisted the information, only presented some of the facts or misled the jury in any way?'

Step 3.   If your client agrees, enact the role-play. It is helpful if you take the role of the support team for the defence and prompt your client where necessary (tell him that you will do this). A good question to ask during the role-play is: 'Would a jury accept your evidence as fact? For example, if someone in court claimed it is impossible to stop using drugs, does that prove that it is impossible? Could the jury find another explanation or viewpoint that would question the accuracy of this claim?'

Step 4.   All arguments presented by the defence should be recorded and summarised in session to question the drug-related belief your client holds. For example, in his role as defence barrister Paul was able to argue that:

- Just because he knew one or two people who still used drugs it did not mean that *he* would not be able to stop using. He agreed that he had been looking at this from a very narrow angle. On reflection he did know people, who are not his friends, who had controlled or stopped using drugs.

- The facts indicate that most people who try drugs stop using eventually. He said that he might be focusing too much on the extreme cases.
- He knew of plenty of famous people who quit using drugs/alcohol.
- Does everyone stop using on his or her first attempt? Perhaps not. He'd heard it could take many attempts. Look at cigarette smokers, there's a whole industry based on how to give up.
- He had actually learnt a lot from trying to stop, clues that might help him in the future.

Step 5.   Use the defence's arguments to develop an alternative belief to the drug-related belief. In Paul's case, the following alternative belief was developed: 'It is possible to stop using drugs. Others have done it. There is nothing unique about me which means I won't be able to. But it will take time and patience'.

Since the aim of the role-play is to help clients examine the *quality* of the evidence supporting a drug-related belief, it can be a particularly useful technique to use prior to reviewing the evidence against a drug-related belief (as described in Chapter 8). Anyone standing in court would expect a comprehensive and rigorous defence. The role-play therefore allows a thorough examination of the facts from all angles, not just from one person's account. It can also be helpful to reverse the role-play so that you as the therapist can challenge the evidence as a way to introduce new perspectives in a less direct manner. Used well, this method can be a productive way of challenging beliefs in a non-confrontational manner and the role-plays are often conducted on a light note with humour.

Historical review

Many drug-related beliefs, particularly positive outcome expectancy beliefs, magnify the positive aspects of using. An interesting question to ask yourself is why this exaggerated view of drug or alcohol use persists even when your client has experienced many negative aspects of using. One explanation is cognitive biasing where the client's favourable view of drugs is reinforced by selective attention to only positive drug-related experiences. In Chapter 7 we noted that 'magnification and minimisation' is an example of a cognitive bias.

Another explanation for the persistence of a drug and alcohol-related belief is that such beliefs are often formed from early experiences of using the drug. For many clients these early experiences may have been perceived as pleasurable and may have carried important meaning (e.g. a first experience of coping or being accepted). So, it can be helpful to explore the importance of these early experiences and their link to current cognitions. An historical review of the belief may highlight that your client's current perception of his use is heavily influenced by these isolated and selected past experiences and is not a realistic perception based on all subsequent drug-related experiences (including the negative aspects).

For example, you might want to carry out an historical review of Sally's belief: 'It's OK to get drunk at social events because everyone likes to drink on these occasions'. Upon asking her when this belief originated (i.e. when she first started thinking this way), Sally mentioned that it probably originated in her teenage years when she started drinking. When asked why she began drinking at that time, Sally said it was to bond with her peer group. They were all drinking to excess and socialising and Sally believed that not drinking would make her stand out as boring and unlikeable.

Whilst an historical review helps place your client's belief in the context of its origin, it is important to bring this review up to date by asking about situations over subsequent years that have supported or contradicted this belief. This is essentially using the techniques described in Chapter 8 to examine the evidence for and against a belief, but with a particular focus on historical events in addition to more recent situations. This can help your client realise that, for some beliefs, the supporting evidence is largely located in the past.

Cognitive continuum

Many drug and alcohol-related beliefs are polarised in that they reflect an extreme viewpoint rather than the middle ground. As you know from Chapter 7, all or nothing thinking is a common cognitive bias. An example is Paul's strongly held belief: 'I am totally out of control of my drug use'. The cognitive continuum technique offers an effective way of tackling this polarised style of thinking as it requires clients to examine all sides of a situation and helps them see things in shades of grey rather than in black and white. All or nothing thinking is particularly problematic as it can leave clients perceiving themselves as stuck in their current behaviour pattern, with limited options and feeling hopeless about change. The following is an example of the cognitive continuum technique used with Paul to work on his belief about being totally out of control.

A control continuum or scale was developed. This involved a horizontal line being drawn on a sheet of paper and the end points labelled 0 per cent (totally out of control of drug use) and 100 per cent (totally in control of drug use). Paul was then asked to place an × where he currently saw himself. In this example, Paul initially placed his × at 10 per cent (feeling only 10 per cent in control of his drug use). Paul was then asked to give his reasons for rating himself at this level. Once the reasons had been identified the therapist used guided discovery to question how Paul's current perception of 'out of control' fitted with other experiences, including those of other drug users (who seemed more 'out of control') and his own past experiences when his drug use was greater. The purpose of the exercise was to get Paul to see in degrees rather than in black and white (which challenged the 'all or nothing thinking' bias) and to explore the possibility that he was more in control of his using than he originally believed (which challenged the content of his original belief). The process of questioning is outlined below.

Therapist: So Paul, you said that you felt only 10 per cent in control of your drug use. You mentioned that the main reason you had for believing this was because you had taken heroin every day this week even though you had been trying not to use anything at all. Is that right?

Paul: Yeah.

Therapist: Can I ask how much heroin you have used on each occasion?

Paul: I used £10 every day.
Therapist: So you're feeling only 10 per cent in control of your drug use because
             you have used every day this week and used £10 on each occasion.
             How does this compare to what you were like in the past.
Paul: What do you mean?
Therapist: In the past, what was your pattern of daily drug use?
Paul: Up until a few months ago I had been using about £20 per day for
             about three years.
Therapist: Have there been times in the past when you have used even more than
             £20 of heroin a day?
Paul: Yes. Just before I went to prison for shoplifting. I was hard at it, 24/7.
             I was using all day every day.
Therapist: Do you know of others who use more drugs than you?
Paul: Yeah. I've seen people in terrible states. Taking anything they can get
             their hands on, losing their minds, letting themselves go, wandering
             around in a daze for days at a time.
Therapist: OK. Let's take another look at our control scale. I would like us to
             take all the things we have just talked about and place them on our
             control scale. For example, on a scale of 0–100 per cent, where 100
             per cent is totally in control of drug use, where would you place those
             who you have seen who are using until they neglect themselves and
             end up in hospital?
[*Paul places an × at the 0 per cent mark.*]
Therapist: If those people were 0 per cent, where would you place the 'you' just
             before you went to prison for shoplifting?
[*Paul marks an × at the 10 per cent level*]
Therapist: And where would you rate yourself when you were more stable for
             those three years using £20 per day?
[*Paul marks an × at the 30 per cent level*]
Therapist: And compared to when you were using £20 a day, where would you
             place yourself today when using only £10 a day?
[*Paul marks an × at the 40 per cent level*]
Therapist: OK Paul. So when we first began today you felt that you were only
             10 per cent in control of you drug use. However, when you were able
             to examine your past patterns of using and compare yourself to others
             it seems that you would now rate yourself as 40 per cent in control
             of your drug use. What do you make of that?
Paul: Yeah. Sometimes I can be a little negative about my using. I guess
             I'm more in control of my using than I think.
Therapist: OK. So what would you have to do in the next few weeks to increase
             your control from 40 to 50 per cent?

The cognitive continuum works well with all the drug and alcohol-related
beliefs that contain the all or nothing thinking cognitive bias. In particular, this
includes negative beliefs relating to the self, as we have found that clients can be
quite negative about the progress they are making or if they lapse following a
period of abstinence. In these instances, it can be helpful to develop the continua
as illustrated in Figure 9.2. The labels in bold represent the initial all or nothing

For negative beliefs about progress (e.g. 'I'm not making any progress'):

_0%_____50%_____100%___

No progress   Some progress   All current
                                                                 goals achieved

For negative beliefs following a lapse (e.g. 'I've used once so I've relapsed'):

_0%_____50%_____100%__

Abstinence   Lapse   Relapse

Figure 9.2 Examples of Cognitive Continua

thinking, which would leave your client with limited options and the potentially overwhelming task of trying to move from one extreme to the other (e.g. from no progress to all current goals achieved). In contrast, the labels added represent the middle ground. These continua illustrate that at the middle ground point, your client would have options about which way to go (e.g. back towards abstinence or more towards relapse) and that this could be carried out in stages. You may want to add more labels to define different parts of the line (e.g. defining 25 per cent and 75 per cent). As you can see from the end of the dialogue with Paul, it can also be helpful to ask clients what they could do to move along the continuum in the more positive direction.

Distinguishing behaviour from the person

We have found that clients often judge and label themselves entirely on a specific behaviour or action (e.g. 'I'm a failure' or 'I'm a bad person') because they can't control their drug or alcohol use. Personal judgements are often based on a set of rules and values that people use to judge themselves and others (Beck, 1976). Unfortunately, when these rules and values are rigid and the judgements are global, this can contribute to negative beliefs about the self and unhelpful beliefs about coping and self-efficacy.

It can therefore be helpful to share with your clients the idea of distinguishing their behaviour from who they are as a person. The message you want to get across is that it can be unhelpful for your clients to define who they are solely on one type of behaviour. There are a number of ways you could do this in relation to substance use:

- Ask your clients to explain the logic behind their negative judgement about themselves so that you get an understanding of what this judgement is based on.

- Ask them why they think they are making global judgements about themselves based on one type of behaviour.
- Ask your clients: 'What are the consequences of defining yourself solely on the basis of your drug/alcohol use?'
- Explore whether your clients' judgement (e.g. that failing to achieve something makes them complete failures as a person) applies to all situations (e.g. failing a driving test) and everyone (e.g. those failing exams or not getting job at interview).
- Ask your clients whether they would judge other people in the same way. Are they judging themselves more harshly?
- Ask them what they would say to a friend who was thinking this way?
- Normalise the experience of regret in most people's lives. Most people – probably everyone – can think of situations or periods when they wish they had acted differently. Whilst the past cannot be changed, the present and future certainly can be.

We have found negative judgements and labels are often expressed by clients who feel that they have done wrong to others because of their drug or alcohol-using lifestyle. In these cases it can be helpful to talk about the substance-using part of them as different or separate from the non-drug-using side. Making this distinction can help clients see that it is the behaviour of using drugs or alcohol that prevents them acting in the ways they would like, rather than a flaw in their character. Point out that their regret in itself suggests that the problem behaviour clashes with who they really are as a person and how they would like to have acted and how they might act in the future.

The downward arrow technique

The downward arrow technique (Burns, 1980) can be used to introduce flexibility into the content of different types of drug and alcohol-related beliefs. This can make it easier for clients to develop alternative ways of thinking. The downward arrow technique can also be used to challenge cognitive biases, for example, to weaken catastrophising, correct all or nothing thinking or reduce overgeneralisations.

When working with substance-related beliefs, using the downward arrow technique starts when a potential drug or alcohol-related belief has been identified and involves asking a series of questions to identify the underlying catastrophic meaning of the belief and to start questioning its accuracy. It basically involves your being curious about your clients' beliefs – what they really mean and why these beliefs is contributing to their substance use. It can be helpful to use the downward arrow technique prior to carrying out other cognitive techniques, particularly if a belief seems to be very rigid or if you are unclear about the links between a certain belief and substance use. Depending on the belief, 'downward arrow' questions may include the following:

- If that is true, what's the worst that could happen?
- What's so bad about that for you?

- If that does happen, what does it say about you? About other people? About the future?
- Why would that be a problem for you?
- How likely is this worst outcome?
- What might other outcomes be?
- How would you cope?

In Simon's case, the downward arrow technique helped him question the catastrophic nature of his drug-related belief ('I can't give up cocaine because my whole social life revolves around it'), which allowed him to start thinking about a more helpful and accurate alternative.

Therapist:	You mentioned that a major reason for you not giving up cocaine was the fact that your whole social life revolved around taking it. Can I ask what would be so bad about not taking cocaine when you went out partying at the weekends?
Simon:	I would not have any fun as everyone else is doing it.
Therapist:	And if you did not take it and everybody else did, why would that bother you … ?
Simon:	I'd stand out. Everyone would notice and it would make them feel awkward because I did not want to join in.
Therapist:	And if that were to happen … ?
Simon:	Then they would not want to hang out with me.
Therapist:	If that happens, what would the consequence be?
Simon:	I'd not be invited out with them.
Therapist:	Why would that be a problem?
Simon:	I'd lose all my friends.
Therapist:	So ultimately, you worry that you may lose the friendship of all your mates if you do not take cocaine with them every weekend.
Simon:	Perhaps that's a little strong. I do see many of them outside of clubbing where drugs aren't the focus. A lot of those friendships were developed before drugs came on the scene and they will be there whatever happens.

As the downward arrow technique often highlights permission-giving beliefs, giving your client a handout of these beliefs and some alternatives may be appreciated (See Appendix 9.1).

Pie charts

The pie chart technique has many useful functions when working with substance use, in particular it can be used to:

- Develop a solution to lifestyle imbalance.
- Examine personal responsibility to change substance use.
- Explore alternative explanations (e.g. why your client began using or cannot stop using substances).

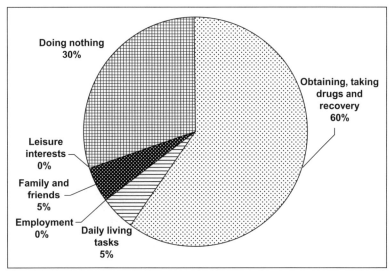

Figure 9.3   Pie Chart 1 – Paul's Typical Week

Pie charts are a graphic problem-solving technique and a technique for developing alternative explanations to unhelpful beliefs about coping/self-efficacy and negative beliefs about the self. They also help challenge cognitive biases by introducing a more flexible way of thinking.

Lifestyle imbalance.   It can be useful to examine the difference between how your client is currently spending his time whilst using drugs or alcohol and how he would like to be spending his time if he was not using. To start with, ask your client to write a list of everything he does during the week, placing items in 5–10 categories. For example, the category of daily living tasks might include eating, washing clothes and general housework. Your client then rates the percentage of time spent engaged in each of these tasks. The list and percentages are then drawn in a pie chart (see Figure 9.3). In our example, the following pie charts were completed with Paul. The first one represents Paul's typical week when using.

Next, ask your client to repeat this for an ideal week where drug use has less importance. The second pie chart (see Figure 9.4) shows Paul's ideal week if he were able to reduce his drug use.

The pie charts are then compared and a plan developed as to how the client might adapt his life to better reflect the second pie chart. After the pie charts were drawn up with Paul, specific goals and plans for how he might adapt his week to look more like his ideal week were made. For example, Paul made a plan to double his weekly contact with friends and family from 5 per cent to 10 per cent.

Personal responsibility.   When stuck in the routine of drinking or drug-taking, and feeling overwhelmed by the prospect of life without substance use, we have found that clients can find it difficult to identify what they can do to help themselves. Developing a list of factors that will contribute to controlling substance use and highlighting their importance in a pie chart can be a very useful exercise as it helps clients see what responsibility they have in controlling their drug or alcohol

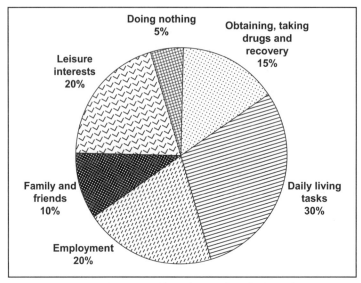

Figure 9.4   Pie Chart 2 – Paul's Ideal Week

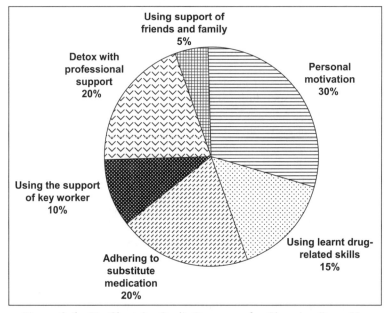

Figure 9.5   Pie Chart 3 – Paul's Resources for Changing Drug Use

use, as well as understanding the role of external resources. You could introduce this technique by saying: 'Now that you are thinking about reducing your use, it might be helpful to explore what factors can help with these changes'. With your clients, make a list of all the factors that may lead to them controlling their drug or alcohol use. It can be helpful to order the list in terms of importance of task, so each item is awarded a percentage grade according to how important it is. Figure 9.5 demonstrates a pie chart completed with Paul. During this task it may be necessary to make suggestions, particularly with regards to your client sustaining any changes made.

With this technique Paul was able to see that 75 per cent of the responsibility to change lay directly with his own actions.

Once the pie chart has been drawn up, each factor can be discussed in detail with regards to how it is actually going to happen. For example, what must your clients do to ensure that their motivation stays high?

Alternative explanations.   A pie chart can also be used to challenge your clients' negative or rigid beliefs about why they started using drugs (e.g. 'I'm a loser') or cannot stop (e.g. 'I'm weak'). Sally, for example, believed that her inability to resist using alcohol was because she was a weak and pathetic person. To work on this unhelpful, negative belief, a list all the factors that contributed to Sally not being able to control her alcohol use was developed. Predictably, the first thing on Sally's list was 'I'm weak'. Sally was asked for more reasons and when the list had been completed, all the items were ranked according to their significance and given percentages by Sally. From this information a pie chart was developed and a discussion then took place to explore Sally's reasons for these ratings. Other possible explanations for why people find it difficult to stop using alcohol were then added to the original list. (You might need to make some suggestions at this point.) Through this discussion, another pie chart was developed. This included all the possible alternatives and led to less weight being placed on the 'I'm weak' explanation. In addition to allowing a consideration of alternative explanations, this technique often helps clients take a more compassionate view of themselves, rather than being censorious about themselves.

Imagery

As discussed in Chapter 7, cravings to use drugs or alcohol can be triggered by a spontaneously occurring image (e.g. of the drug, of stimuli associated with the drug or of actually using the drug/drinking alcohol). The following steps describe how to assess and work with images that relate to substance use.

Step 1: Assessment.   It can be helpful to start by focusing on one or two recent episodes of using drugs or alcohol and asking your clients whether they experienced any images or pictures in their mind when craving and before using. You might want to prompt about images of the drug or of using. If your clients didn't have an image on these occasions, you could ask whether they have ever experienced images. Once an image has been identified, ask if this is a recurrent image. If it is, it can be helpful to identify the underlying meaning by asking 'What does this image mean to you?' or 'What memory does this image represent?'

Step 2: Information exchange.   As this may be the first time that your clients have discussed imagery it is important to spend time normalising the experience of images. This should highlight how common images are, how unpleasant they can feel and that they may take different forms – visual, auditory, olfactory or tactile. This may also address any worries your clients have about experiencing images (e.g. 'It feels like I'm going mad').

Step 3: From images to challenges.   Four ways of working images are described below:

1. *Images leading to belief challenge:* Like drug-related beliefs, drug-related images carry meaning. For example, one client had a visual image of himself lighting a crack pipe, and this image triggered cravings. Exploration of the meaning behind this image uncovered a new drug-related belief: 'Smoking crack is great.' Once the meaning of the image had been established – image of lighting the crack pipe = smoking crack is great – the evidence for and against the drug-related belief was examined using the techniques described in Chapter 8. This involved examining how true it was that smoking crack is always great. An alternative, less distorted belief was then generated: 'Smoking crack is hardly ever great. It only seems that way when you are craving'.

2. *Image of more realistic outcome:* Sometimes it is possible to alter the original image slightly to illustrate a different meaning. For example, the client described above, who saw himself piping crack cocaine, changed the image to watching himself stuff hundreds of pounds into a big pipe and burning it. This new image evolved from a discussion with the client about the disadvantages of using crack cocaine ('I'm burning my life savings'). Another client was able to change his image of seeing himself phoning a dealer from a call box (= 'the drugs are on their way') to seeing himself in the same call box, waiting in the dark for hours (= 'this is a waste of time and they don't care about me'). This second image was arrived at through further questioning and was a more realistic account of what happened on most occasions when he tried to phone his dealer.

3. *Frozen images:* Substance-related images often involve the client watching himself taking the drug. Typically, these images represent the moments before or during experiencing the pleasurable effects of the drug. For example, clients often report seeing themselves lighting a crack pipe, enjoying a glass of wine or watching as the heroin leaves the syringe to enter a vein. These images have been stuck at the 'best' moment in the drug-using cycle. It can therefore be helpful in session to run these images on in time to later moments that do not carry the same exaggerated positive perception of drug use. This could include the moment when your client sees himself in bed feeling miserable from the effects of using crack, explaining to his boss why he has to take a day off sick because of a hangover or seeing the damage left on the skin from injecting. Discussion in session can help change the meaning of the original frozen image to a new meaning associated with the updated image (e.g. 'Using crack for a couple of hours is not worth the two days I spend depressed', 'Alcohol is going to get me sacked' or 'I'm destroying myself with heroin'). The next time the clients experience the frozen images they can remind themselves, perhaps using a flashcard (see Chapter 11) of the new, alternative image.

4. *Ideal coping/mastery:* This technique requires your client imagining herself coping with a drug-related high-risk situation. One client had a repeated image of herself scoring drugs in the local market (underlying meaning = 'I can't go there without scoring'). As the market was where she bought cheap food, it was not helpful for her simply to avoid the location. In session she

worked on a new image where she saw herself shopping and being able to ignore the drug dealers.

Summary

This chapter has described a range of interventions that can be used to tackle unhelpful drug and alcohol-related cognitions. The techniques described here and in Chapter 8 offer a number of ways to demonstrate to your clients that there are alternative perspectives to consider. The techniques can be used to tackle the content of drug and alcohol-related beliefs and to challenge cognitive biases reflected in these beliefs. The techniques aim to support your clients in adopting a more flexible, objective and helpful thinking style. In Chapter 10 we introduce the use of behavioural experiments, which encourage your clients to test the validity and helpfulness of the alternative explanations generated.

Appendix 9.1: Common permission-giving beliefs and alternatives

Common Permission-giving Beliefs	Alternative Responses
If I don't use, I will never get any sleep	If I use, it may knock me out quickly but I never feel properly rested in the morning and my sleep is always broken during the night
Only weak people get addicted, it won't happen to me	I'm like anyone else. No one sets out to be addicted to drugs/alcohol. It could easily happen to me
Because I used yesterday, it means that I have no control over my use	Just because I used drugs on one day it does not mean that I will use on another day or that I have forgotten how to control my use.
My drug use is out of control	My drug use may sometimes feel out of my control but that's just a feeling since I know how to slow it down and stop it
Everyone thinks I'm a junkie so I might as well prove them right	It's true that many people may not believe I can be drug/alcohol-free but I'm trying and that's what matters
I'll give up tomorrow	Don't put off things that you can do today. What am I waiting for? Just do it
I'll never be able to control my cravings without using	Cravings come and go, regardless of whether I use
Methadone has never stopped me feeling rough, so I have to use on top of my script	The reason why methadone is not holding me is that I'm using on top and need a higher script to hold me
I might as well carry on using until my money runs out	Stop using and treat myself to something lasting that I need
I'll never be able to get through the day without using	It's never as bad as I make out. I'll get through the day OK if I keep focused on the tasks at hand
Just one won't do any harm	It's never just one. Stop kidding yourself. Once I have one I don't stop
These withdrawals feel so bad I'll have to use	The withdrawals are uncomfortable and I can't stand them but they will go. Stay in there.
It's been such a long time since I've used. I've obviously got it under control so one won't hurt	I've done really well to stay off drugs/alcohol so why risk it now. I've been down this round many times before. It does not work
Damn, I've had a night on it. I'm useless and might as well carry on using	Yes I've been using but that does not mean I have to carry on.

Common Permission-giving Beliefs	Alternative Responses
I've had a stressful day	I've had a stressful day and deserve to treat myself but not by using. I don't need to treat myself in this way
Everyone is using	It sometimes seems like everyone is using but that's probably not true and that also does not mean that I should use
If I have a hit I won't be harming anyone	If I use I will be harming myself. I will lose what I've achieved
The satisfaction I'll get from this is worth the risk	Don't test myself. I've got too much to lose and it's not worth a few minutes of pleasure
I have to use otherwise I won't be able to concentrate on my work	Using will only make me feel that I'm concentrating but it actually makes me less productive

Chapter 10

Behavioural Experiments

Overview

When exploring clients' reasons for using/not using drugs or alcohol there will be occasions when they might not know the answer to a particular question and where more evidence is needed to help them answer it. As CBT actively encourages guided discovery, the therapist and client can try to answer these questions by setting up an experiment. These behavioural experiments (BEs) are, in short, situations that help test whether your clients' beliefs are true or not. Cognitive interventions often set the scene for change in substance-related cognitions, but behavioural experiments are usually needed to help consolidate the belief change.

Experiments can be observational (e.g. 'Next time you are there just see what really happens') or more usually involve manipulation of the situation to test a particular belief (e.g. 'Next time you are craving, use this craving management technique [e.g. a flashcard] and then see whether your predictions are true that nothing you do seems to soften the impact of cravings'). In many cases, BEs act as a way of testing unresolved questions from therapeutic sessions. For example, a client may see how an alternative explanation fits with the evidence discussed in a session but remain unconvinced that it is really true. In this case, a well-constructed BE will help clarify the situation one way or another (e.g. 'I can stop cravings by using the craving management technique'). This chapter describes how to set up a BE and covers five common experiment themes relevant to overcoming problem substance use.

Applied Cognitive and Behavioural Approaches to the Treatment of Addiction: A Practical Treatment Guide By Luke Mitcheson, Jenny Maslin, Tim Meynen, Tamara Morrison, Robert Hill and Shamil Wanigaratne

How to set up an experiment

Bennett-Levy *et al.*'s (2004) *Oxford Guide to Behavioural Experiments in Cognitive Therapy* is an excellent guide to the process of designing a BE and has influenced the information presented in this chapter. Due to the complexity of addiction clients' presenting problems there is often limited time for such work. We therefore find the following basic steps and related worksheet a useful guide to designing all experiments with substance use (the template is from Clark, 1999, p. 18). The worksheet in Figure 10.1 gives details of a recent experiment undertaken by Sally to illustrate the process. The steps below map onto the worksheet (Appendix 10.1).

The aim is to complete steps 1–3 in preparation for the experiment.

Step 1: In column 1 identify a situation where the drug-related thoughts will be triggered.

Step 2: Write down in column 2 the specific drug-related thought(s) to be tested, including strength of ratings.

Step 3: In column 3 write the details of how the drug-related thought(s) will be tested – the actual experiment.

Steps 4 and 5 are completed in the session after the experiment has taken place.

Step 4: In the outcome column the client describes the results of the experiment with reference to the belief tested.

Step 5: The fifth column records what was learnt from the experiment, including any alternative beliefs. The original beliefs can be rated again in this column and a summary made of what was learned – the take home message.

When designing the experiment always identify obstacles that might interfere with the collection of the information needed. How might the client deal with

Situation	Prediction What do you think will happen? How would you know ? Rate belief (0-100)	Experiment What will you do to test the prediction?	Outcome What actually happened? Was the prediction correct ?	What was learned Balanced view? (Rate belief 0-100) How likely is what you predicted to happen in the future (Rate 0-100)
Going to friend's party	Need to drink alcohol to get through this evening without feeling overwhelmed (90%) I will not be able to enjoy myself if I don't drink (90%) Other people will not find me interesting or fun if I don't have a drink (100%) I will constantly be worrying about how I'm being if I don't have a drink (90%)	Go to party and don't drink any alcohol. See what happens	Went to party without drinking and felt very nervous. Stuck close to my friend for support. Soon involved in a group conversation and met a very interesting woman who had very similar experiences to me. Forgot about worries for a time and still did not take a drink	Felt overwhelmed at first but this eventually calmed. Also enjoyed myself when involved in interesting conversation. Person seemed to enjoy conversation. All this without a drink. Can enjoy a social occasion without a drink (80%) but need friend's support

Figure 10.1   Sally's Behavioural Experiment Worksheet

these? As the example above demonstrates, BEs are commonly used to test drug-related beliefs that either exaggerate the positive aspects of using or undermine the person's ability to cope without substance use. BEs can also be used to test alternative beliefs that are perhaps less positive about the use of drugs or focus on how the client is able to cope without drugs. These are usually control beliefs. These alternative beliefs, elicited from the client before the experiment is done, can be included in the template and placed in the second column under predictions. They are tested in the same way.

Five common behavioural experiments used in working with problem substance use

This section highlights some common BEs used in testing beliefs related to overcoming problem substance use. We describe these in terms of five themes. It is not an exhaustive list but acts as a guide to developing your own experiments.

Questioning aspects of the drug experience

BEs are often used to challenge situations where the client exaggerates the benefits of using or catastrophises the consequences of not using. This type of experiment is illustrated in Figure 10.1.

Sometimes people who are trying to remain drug-free worry about not being able to cope with unexpected and overwhelming cravings or withdrawal states. In this case, they may keep a small supply of the drug or alcohol in the house or keep the dealer's phone number in case they have to use it in an emergency. Unfortunately, behaviour like this only makes them feel less in control of their drug use and keeps alive the idea that they still use drugs/alcohol. A BE may be needed to demonstrate this. For example, in order to test the belief 'I have to keep drugs in the house in case I can't cope' and discover whether the alternative belief, 'Keeping drugs in the house only serves to place temptation in my way and keeps drug-related thoughts alive in my mind', is more realistic, a client was asked to monitor the frequency of cravings, urges to use drugs and drug-related thoughts during a weekend of keeping a supply of drugs in the house and one of not. In this case, the client discovered that he felt more pressure to use drugs when the drugs were in the house.

BEs can also be used to change risky substance-using practices and promote safer ways of using. For example, a client injected heroin rather than smoked it because he believed that injecting would deliver much faster results in relieving his withdrawal feelings. He agreed to test this and to monitor how long it took from time to prepare the drug until the effects began to relieve his withdrawal sensations. The client was surprised to find that injecting took longer since he spent more time preparing the heroin for injecting and needed over 15 minutes to search for an appropriate vein. This experiment helped this client to drop intravenous drug use.

Clients often believe that the mere presence of a drug-related thought means that they will use substances. It can therefore be helpful to discuss with the client that drug-related thoughts are mental events often automatically triggered by internal/external situations. As they are only thoughts the client does not have to act on them and use drugs. A BE can be an effective way of demonstrating this. For example, a client who believed she used crack every time she experienced drug-related thoughts was asked to review the last week of her drug use. This review highlighted one occasion when the client remembered having drug-related thoughts and images but did not use. After discussing the possibility that drug-related thoughts were mental events that did not necessarily lead to using, the therapist and client decided to set up a BE. They identified an alternative prediction based on their discussion: 'Thoughts of using come and go during the day but it does not mean I have to act on them'. To test the new belief the client was to employ coping skills (attention-switching exercises/alternative activities/ reading coping statements written on flashcards) every time she was aware of drug-related thoughts during the week. Even though the client still used crack during the week, she did discover that on two days the coping skills stopped her from acting on drug-related thoughts.

For clients who are preoccupied with self-monitoring for physical and emotional feelings associated with withdrawal states, BEs can be used to demonstrate that mentally absorbing activities can sometimes lessen the perceived experience of these unpleasant events. For example, Paul said that his withdrawal feelings were usually unbearable between waking at 8 am and collecting his methadone from the pharmacy at 11 am. Paul reported that he usually spent this time confined to the house, unoccupied and monitoring his worsening symptoms. He said that this often resulted in his scoring heroin. The therapist explored with Paul the possibility that his perception of the unpleasant withdrawal feelings may be intensified because of his constant self-monitoring. Paul was able to identify occasions when this may have happened. In order to test this idea, the therapist and Paul developed a list of morning tasks that Paul could do to occupy himself before collecting his methadone. A BE was then set up to test the thought: 'Absorbing myself in activities will lessen the experience of withdrawal'. During the next week, between waking and going to the pharmacy, Paul involved himself in these tasks, which included taking his dog for a walk, buying a newspaper and reading the sports section. In the next session, Paul reported that he had experienced withdrawal states but had found that on most mornings these simple activities provided some distraction and lessened his negative experience of withdrawal. He concluded that self-monitoring of symptoms only made them feel worse.

Adopting a non-drug-using lifestyle

The time spent obtaining, preparing, becoming intoxicated and recovering from regular substance use can often limit opportunities for other enjoyable and vocational activities. Also, since many activities have been conducted under the influence of substances, the client may not believe that they can do something without the support of the drug or alcohol. Since recovery can often involve dramatic changes to lifestyle and identity, BEs can provide a way for the clients to discover new interests for personal development and help build confidence in being able to deal with situations without relying on their drug for support. For example, Sally originally believed that she would not be able to cope with or enjoy going to a party without drinking. The BE in this case was able to demonstrate that Sally could function at a social event without the support of alcohol and further evidence that someone enjoyed talking to her. Furthermore, BEs can be used to test beliefs that have become barriers to behaviour change. For example, a client who believed 'I can't do anything when I've got a hangover' found out that this was not always the case since swimming was useful in recovering from a hangover. (These ideas are explored in more detail in Chapter 11.)

Craving experience

Many of our clients experience cravings and may have developed beliefs about not being able to manage without resorting to drug or alcohol use. This pessimistic interpretation may also have arisen because the client has made many unsuccessful attempts to manage cravings in the past. If this is the case, the client may also be sceptical that any intervention can work. In this context, it can be helpful to design experiments to test a client's belief about cravings and being able to manage them. Often these experiments are designed to collect evidence to test one of two theories, where Theory A is the drug-related thought and Theory B is an alternative, less distorted interpretation of the situation.

For example, Sally used craving management techniques to test Theory A: 'I always have to have a drink when I experience cravings' and Theory B: 'Craving feelings fade if I don't drink'. Other examples of thoughts that can be tested in the context of using cravings management techniques include: 'If I don't use cocaine for a whole day, I'll get cravings that will last all day and I'll have to use' or 'My cravings will get worse if I do not use'. Many of the behavioural interventions in Chapter 11 can be used to test predictions like these.

Intolerance of negative mood

Many people use drugs in order to avoid distressing emotions (e.g. depression, anger, panic, boredom). In this case, clients will probably have drug-related beliefs that explain why they believe that drugs/alcohol help them deal with these emotions. For example, Sally believed that alcohol relieved her symptoms of anxiety and Paul said that heroin was a good way of dealing with boredom. In these cases, it can be helpful to develop BEs that test whether the clients' predictions are true or whether there is an alternative view that is less favourable to managing mood states by using drugs or alcohol. Since managing emotions is an important area in addictions work, we consider this issue extensively in Chapter 12.

Testing out control of drug use

BEs are often used to test whether using a drug-related coping strategy will help reduce substance use. These experiments often help test drug-related predictions (e.g. 'I can't turn down the offer of a free smoke'; 'My methadone doesn't work, so I have to use heroin to top it up'; 'I will not be able to cope with [an event] if I don't use'). Once the prediction has been noted and rated, the client is asked to employ some coping strategies during the week to help limit use and test the predictions. In the examples just given the coping strategies could involve employing drug refusal skills, requesting an increase in methadone prescription and noting the effects or using craving management techniques.

Finally, BEs play an important role in collecting evidence to corroborate alternative drug-related beliefs which have evolved from in-session discussions. For example, in Chapter 9, in relation to reviewing counterevidence, Simon concluded that he could have an enjoyable time clubbing without taking drugs. To test whether this new belief was accurate, it was decided that Simon would not take cocaine on the next two occasions he went clubbing. He was also asked to rate his level of enjoyment of the occasion and give evidence to support his rating. When Simon returned the following week, he had completed the task. On both occasions Simon had refrained from taking cocaine and had found that he was still able to enjoy his evening, confirming the validity of his new belief ('I can enjoy myself clubbing without using cocaine').

Good practice points when using behavioural experiments

BEs require the foundation of a good therapeutic relationship since the client will be asked to try something new and potentially anxiety-provoking. BEs should be clearly related to testing beliefs from the formulation and should always be collaborative. For obvious reasons, you as the therapist may not be able to attend *in vivo* experiments. Therefore, BEs in addiction are often homework assignments. As they are an essential part of this work, care and time should be taken to make clear that BEs are integrated into most sessions and into the therapeutic process as a whole. Always leave enough time in subsequent sessions to go through the details and results of experiments. To gain the maximum benefit from the experiments the basic process should involve a thorough planning stage. This planning time is necessary to define what is being tested and what resources will be needed, especially if the experiments involve others (e.g. others being employed to help restrict access to cash). Next comes the testing stage, followed by observation of the results. The final stage should allow for enough time to reflect on what was learnt. Often, one BE will lead to further experiments as more information becomes available. Be clear about what you are testing, since complicated BEs are likely to confuse the client. BEs can be used for verification of the formulation and further socialisation to the model. For example, 'Let's see if it is true that these drug-related thoughts are more frequent in situations when you have cravings'. A BE is a good way to increase skill acquisition and generalisation of skills from session to everyday life. It is important to initiate BEs in the course of treatment since the client will be relying on this type of enquiry after treatment termination to sustain behaviour change. It is often helpful to include the lessons learnt and the practice of BEs in the relapse prevention plan. As a therapist, you should acknowledge and offer praise and appreciation for your clients' attempts at conducting these experiments.

Summary

BEs are a powerful tool for changing thinking because they actively involve clients in testing the veracity of their beliefs through evidence gained from actual experience. The key is constructing BEs that are unambiguous and simple to do. Working with clients to develop BEs can enhance a collaborative relationship and reinforces the idea that they need to be active between sessions. Ultimately, this process can help clients become their own therapists, able to identify and work with a range of self-defeating cognitions which could be crucial for longer-term recovery management.

Appendix 10.1: Behavioural experiment worksheet (Clark, 1999)

Situation	Prediction *What do you think will happen?* *How would you know?* *Rate belief (0–100)*	Experiment *What did you do to test the prediction?*	Outcome *What actually happened?* *Was the prediction correct?*	What was learned *Balanced view?* *(Rate belief 0–100). How likely is what you predicted to happen in the future?* *(Rate 0–100)*

Chapter 11

Behavioural Interventions

Overview

In Chapter 10 we introduced you to behavioural experiments; in this chapter we deal with behavioural interventions. It is important to understand the difference between these two terms or concepts. Behavioural experiments are primarily used to help clients check and assess aspects of their usually distorted thinking, and this follows directly from work looking at cognitions. Behavioural interventions, on the other hand, are used to break the cycle of continued drug or alcohol use by intervening at the behavioural level. This means changing unhelpful behaviours that have been identified in the client's formulation (i.e. those behaviours identified in the situation-level formulation introduced in Chapter 5 and Appendix 5.1). Unhelpful behaviours include the substance use itself, as well as other behaviours that contribute to drug and alcohol use, such as associating with drug-using acquaintances, not engaging in any meaningful activities and engaging in specific activities to acquire the substances.

Changing unhelpful or substance-related behaviours essentially involves doing something different. Rather than just talking with clients about what not to do, we need to help them identify what they could do instead. So we are talking about replacing unhelpful behaviours (related to substance use) with more helpful behaviours (that are less compatible with substance use). This can help the client gain a greater sense of personal efficacy and control.

How to use this chapter

This chapter focuses on behavioural strategies that are used to help clients manage their cravings without using substances and to help them change other undesirable behavioural patterns. Many of the strategies discussed are described in Beck *et al.* (1993). It is not intended that the strategies be used in the order presented or that every strategy will be helpful or relevant for every client. Instead, the strategy

Applied Cognitive and Behavioural Approaches to the Treatment of Addiction: A Practical Treatment Guide By Luke Mitcheson, Jenny Maslin, Tim Meynen, Tamara Morrison, Robert Hill and Shamil Wanigaratne
Copyright © 2010 John Wiley & Sons, Ltd.

you share with a client will be guided by that person's individual formulation. The strategies discussed here can also be integrated into the behavioural experiments described in Chapter 10.

The following four behavioural interventions most commonly applied to substance use problems form the focus of this chapter:

1.   Stimulus control
2.   Craving management
3.   Problem-solving
4.   Activity scheduling

Stimulus control

For many clients, substance use can feel like an automatic response to certain situations (i.e. high-risk situations [HRS] or triggers). These can be internal or external (see Appendices 5.2 and 5.3 for client worksheets). Internal triggers are different emotional states and external triggers (HRS) are things in the environment, such as people, places, events, objects and activities. In these situations clients may believe they have little or no control over their drug or alcohol use. Therefore, in the early stages of your work together it can be useful to focus on ways to avoid or change the triggers. This can result in clients beginning to feel more confident and in control of their use. Changing triggers in the environment is known as stimulus control. After identifying the triggers with your clients and integrating them in the formulation, it can be helpful to discuss and problem-solve how they can *avoid* or *change* these triggers (or stimuli). In the section on craving management below we give a more detailed explanation of identifying triggers.

Examples of triggers to avoid
•   Pubs and off-licences
•   Streets or neighbourhoods where dealers live
•   People associated with drug or alcohol use

Examples of ways to change triggers
•   Change routines that precede substance use (e.g. going home from work at lunchtime to have a hit)
•   Change the location to meet friends (e.g. at a café rather than a pub)
•   Listen to different music
•   Don't have spare cash at hand
•   Remove alcohol from the house
•   Remove drug-using paraphernalia (pipes, bongs, stash box, etc.)

Stimulus control could be a useful initial intervention with Paul. Paul is committed to reducing his weekly illicit heroin and crack use. Unfortunately though, he is finding this hard to achieve. When Paul's pattern of use is reviewed with a drug diary (see Appendix 5.4) there appears to be heavier use on the day(s) after he receives his benefit. Having identified this trigger or HRS (i.e. benefit day and money in his pocket) Paul is asked whether anything in the past has stopped him spending money on drugs on benefit day. Paul remembers one occasion when he paid a court fine on that day and this had significantly reduced his use that week. Using this information Paul used a behavioural experiment (see Chapter 10) to test whether changing and avoiding the HRS would reduce his drug use. Paul's stimulus control strategy was to limit his available cash on benefit day by making sure that when he received his benefit he immediately paid all outstanding bills and bought groceries for the week before he allowed himself to buy any drugs. Paul found that this simple strategy did reduce his weekly drug use.

When to use stimulus control. Avoiding triggers can be a useful first step for clients wanting to make changes to their substance use. It can help people make the initial break from a pattern of regular, heavy use. It can also benefit individuals who have a strong drug-related belief that they cannot exert any control over their substance use. In the latter case, avoiding or changing certain triggers could be framed as a behavioural experiment to test beliefs about lack of control; for example, if clients say, 'I have no control over my drug use', this could open a discussion about how they could go about testing this belief. However, stimulus control should not be the only behavioural intervention used for substance use, as it has a number of shortcomings. For example:

- Some triggers are difficult to change (e.g. collecting social security benefit or wages).
- Other triggers may occur unexpectedly (e.g. a friend dropping by).
- Emotional triggers cannot be avoided, as emotions are a normal part of human experience.
- Avoiding triggers as a long-term strategy may maintain unhelpful beliefs about lack of control and confidence in managing difficult situations and emotions without substance use.

For clients to make longer-term changes and decrease the likelihood of relapse, they need to be able to manage triggers and cravings when they arise.

Craving management

Cravings can be experienced as intense, confusing and unpleasant. They often seem sudden, unexpected and uncontrollable. They can serve as the mediator between triggers and substance use.

Trigger → Craving → Substance use

Clients do not report experiencing cravings before every episode of substance use. For some, the craving may be more subtle, particularly if they are using substances very regularly. Therefore, the craving may only be experienced when they make efforts to reduce or stop using.

As many triggers to cravings cannot be changed or avoided, it is important that clients learn strategies to manage cravings. Craving management strategies do not aim to stop the individual from experiencing cravings altogether. Instead, the aim is to equip clients with strategies to prevent cravings leading to substance use. This can result in cravings being perceived as more controllable and predictable.

When to use craving management.   Craving management can be used as an intervention for clients wanting to reduce or stop their substance use. It is particularly helpful for clients who report strong physical cravings. Ideally, craving management should be carried out in the earlier stages of treatment, but it can also be integrated into work focused on relapse prevention. A number of strategies can be used to help people manage their cravings. However, clients will vary according to:

- What strategies they find helpful.
- When they find certain strategies helpful.
- How many strategies they find helpful.

Four steps to managing cravings

Craving management takes place over a number of sessions. It can be broken down into four main steps. This can be a useful outline to follow in your work with clients. The four steps are:

1.   Understanding the individual's experience of craving.
2.   Identifying triggers to craving.
3.   Normalising the experience of craving.
4.   Practising strategies to manage cravings.

Understanding the individual's experience of craving.   The first step is to help clients develop a greater understanding of their craving experience. Cravings tend to consist of physical sensations, emotional feelings and thoughts about using. Examples include:

- *Physical* – heart racing, butterflies in stomach, sweaty, shaky, tense
- *Emotional* – agitated, nervous, excited, frustrated, irritated, anxious
- *Thoughts* – 'I need some …', 'I have to get some' … , 'I want some …', 'I can't think about anything else', 'This craving is really strong', 'This craving is getting worse'

In addition, clients often describe experiencing certain tastes and smells associated with their substance of choice. They also talk about their 'mind racing' with thoughts about using and often report powerful images of themselves using, or of the substance itself or related paraphernalia.

It is important to ask clients about all these different experiences. To do this, you could explore what a typical craving is like, or talk about their most recent craving. Useful questions to ask when exploring experiences of craving are listed below.

Questions to explore craving experiences
- What is a typical craving like for you?
- When was the last time you had a craving?
- How does your body feel? How do you feel physically?
- What can you taste? What can you smell?

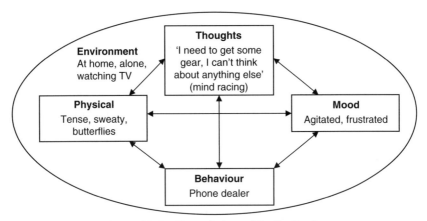

Figure 11.1 Formulation of Paul's Craving

- How do you feel emotionally?
- What is going through your mind? What are you saying to yourself?
- What images do you have?
- Does your mind race with thoughts about using?

Your client's experiences of craving can be formulated using the five-part model. As an example, Paul's craving experience is described in Figure 11.1. Clients often report that drawing out their craving experience makes it seem more manageable.

Identifying triggers to craving. As discussed, triggers can be internal (e.g. different physical or emotional states) or external (e.g. people, places, events, objects and activities). There are a number of ways to identify a client's triggers and these can be used to identify both internal and external triggers. Chapter 5 has highlighted how both internal and external triggers can be assessed using the worksheets in Appendices 5.2 and 5.3.

Most importantly, ask your clients: 'What do you think are the triggers to your cravings?'

You could explore with your clients a specific time when they had a craving. This could be the most recent time or a time they can remember clearly. Ask them:

- Where were you?
- Who were you with?
- What were you doing?
- When was this (i.e. day, time)?
- How were you feeling?
- What were you thinking about?

You could ask specific questions to identify triggers, such as:

- When do you experience cravings?
- Do you experience more cravings when you are:

- with certain people?
- in particular places?
- at certain times?
- doing certain things?
- feeling a certain way?

This information can be gathered from drug/alcohol diaries (see Chapter 5 and Appendix 5.4). The information in the situation column will give clues about potential external triggers and the information in the mood column will give clues about the internal triggers.

It can be helpful to explore a number of different situations when your client experienced a craving to identify the full range of triggers, and to write these down. Once this list has been compiled it can be used to record the corresponding coping responses to deal with the trigger. When new triggers (and corresponding coping responses) are identified they can also be added to the list. This list is useful at a later stage when reviewing relapse prevention strategies.

Normalising the experience of craving.   It can be helpful to share the following information with clients:

- Cravings are *normal* – everyone will experience cravings during their lifetime.
- Cravings are *common* – they are to be expected when people have been using regularly.
- Cravings are *time-limited* – they occur, peak and pass.
- Cravings are a *sign of change* – for some people cravings can be interpreted as an indication that they are desisting from using.

Talking with clients about these issues can be used to identify and test any inaccuracies they have about the nature of craving. This process can be guided by the steps outlined in Chapters 8 and 10.

Practising strategies to manage cravings.   The final step in craving management is to share with clients different strategies that people have found helpful in managing their cravings. A good starting point is to reframe the craving as a warning to clients that they need to do something different, as they may be at risk of using. It is also good practice to start by discussing with your clients what works for them and what ideas they have about managing cravings. For example, you could ask:

- What are you currently doing to cope with cravings? How helpful is this?
- What have you done in the past to manage cravings? How helpful was this?
- What else do you think would help you manage cravings?
- What would you suggest to a friend who was asking your advice about ways to manage cravings?

There are various craving management strategies that you can then share with clients. These include:

- Attention-switching exercises
- Relaxation techniques
- Urge surfing
- Recalling negative consequences
- Positive self-talk
- Flashcards

Attention-switching exercises.   These involve your client thinking about something unrelated to or incompatible with drug or alcohol use. These techniques aim to change the focus of attention in the short term away from internal experiences (i.e. craving and thoughts about using) and onto external events. By switching attention, these brief interventions will help your clients discover that cravings and substance-related beliefs are temporary if ignored, and that they can do something to lessen their intensity. It is useful to draw up a list of these activities with your clients. Examples include:

- Doing physical exercise (e.g. walking, running, cycling, going to the gym, swimming).
- Talking to someone (a friend, family or sponsor) face to face or by phone.
- Going out (e.g. to the library, museum, café, park, cinema).
- Listening to music not associated with using.
- Watching a TV programme or film.
- Reading a book, newspaper or magazine.
- Playing a game (e.g. cards or computer games) or doing a puzzle.
- Taking a bath or shower.
- Doing some housework.
- Describing to themselves their surroundings (e.g. what they can see, hear and smell) in detail.
- Reciting a song, poem, rhyme or prayer.

With encouragement clients are likely to come up with ideas of their own. It is important to remember that different activities work for different people, so it is useful to share these ideas with your clients and then allow them to choose which ones they will try. Ideally, your client should select more than one activity, as each one may be useful for a short time only. Trying different techniques could be set as homework. If your client does practise these techniques outside the session it is important to monitor the effectiveness of the activity chosen and review the outcome in subsequent sessions.

Relaxation techniques.   This involves a set of techniques aimed at reducing physical and emotional stress. Relaxation can be a useful strategy for managing the physical sensations and emotions associated with a craving. Furthermore, these techniques can demonstrate to your client the short-lived nature of cravings and the client's ability to control their intensity.
   A variety of relaxation techniques have been developed. Describe each of these to your clients and ask which they would like to try first.

Relaxation like all skills requires practice. It can be helpful to practise it first in session, before asking the client to practise it regularly at home. A summary of some of the techniques is given in Appendix 11.1. You can give this to your client. It is useful to practise the technique again in your next session to ensure your client is using it properly.

Progressive muscle relaxation is aimed at relaxing the body and involves tensing then relaxing different muscle groups. Each muscle group is tensed and relaxed in turn, several times. By tensing a muscle prior to relaxing it, the difference between tension and relaxation is highlighted, and the sensation of relaxation is magnified. A possible script for progressive muscle relaxation is suggested below. Clients tend to feel less self-conscious if you do this with them.

Progressive Muscle Relaxation

Many people find relaxation a useful thing to do. Relaxation can help your body unwind and your mind to feel more at ease. Relaxation can be helpful if you are craving and find yourself feeling tense, stressed or anxious.

First of all, sit in a comfortable position. Sit right back in the chair so your back is supported by the chair. Your legs should be uncrossed and your feet flat on the floor. Let your hands rest on your lap. If you like, close your eyes.

We'll start with our hands and arms. Clench your fists and tense your arms. Hold for five seconds and feel the tension in your hands and arms. Then slowly relax your hands and arms. Relax for ten seconds and notice the difference between tension and relaxation in your hands and arms. (Repeat twice.)

Now we'll work on our shoulders. Hunch your shoulders by lifting them towards your ears. Hold for five seconds and feel the tension in your shoulders. Then slowly relax your shoulders. Relax for ten seconds and notice the difference between tension and relaxation in your shoulders. (Repeat twice.)

Now we'll work on our stomach. Pull in your stomach tight. Hold for five seconds and feel the tension in your stomach. Then slowly relax your stomach. Relax for ten seconds and notice the difference between tension and relaxation in your stomach. (Repeat twice.)

Now we'll work on our feet and legs. Curl your toes and tense your legs. Hold for five seconds and feel the tension in your feet and legs. Then slowly relax your feet and legs. Relax for 15 seconds and notice the difference between tension and relaxation in your feet and legs. (Repeat twice.)

Now we'll work on our face. Screw up your face as tight as you can. Hold for five seconds and feel the tension in your face. Then slowly relax your face. Relax for 15 seconds and notice the difference between tension and relaxation in your face. (Repeat twice.)

Now just sit back and relax. You may notice your body feeling heavier. Continue to let your whole body relax and sink deeper into the chair. (Continue for five minutes or more.)

When you are ready, slowly open your eyes ...

Deep breathing aims to relax the body through slower and deeper breathing. When we feel tense, our breathing tends to become quicker and shallower. Deep breathing exercises are carried out for about five minutes. You could say to your client:

> Sit in a comfortable position. Sit right back in the chair so your back is supported. Your legs should be uncrossed and your feet flat on the floor. Let your hands rest on your lap. Close your eyes and concentrate on your breathing. Notice each in breath and each out breath. Breathe in through your nose for about two seconds and out through your mouth, again for about two seconds. As you breathe in, imagine your stomach inflating like a balloon. And as your breathe out, imagine your stomach deflating like a balloon and all your tensions being breathed away.

Imagery aims to relax the body by relaxing the mind. It involves asking clients to imagine themselves somewhere relaxing and safe. This could be somewhere they have been to or somewhere that is completely imaginary. Ask them to close their eyes and conjure up the image in as much detail as possible, then describe it to you. Ask them to notice the warmth, the light, the sounds and the smells. This image can be 'rehearsed' out of session and conjured up when they have a craving.

If your client has difficulty thinking of somewhere, you could make a suggestion, for example, on a beach, by a river, in a forest, by a waterfall, in a field, by an open fire or wrapped up in a duvet. If clients have difficulty imagining any of these places, then ask them to choose one from your list and describe it to them in detail.

Clients may find it easier to learn relaxation techniques by practising at home when they are not craving before generalising to times when they are craving. If a client has physical problems (e.g. with their back or neck), progressive muscle relaxation may not be advisable and they should consult their GP before attempting it. If a client experiences panic attacks, relaxation exercises may prove counterproductive as some clients become over-aware of their body. Consider consulting a psychologist/therapist about this first.

Self-soothing involves doing something that is soothing to one of the five senses (sight, hearing, smell, taste, touch). Again, ask clients for their ideas as different people will find different activities soothing and enjoyable. Some self-soothing activities may overlap with the attention-switching activities. Examples include:

- *Sight* – favourite TV programme or film, a flower, relaxing picture, photograph
- *Hearing* – favourite music, recording of natural sounds (e.g. waves breaking on the shore), birds singing, wind chimes
- *Smell* – scented candle, incense sticks, essential oils, baking/cooking, flowers, perfume, clean clothes
- *Taste* – food, drink
- *Touch* – warm bath or shower, comfortable clothes, massage, hug, comfortable chair

Urge surfing. The idea here is for the client to experience a craving without fighting it or giving in to it. The analogy of a wave is useful when talking to clients about the duration of a craving. Explain that cravings occur, peak and pass, like waves breaking on the shore. As a surfboarder surfs over the wave, the client's task is to 'surf' over the craving.

Figure 11.2   Craving Wave

To socialise your clients to this, it can be helpful to ask them to think of a time they had a craving and did not use. Ask them what happened. Did the craving escalate and peak? When did it pass? This conversation is particularly useful when clients believe their cravings are constant – this is a drug or alcohol-related belief that can be tested through a behavioural experiment. You could also have this conversation at an earlier point (e.g. when normalising the experience of craving).

A 'craving wave' can be drawn to demonstrate the course of a craving (see Figure 11.2). Explain that the peak of the wave, between the two crosses, is the hardest part of the craving to surf, but that the craving does pass with time. Ask clients to sit with the craving and focus on how it feels as it passes through their body. Suggest that they acknowledge that it is a craving and remind themselves that though the craving may be unpleasant, it is time-limited. They could also use some of the strategies previously described, such as relaxation and imagery, to help them 'urge surf.'

Urge surfing is an extension of the delay tactic, which involves delaying a decision to use by 10–20 minutes (or longer), by which time the craving has often passed. Urge surfing can be framed as a behavioural experiment to test beliefs about the unlimited duration of cravings (e.g. 'this craving will only get worse and worse'). An experiment could be set up to find out whether the craving does pass.

We have found that clients who successfully stop using drugs or alcohol often employ urge surfing as a longer-term strategy. It is particularly useful in preventing relapses, as it can be used regardless of when or where a trigger occurs. Clients often bring the idea of urge surfing to their everyday activities, so they are able to continue with what they were doing even if they get a craving, as they know that with time it will pass.

Recalling negative consequences.   Recalling the disadvantages of using substances and the advantages of not using is another important craving management technique. When people are craving, they tend to focus on the good things about using, as this information is consistent with their drug-related beliefs which are activated prior to and during a craving. Therefore, clients need to remind themselves of all the negative consequences of using, in both the short and long term, and their reasons for wanting to stop or control their use. This technique is similar to the advantages and disadvantages technique used to enhance motivation to change (see Chapter 4).

It can be useful if clients write out in session the negative consequences of using, as they may have difficulty recalling this information when they are craving. They can then keep this list with them or put it somewhere where they can see it. For example, clients wanting to reduce their alcohol use could put it on the fridge or on the drinks cupboard. Clients wanting to stop drug use could put it by the phone or inside the front door, so they see it before going out to score.

Another technique that uses visualisation to recall the negative consequences of substance use is the 'red box'.

The Red Box Technique

Ask your clients whether they would like to try a technique that may assist them in dealing with cravings or high-risk situations. Then say to them:

Imagine something that you have *freely* done when under the influence of drugs or alcohol (not something that someone has done to you). The thing I want you to imagine is something that causes you some degree of embarrassment, not so much that you cannot bear thinking about it, but something that may make you shake your head and say, 'I can't believe I did that'. I don't want to know what this situation or image is. Picture the situation in as much detail as possible and think about what it feels like to remember this.

Now imagine a square box. Put that picture and feeling in the box. Put the lid on and paint a red cross on the lid of the box.

Next time you find yourself in a situation where all your reasons for not using are ineffective or where you find yourself in a high-risk situation, smash open the box and replay the picture and re-experience the feeling. Say to yourself, 'This is my relationship to drugs/alcohol. This is what drugs/alcohol do to me.'

This should give you enough time to reconsider what is happening and to get you out of the situation or mood you are in. Remember, your brain may be trying to fool you into using by remembering the good times and forgetting the bad. Remembering things that have really happened to you makes it much harder for your brain to fool you!

If you use your image a lot and you feel it is beginning to lose its emotional power, replace it with another. Remember and use the image only when you need to.

Positive self-talk. This aims to counter the drug-related beliefs that occur when someone is craving. This can be useful as thoughts about using are often experienced as powerful, strong and urgent. Positive self-talk consists of positive statements that help the client manage a craving without using. These statements may reflect the control beliefs described in Chapter 5 and the negative consequences of using (see above).

Help your client generate a list of positive self-talk statements which challenge the drug-related beliefs. The actual statements your client finds helpful will vary according to the individual. Again, it can be helpful to write these down in your session. Examples include:

- I can't have just one hit.
- I'll feel like I've let myself down if I have a drink.

- This craving is horrible, but it will pass.
- I've coped with feeling this way before.
- I can beat this.

Flashcards. Flashcards can be a very effective tool to combat cravings and thoughts about using. The idea here is for clients to carry the flashcard with them (in their pocket, wallet or handbag) and read it quickly when thoughts about using begin.

The key coping statements will vary according to the individual. It may be the most important negative consequences of using, the most helpful positive self-talk statements or some other statement the client finds useful, such as goals and values. Flashcards are slightly different from the list of negative consequences and self-talk statements as only the key coping statements are written on a flashcard so they can be read quickly, at any time and any place, e.g. 'Don't listen to the thoughts. Leave NOW before it's too late'. Clients can write the card while in session, or they may prefer the statements to be typed and stuck on a card. Alternatively, some clients choose to carry a photo of someone important to them, as looking at the photo feels like a statement itself.

Managing cravings in session. For a number of reasons it can be useful for clients to practise the strategies in session before trying them out at home. This can help ensure the client has understood the strategy and knows how to use it (e.g. when learning relaxation or using positive self-talk). Trying strategies out in session also increases the clients' confidence in their ability to use the strategy and in the strategy itself (e.g. distracting themselves by talking about something else when they are experiencing a craving).

Cravings can be induced in session by asking clients to imagine they are using or about to use, or by bringing triggers to cravings to the session (either imagined or actual, depending on the trigger). As previously mentioned, practising the strategies in session can be framed as a behavioural experiment to test beliefs about the duration and controllability of cravings, and about the potential helpfulness of different strategies. If you do induce cravings in session, it is important that your client has agreed to this and understands the rationale for doing so. Check with clients before the session ends that the craving has subsided and/or that they have a coping plan in place after leaving the session (i.e. about where to go, what to do and what strategies to use).

Some clients have a belief that talking about cravings will induce one and inevitably lead to them using. This belief can be tested in session to find out whether talking about cravings does act as a trigger and to test other ways of managing the craving that does not involve using.

Summary of craving management
- Craving management is a behavioural intervention that aims to increase awareness, predictability and manageability of cravings.
- It consists of a 'toolkit' of strategies.
- Your client needs to be equipped with a number of well-rehearsed strategies in order to select one or two to use in any given situation.

- Whilst carrying out craving management, it can be helpful to adopt an attitude of curiosity.
- Encourage your client to try each strategy more than once and not give up if the first attempt at using a strategy is not effective.
- It can be useful to adopt a trial-and-error approach to finding out what strategy or combination of strategies works for which triggers.

Problem-solving

Daily problems are unavoidable – they arise in our environment, in dealings with other people and from our thoughts and behaviour. There are different ways to solve problems. Some are helpful, while others are less helpful. First responses are often based on emotions or instincts, with little consideration of the potential consequences.

Avoiding problems tends to be a less helpful strategy in most circumstances. Avoidance as a problem-solving strategy aims to alleviate the stress and worry associated with a problem by not addressing it. However, if this works, it is usually only in the short term, as putting things off comes with its own stresses and worries since the problem is still there and may be getting worse.

It is well documented that substance use is associated with avoidance. In addition to using substances to avoid experiencing difficult thoughts, feelings and memories, clients often talk about using substances as a way to avoid thinking about everyday problems that need to be addressed, and the stress and worry associated with these. There are many reasons why clients choose to avoid addressing daily problems, for example:

- There is no obvious solution (e.g. to finding a job).
- The solution involves doing something anxiety-provoking (e.g. meeting new people).
- The solution seems to be out of clients' control (e.g. their partner arguing with them).
- The solution involves facing up to the reality of their current situation (e.g. their debts).

Problem-solving as an intervention means just that – solving problems. Most can be addressed and solved to some extent. Some problems can be completely solved and some can be solved in stages. Other problems may need to be solved later. There is usually more than one solution to every problem. So, as a behavioural intervention, problem-solving is about effectively addressing and solving problems. The aim is to teach clients this strategy and then help them apply it to the different problems they encounter in their daily lives. At a cognitive level the decision to problem-solve helps to shift an individual's locus of control from the external to the internal, resulting in increased self-efficacy.

When to use problem-solving. Problem-solving can be used to help clients change environmental factors and unhelpful behaviours that might be maintaining the substance use, as this approach enables them to come up with alternative ways of behaving. For example, clients may be able to problem-solve ways to reduce social isolation or to limit how much they spend on drugs. Problem-solving can also be used to help your clients develop stimulus control strategies, by identifying different ways to avoid or change environmental triggers to substance use. For example, clients might be able to problem-solve ways to avoid people associated with drug use or change their routine. Problem-solving can also have a beneficial impact on mood (this is discussed in more detail in Chapter 12).

Stages of problem-solving.   Effective problem-solving can be broken down into five stages:

1. Identify the problem.
2. Identify all possible solutions.
3. Choose the best solution.
4. Prepare.
5. Carry out and review.

Effective problem-solving occurs when these stages are gone through methodically. We recommend that you teach clients each of these stages and practise solving problems in session before asking them to do this at home. Appendix 11.2 summarises the stages and can be given to your client. The five stages are outlined below and illustrated using Simon's issues.

Identify the problem.   The first stage is to *identify* the problem and *name* it. This is most easily done by using the client's formulation to identify potential environmental and behavioural problems. Alternatively, the client may bring a particular problem to the session. Sometimes this problem is easily identifiable. At other times, the client may talk vaguely about a potential problem (e.g. 'I can't cope at the moment'; 'It's too difficult') in which case, you need to understand what lies behind these statements so you have a specific problem (or problems) to address.

You could ask: 'What specific things do you feel unable to cope with?' (e.g. paying bills or seeing friends without drinking alcohol); 'What particular things are you finding too difficult at the moment?' (e.g. not having enough money to buy food; arguing with partner); 'What would you be doing differently if you were coping?' (e.g. paying the rent on time or finding time for oneself). If you end up with more than one problem to address, then you need to complete the five stages for each problem.

The problem needs to be *clearly defined* so it is *concrete* rather than abstract. A broad and abstract problem can be broken down into specific, manageable parts. Gather as much information and as many facts as you can. For example, if your client is talking about being unable to cope with paying bills, you could break this down into what the difficulties are (e.g. not having enough money or having the money but putting off paying). This problem could then be broken down further (e.g. clients might not have enough money because they have lent it to a friend; they have spent their money on drugs; their bills are very high).

Further exploration of Simon's cocaine use while out with his friends led to him stating that he 'would find it too difficult to not use cocaine with them' (a vague statement about a potential problem). When asked what specifically he would find too difficult, he revealed that he found it difficult to say no when someone offered him a line (specific problem), but having a line or two from someone else led to his buying his own drugs. Further questioning about what specifically concerned him revealed that when he had said no in the past, he was asked why and he did not know how to answer without going into detail about the negative side to drug use (concrete and specific problem). He did not want to talk about the negatives while on a night out as it might 'bring everyone else down', but seemed less concerned about talking to his close friends about it at another time.

Identify all possible solutions.   This involves identifying all possible solutions to the specific problem. With your client, write down as many ways as you can both think of. At this stage, do not judge whether the solutions are good or bad. Try throwing in a few 'off the wall' solutions to demonstrate that creativity is key at this stage and that nothing should be ruled out. Ask your client to view the problem as an outsider who is advising a friend about what to do. This can help generate more solutions. Also encourage your client to think of solutions that have worked for him before. Perhaps he can think of something that worked well for him in a similar situation, or even ask friends about solutions that have worked for them in similar situations.

Simon and his therapist identified the following solutions to the problem of what to say if friends ask why he does not want a line:

1. Tell them I am not feeling well.
2. Tell them I've just had a line.
3. Tell them I want a break from it tonight.
4. Tell them I don't feel like it.
5. Tell them it's none of their business.
6. Tell them I am trying to cut down.
7. Tell them it's a long story and I won't bore them with it now.
8. Tell them about the impact it's having on my mood and work.

Asking Simon what he would advise a friend helped him generate ideas, and his therapist also made a few suggestions.

Choose the best solution.   The next stage is to look through the solutions and for your client to pick the one he thinks is the best. A good starting point is to eliminate the least practical and riskiest ones. For the rest, consider the pros and cons and the short- and long-term consequences of each. If there are a few potentially good solutions, you can number them in order of how helpful your client thinks they will be. This will give him more than one option and an element of choice. The solution that maximises the most positive consequences and minimises negative consequences is the one to try first.

Simon ruled out the first three solutions as he did not want to lie to his friends. He also ruled out the fourth because he thought it would lead to further questions and the fifth because he thought it sounded rude. After considering the pros and cons of the remaining three solutions, he decided they were all possible and rated them in the following order:

1. Tell them it's a long story and I won't bore them with it now.
2. Tell them I am trying to cut down.
3. Tell them about the impact it's having on my mood and work.

Prepare.   It is important that your client does some preparation before carrying out the chosen solution as this will maximise the chances of success. There are two aspects to this. The first is to identify the resources available that will help the client implement his solution, such as enlisting the help of others, gathering information, breaking the solution down into smaller steps or completing some other task prior to tackling the solution. The second is to think of potential obstacles to carrying out the solution (i.e. what might prevent the plan from happening?) and ways to overcome these (i.e. what can be done to overcome these?). This may involve role-playing the situation in session (particularly useful if it involves interpersonal skills) and having a second solution in reserve as a back-up.

Simon identified his girlfriend as someone who could support him in trying the first solution (available resource). In addition to offering him general support, she could help divert the conversation away from drug use. Simon also identified two potential obstacles to carrying out the first solution. First, as he hadn't said this before he was concerned it wouldn't sound natural. Second, his friends might continue to ask why he didn't want a line. Overcoming this obstacle involved Simon role-playing with his therapist to practise saying 'It's a long story, I won't bore you with it now' and to responding to further questioning. The therapist took Simon's role to start with to model this 'refusal' skill, while Simon role-played his friend. They then swapped roles.

Carry out and review.   The final stage of problem-solving is to carry out the solution by putting it into action. The client needs to keep a check on whether the solution is working. If it's not effective or only partly effective, he needs to think about what needs to be overcome, how he might change what he is doing and whether he needs to try a different solution. After carrying out the solution, evaluate how effective this solution was with him. What were the consequences? Could he use this solution in the future for the same or a similar problem? What could he have done differently?

Simon generally found this a helpful way to respond to his friends' questions about why he didn't want a line. However, while responding in this way and checking its effectiveness, he realised that he also needed to change the topic of conversation in order for this solution to be fully effective. Simon concluded that using this solution would be a helpful strategy which he could use in the future as the consequence was that his friends didn't pursue this line of questioning further.

In general it is better to stick to solving one problem at a time. If a problem cannot be solved immediately, help your client identify a time when it can be addressed. Clients should be encouraged to focus on addressing problems that they themselves can change rather than trying to change other people. Remember that there will be some situations when the best solution is to do nothing, or the problem cannot be solved and your client may need support around this. It is important to stress that positive experiences of problem-solving play a fundamental part in any personal development. Success at problem-solving can therefore be experienced by clients as a definite step on the road to recovery.

Activity scheduling

Activity scheduling is a behavioural intervention that originated from cognitive behavioural therapy for depression (e.g. Beck, 1976). As you know from previous chapters, what we do (our behaviour) impacts on our mood and thoughts. When people are using substances, their activities tend to focus on their drug or alcohol use, and they often stop doing activities that they enjoy or give them a sense of achievement. Furthermore, when people cut their substance use, they often find themselves more isolated, as they avoid people and places that are associated with using. As Figure 11.3 illustrates, Paul's behaviour (staying at home, not pursuing interests) reinforces his drug-related beliefs ('drugs are all I have in life'), has a negative impact on his mood (he feels bored and lonely) and view of himself ('I'm such a failure'), and therefore maintains the substance use (use heroin/crack to pass the time).

The aim of activity scheduling is to increase the client's repertoire of meaningful activities (hobbies, interests, socialising, work). These activities will provide an environment that positively reinforces non-substance-related behaviours and will help break the negative cycle illustrated in Figure 11.3 by intervening at the behavioural level. In addition, increasing meaningful activity challenges drug-related beliefs and negative thoughts about the self by providing evidence against these cognitions. Activity also provides a way of switching attention, which is one way of managing cravings. In a wider context, activity scheduling acts as the main intervention to present your client with opportunities to engage in meaningful activities to aid recovery (e.g. occupational, leisure, educational and social interests).

When to use activity scheduling. Activity scheduling is a useful intervention to use when clients are not engaging in many activities other than using substances.

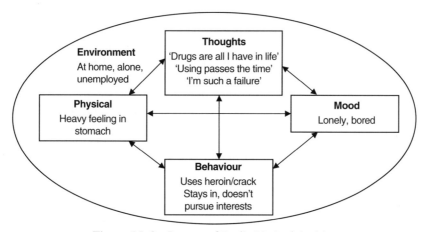

Figure 11.3 Impact of Paul's Limited Activity

You could specifically ask your clients: 'What do you do throughout the week?' or 'How do you spend your time?' If they come up with a limited number of activities, this might be a helpful intervention to try. You could also ask: 'What impact has substance use had on your activity levels/social life/motivation to pursue your interests?' In addition to asking questions like these, activity scheduling is worth considering if your client talks about feeling bored, lonely or depressed.

Four steps to activity scheduling

There are four main steps to activity scheduling:

1. Rationale.
2. Activity monitoring.
3. Learning from the diary.
4. Scheduling activities.

As with previous interventions, it is useful to go through each of these steps with your client to maximise the usefulness of this intervention. These four steps are outlined next and illustrated using Paul's issues.

Rationale.   If you identify a lack of meaningful activity as being an important behavioural factor in the substance use, you can add this to the client's formulation to demonstrate how it contributes to the maintenance cycle (as outlined in Figure 11.3). This will provide you and your client with a rationale for working on increasing activity levels. In particular, point out to your clients that a lack of activity is contributing to their feeling bored, depressed and lonely. To highlight this, you could ask them to compare how they feel after staying at home compared to how they feel if they go out. Also make explicit the link between a lack of activity, drug-related beliefs and the subsequent substance use (as described above). Explain that you would like to work with them around slowly increasing their activity levels to see if this leads to any changes in their mood and their substance use. Ask them to repeat the rationale, to check your explanation and their understanding.

Paul's formulation highlights that boredom is a common (internal) trigger to heroin and crack use. He has a belief that the boredom will become 'unbearable' and this leads him to use drugs. The boredom is also, in part, maintaining Paul's contact with his drug-using friends (an external trigger to drug use).

Activity monitoring.   After going over the rationale for activity scheduling, the next stage is to monitor in detail what the client is already doing, so you can look for patterns between current activity levels, substance use and mood. An activity diary is used to monitor activity (see Appendix 11.3). Completing this diary will help demonstrate the rationale and highlight where changes in activity might be needed (e.g. where there is a lack of structure to the day). It can be helpful to introduce an activity monitoring diary as follows:

• This is an activity diary. It aims to look in detail at your daily activity and your mood over a one- or two-week period.

Time	Monday	Tuesday	Wednesday	Thursday	Friday	Saturday	Sunday
6–7 pm	Watched TV 7	TV 6	Super-market 3	Shower 3	Watched film 2	Went for walk 2	Watched TV 5
7–8 pm	TV 7	Friend visited 3	Cooked and ate, TV 4	Walk and bought chips 2	Phoned Mum 2	Tidied flat 3	Read paper 4
8–9 pm	TV 7	Used brown and white 1	TV 5	Home, TV 3	Bought fish and chips 1	Cooked and ate, TV 3	Watched TV 7
9–10 pm	TV 7	Used brown and white 1	TV 6	TV 5	Watched TV 4	TV 5	TV 8
10–11 pm	TV 8	TV, with friend 2	TV 7	TV 6	TV 5	TV 7	TV 8

Mood rated: boredom; 10 = worst it could be.

Figure 11.4 Extract from Paul's Completed Activity Diary

- You need to complete for each hour what you were doing and how you were feeling.
- Ideally, it should be completed at the end of each hour, or as close to that as possible, so you're not relying on your memory.
- This can seem time-consuming at first and like a chore, but people usually get the hang of it quickly and find it doesn't take long at all.
- This diary will help us identify patterns between what you do, how you feel and the substance use. It will also help us identify what you could be doing differently.
- You only need to write one or two words to describe what you were doing.
- Even if you are just sitting down, you should record that.
- You only need to rate your mood between 0 and 10. Which mood would you like to rate?

With regards to mood rating, ideally you want them to rate a mood that commonly triggers substance use. You could refer back to their formulation, or ask them which mood bothers them the most. They need to rate the mood on a scale of 0 = not at all, 10 = worst it could be.

Ask your client to practise completing the diary in session for the day so far, to check they've understood how to complete it. Figure 11.4 shows an extract from Paul's diary. We have found it easier to ask clients to rate one mood. However, an alternative is to ask your client to rate pleasure (enjoyment) and mastery (achievement), again on a scale of 0–10.

Learning from the diary. When your client brings a completed activity diary to your session, the next step is to look for patterns with your client. You are looking for links between activity, mood, substance use and times of the day. Pay particular attention to the times when a lack of meaningful activity preceded drug or alcohol use, or was associated with a worsening in your client's mood. The following list suggests questions to ask your client to help identify patterns.

Questions to identify patterns in the activity diary
- Did your mood change during the week? What patterns do you notice?
- Were there certain times of the day or week when you felt worse?
- Were there certain times of the day or week when you felt better?
- Did the activity you were doing affect your mood? How?
- Did the activity you were doing affect your drug use? How?
- What activities made you feel better? Why do you think this was?
- What activities made you feel worse? Why do you think this was?
- Did your mood affect your drug use?

What patterns do you see in Paul's diary extract (Figure 11.4)? He is more likely to feel bored while at home watching TV. He felt less bored when he was with a friend; however, this involved using drugs for some of that time. Paul also felt less bored when watching a film, going for a walk, buying fish and chips, shopping, cooking, tidying his flat, talking on the phone and reading. All these activities he did by himself.

The pleasure and mastery scale used in treatment is not only valuable in itself, it can also be used as a means of encouragement towards recovery.

Scheduling activities. The final step is to schedule in activities for the coming week. People need a balance of enjoyment and achievement in their lives and scheduling activities helps ensure this balance is achieved. Scheduling activities in advance also increases the number of activities carried out over the week, gets round the need for repeated decision-making ('What shall I do next?') and makes it more likely that activities will be carried out. Scheduling in activities can also reduce an overwhelming number of tasks into a smaller manageable list (e.g. if someone has daily chores to catch up on).

The diary format that was used to monitor activities over the previous week can be used to schedule in activities. It is used as a diary for the week to come, so activities are actually written into the diary. To help plan activities, use the completed monitoring diary and the patterns identified as a guide to which activities your client needs to be doing more or less, and when. Some useful questions to ask your client to help him think of activities to schedule are listed below.

Questions to identify activities
- Looking at your completed monitoring diary, what activities make you feel less bored/lonely/depressed? Can you think of any others?
- Looking at your completed diary, what activities make you less likely to use? Can you think of any others?
- When in the day do you need to do something different?
- What other activities would you like to do?
- What activities do you enjoy doing?
- What activities did you used to enjoy doing?

- What activities do you need to do (e.g. housework)?
- What do people you know do?
- What would a friend suggest you do?
- What activities would you suggest to a friend?

So what activities could Paul schedule in? He needs to be spending less time watching TV, although watching something of interest, such as a chosen film, could be scheduled in. He could also schedule in cooking each evening, shopping, going for a walk more regularly or phoning friends and family. There are likely to be other activities and tasks that he could do that aren't listed in the completed diary, but that could be elicited by asking the questions above. Paul seems to feel less bored when doing an activity with someone. However, if he plans to see other people, he needs to schedule in non-drug-related activities during this time.

In general, Paul needs to schedule in a greater variety of activities and more activities with others. However, two problems may arise. First, Paul's lack of money may prevent him from engaging in some activities. Second, Paul's social network consists of others who also use drugs. These problems would need to be tackled, using the problem-solving approach outlined above. Paul would also benefit from some craving management work, as he may continue feeling bored at times and boredom is a trigger for his cravings.

We believe activity scheduling plays a fundamental part in the recovery process and should be an essential part of any treatment plan. To help engage your client in this, try adopting a spirit of curiosity or collaborative empiricism to testing different activities and examining their impact on substance use and mood. A graded approach to testing activities can be helpful. Initially, your clients may only feel confident in carrying out simpler or more familiar activities. To maximise the chances of success, break down activities and tasks into small, manageable steps. This is particularly helpful for tasks that have to be done (e.g. household chores that give a sense of achievement once completed, but little enjoyment). Increasing social capital can be an important part of recovery, so encourage your clients to do some activities with other people. Clients often talk about lack of money stopping them doing more activities and it can be helpful to problem-solve this with them.

Summary of behavioural interventions

Behavioural interventions aim to change unhelpful behaviours such as substance use and other behaviours related to this. Making behavioural changes has a positive impact on mood, physical sensations, drug-related beliefs and the environment. Behavioural interventions can be used as a starting point to help clients gain a sense of control and confidence over their substance use. These interventions can also be integrated into behavioural experiments to test the accuracy of drug or alcohol-related beliefs. Key behavioural interventions include stimulus control, craving management, problem-solving and activity scheduling. You may use any number of these with your client, and they are sometimes best used in combination (as highlighted in Paul's case). The chosen interventions will be guided by your client's own formulation and goals, and a collaborative and curious approach will create an atmosphere that increases the likelihood of your client trying out the different strategies suggested. The interventions will also provide you and your clients with further information about the function and consequences of their substance use. Any new information, particularly regarding drug or alcohol-related beliefs (i.e. the reasons for using) should be integrated into an ever-evolving formulation.

Appendix 11.1: Relaxation techniques handout

Progressive Muscle Relaxation

Many people find relaxation a useful thing to do. Relaxation can help your body unwind and your mind to feel more at ease. Relaxation can be helpful if you are craving and find yourself feeling tense, stressed or anxious.

First of all, sit in a comfortable position. Sit right back in the chair so your back is supported by the chair. Sit with your legs uncrossed and your feet flat on the floor. Let your hands rest on your lap.

We'll start with our hands and arms. Clench your fists and tense your arms. Hold for five seconds and feel the tension in your hands and arms. Then slowly relax your hands and arms. Relax for ten seconds and notice the difference between tension and relaxation in your hands and arms. (Repeat twice.)

Now we'll work on our shoulders. Hunch your shoulders by lifting them towards your ears. Hold for five seconds and feel the tension in your shoulders. Then slowly relax your shoulders. Relax for ten seconds and notice the difference between tension and relaxation in your shoulders. (Repeat twice.)

Now we'll work on our stomach. Pull in your stomach tight. Hold for five seconds and feel the tension in your stomach. Then slowly relax your stomach. Relax for ten seconds and notice the difference between tension and relaxation in your stomach. (Repeat twice.)

Now we'll work on our feet and legs. Curl your toes and tense your legs. Hold for five seconds and feel the tension in your feet and legs. Then slowly relax your feet and legs. Relax for 15 seconds and notice the difference between tension and relaxation in your hands and arms. (Repeat twice.)

Now we'll work on our face. Screw up your face as tight as you can. Hold for five seconds and feel the tension in your face. Then slowly relax your face. Relax for 15 seconds and notice the difference between tension and relaxation in your face. (Repeat twice.)

Now just sit back and relax. You may notice your body feeling heavier. Continue to let your whole body relax and sink deeper into the chair. (Continue for five minutes or more.)

Deep Breathing

Sit in a comfortable position. Sit right back in the chair so your back is supported. Sit with your legs uncrossed and your feet flat on the floor. Let your hands rest on your lap. Concentrate on your breathing. Notice each in breath and each out breath. Breathe in through your nose for about two seconds, and then out through your mouth, again for about two seconds. As you breathe in, imagine your stomach inflating like a balloon. And as you breathe out, imagine your stomach deflating like a balloon and all your tensions being breathed away.

Self-Soothing

Self-soothing involves doing something that is soothing to one of the five senses (sight, hearing, smell, taste, touch).

Examples include:
- **Sight** – favourite TV programme or film, a flower, relaxing picture, photograph
- **Hearing** – favourite music, recording of natural sounds (e.g. waves breaking on the shore), birds singing, wind chimes
- **Smell** – scented candle, incense sticks, essential oils, baking/cooking, flowers, perfume, clean clothes
- **Taste** – food, drink
- **Touch** – warm bath or shower, comfortable clothes, massage, hug, comfortable chair

Appendix 11.2: Effective problem-solving handout

Effective problem-solving can be broken down into five stages:

1. Identify the problem.
2. Identify all possible solutions.
3. Choose the best solution.
4. Prepare.
5. Carry out and review.

Identify the problem

The first stage is to *identify* the problem and *name it*. Sometimes there is a specific problem that is easily identifiable. At other times, a potential problem may be vague – for example, thinking 'I can't cope at the moment', 'It's too difficult' or any other number of things. In this instance, you need to understand what is behind these statements so that you have a specific problem (or problems) to address. You could ask yourself: 'What specific things do I feel unable to cope with?' 'What particular things am I finding too difficult at the moment? or 'What would I be doing differently if I was coping?' If you end up with more than one problem, you need to complete the next stages for each problem. The problem needs to be *clearly defined* so it is *concrete* rather than abstract. A broad and abstract problem can be broken down into *specific*, manageable parts.

Identify all possible solutions

This involves identifying all possible solutions to the specific problem. Write down as many ideas that you can think of. At this stage, do not judge whether each solution is good or bad. It can be helpful to suggest a few 'off the wall' solutions as these can generate creativity, which is important at this stage. Nothing should be excluded. Try viewing the problem as an outsider who is advising a friend about what to do. Think of solutions that have worked before or solutions that worked well in a similar situation. You could even ask someone about solutions that have worked for them in a similar situation.

Choose the best solution

The next stage is to look at the solutions and choose which you think is the best. A good starting point is to eliminate the least practical or too risky suggestions. Consider the pros and cons of the rest, and the short- and long-term consequences of each one. If there are a few potentially good solutions, it can be helpful to put them in order of how helpful you think they will be. Then you will have more than one to choose from. The solution that maximises the most positive consequences and minimises negative consequences is the one to try first.

Prepare

It is important that you do some preparation before carrying out your chosen solution as this will maximise the chances of success. Preparation has two aspects. The first is to identify the resources that will help you carry out this solution, such as enlisting the help of others, gathering information, breaking the solution down into smaller steps or completing some other task prior to carrying out the solution. The second is to think of potential obstacles to carrying out the solution (i.e. what might prevent the plan from happening?) and ways to overcome these (i.e. what can be done to overcome these?). This may involve having a second solution in reserve as a back-up.

Carry out and review

The final stage of problem-solving is to carry out the solution by putting it into action. You need to keep a check on whether the solution is working. If it's not effective or only partly effective, you need to think about what needs to be overcome, how you might change what you are doing and whether you need to try another solution. After doing this, evaluate how effective it was. What were the consequences? Could you use this solution in the future for the same or a similar problem? What could you have done differently?

Appendix 11.3: Weekly activity diary

Please write in each box: (1) activity – what you did
(2) mood rating (0–10)

Mood I am rating is: _____

Time	Mon.	Tues.	Wed.	Thurs.	Fri.	Sat.	Sun.
7–8 am							
8–9 am							
9–10 am							
10–11 am							
11–12 pm							
12–1 pm							
1–2 pm							
2–3 pm							
3–4 pm							
4–5 pm							
5–6 pm							
6–7 pm							
7–8 pm							
8–9 pm							
9–10 pm							
10–11 pm							
11–12 am							
12–1 am							

Chapter 12

Working with Emotions

Overview

Two of the criticisms often levelled at CBT are that it is formulaic and that it underestimates the role of emotions. By now we hope that you will see that any formulas in CBT are there to guide you and not simply to direct you. This chapter builds on this work and explores a number of individual approaches for dealing with emotions.

This chapter demonstrates how emotions (also known as 'moods' or 'feelings') play a key role in triggering and maintaining substance use. As previous chapters have explored, emotions serve as internal triggers to substance use and are also a consequence of using substances. Therefore, when working with substance use, we need to focus interventions at the emotional level, in addition to targeting drug-related cognitions and unhelpful behaviours.

How to use this chapter

Previous chapters have described a range of cognitive and behavioural interventions that aim to help people reduce their substance use. These interventions also have an impact on an individual's emotional experience and can therefore be used to help clients manage difficult emotions in ways that do not involve using

Applied Cognitive and Behavioural Approaches to the Treatment of Addiction: A Practical Treatment Guide By Luke Mitcheson, Jenny Maslin, Tim Meynen, Tamara Morrison, Robert Hill and Shamil Wanigaratne
Copyright © 2010 John Wiley & Sons, Ltd.

substances. This chapter aims to make explicit how you can use the interventions described in previous chapters to help clients manage difficult emotions as they arise, without using drugs or alcohol. This approach to working with emotions can be broken down into four steps:

1. Understanding and normalising emotions.
2. Identifying links between emotions and substance use.
3. Identifying and labelling emotions.
4. Strategies to manage emotions.

It should be noted that this chapter does not focus on directly treating the underlying emotional factors and co-morbid mental health problems. Ongoing emotional difficulties indicate the need for more specialist assessment and intervention, particularly if these difficulties persist when the substance use has become less problematic.

Understanding and normalising emotions

When working from a cognitive behavioural perspective, we have found it helpful to understand emotions in the following way:

- *Emotions are useful* – as adaptive social creatures we need to experience emotions in order not only to keep us safe but to help us monitor and assess what is valuable and what is not, what may need to change and what can be kept.
- *Emotions are normal* – we are all born with the readiness to experience different emotions and we all experience emotions, at least to some degree, every day. When difficult emotions become intense and more frequent, they can be experienced as distressing.
- *Emotions are 'felt' experiences* – describing emotions can be difficult as, unlike our thoughts and beliefs, they do not present in verbal or spoken form. Sometimes we may not have words that adequately fit with our emotional experience. In addition, people may use different labels to describe a similar experience, or the same ones to describe different experiences.
- *Emotions manifest physically* – there is usually a link between how we feel emotionally and how we feel physically. For example, someone feeling anxious (emotion) may describe feeling sweaty and shaky (physical); someone feeling depressed (emotion) may describe feeling tired and heavy (physical); and someone feeling angry (emotion) may describe feeling tense and hot (physical).
- *Emotions are a means of communication* – expressing emotions can help us communicate more effectively with other people, as they are more likely to receive the message we intended to communicate if we describe how we are feeling. Emotions also provide us with information about our reaction to a situation or event and this guides our response. For example, difficult emotions may warn us that we need to do something different. What we do in response to an emotion can be helpful or less helpful.

Figure 12.1 Continuum of Emotion – Different Labels

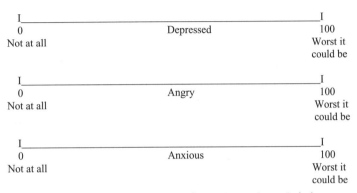

Figure 12.2 Continuum of Emotion – Same Label

- *Emotions come and go* – like cravings, emotions occur, peak and pass. The 'wave' analogy used in Chapter 11 to describe cravings can also be used to describe emotions.
- *Emotions are not dichotomous* ('all or nothing') – people feel varying degrees of emotion. Different labels may be used to describe the different degrees of an emotion (see Figure 12.1) or the same label can be described to varying degrees (see Figure 12.2).

As a first step, it can be useful to share this way of understanding emotions with your client. In particular, it is important to normalise the experience of difficult emotions. Conversations about emotions can be started by asking clients: 'Why do you think we experience emotions?' You can then share the above points and ask for their feedback.

Identifying links between emotions and substance use

The second step is to discuss the link between emotions and substance use. We have found it helpful to understand the link between emotions and substance use in two closely related ways:

1. Emotions as a trigger to substance use.
2. Emotions as a consequence of substance use.

Emotion →	Belief →	Behaviour
Low mood	'Crack will lift my mood'	Crack use
Boredom	'Drinking alcohol is something to do'	Alcohol use
Anxiety	'Heroin will relax me'	Heroin use
Anger	'Cannabis will chill me out'	Cannabis use
Happy	'Cocaine will heighten my mood'	Cocaine use

Figure 12.3   The Role of Beliefs in Linking Emotions to Substance Use

Emotions as a trigger to substance use

The experience of difficult emotions can serve as internal triggers to substance use. By internal we mean that the trigger resides within the individual. The link between emotions and substance use (i.e. the behaviour) is *mediated by drug/ alcohol-related beliefs*. Some examples of beliefs that link emotions to substance use are listed in Figure 12.3. Substance use is often used as a way of pushing emotions away, as an attempt to avoid experiencing emotions in the first place or as an attempt to stop the emotions becoming too intense or overwhelming. People believe that the drug will bring them short-term, immediate relief (i.e. a quick fix) from the distressing emotions they may feel. It should also be noted that the experience of positive emotions could also trigger substance use (e.g. drinking alcohol as a way of enhancing the happy mood associated with an important event).

The emotions that trigger substance use will have their own triggers. These are likely to be cognitive, behavioural and environmental. For example, low mood could be associated with negative thinking patterns (cognitive), boredom could be associated with a lack of meaningful activity (behavioural) and anger could be associated with arguments at home (environmental).

Emotions as a consequence of substance use

Emotional experiences are a consequence of using substances. Substance use can lead to positive emotions, such as euphoria, along with a range of difficult emotions, such as low mood, anxiety and irritability. These emotional consequences are due to biological changes (e.g. dopamine or serotonin depletion following chronic stimulant drug use) and/or cognitive responses (e.g. negative thoughts about oneself for having used). Emotional consequences can also be related to other behaviours and environmental circumstances associated with substance use (e.g. social isolation where a possible emotional consequence is loneliness and low mood), lack of meaningful activity where a possible emotional consequence is boredom and low mood, and not having enough money to pay bills where a possible emotional consequence is stress and anxiety. Furthermore, using substances to bring immediate relief from distressing emotions does not make the difficult emotions go away in the longer term. Substance use also prevents the person finding alternative ways to manage emotions, which can undermine their confidence in dealing with these normal human experiences.

Emotion	Belief	Behaviour	Emotional consequence
Low mood	'Crack will lift my mood'	Crack use	Low mood (from the 'crash')
Boredom	'Drinking alcohol is something to do'	Alcohol use	Boredom (from staying in to drink)
Anxiety	'Heroin will relax me'	Heroin use	Anxiety (from withdrawal)

Figure 12.4 The Emotional Consequences of Substance Use

As the situation-level formulation based on the five-part generic cognitive model discussed in Chapter 5 highlights, substance use is understood as a vicious cycle with many feedback loops. The emotional consequences of substance use clearly demonstrate this, as the emotions resulting from substance use can in turn trigger further substance use, as highlighted in Figure 12.4.

Some clients tell us that their experiences of difficult emotions decrease in intensity once they have reduced or stopped using. For example, clients talk about feeling less anxious when they stop drinking alcohol or feeling less depressed when they stop using crack. Other clients report an initial increase in difficult emotions while reducing substance use or during the initial stage of abstinence. For example, clients have described feeling more irritable when reducing cannabis use or lonelier when reducing heroin use.

When discussing the link between emotions and substance use, it can be useful to start by asking clients what they understand about this link. You could then bring in the above points, if they haven't already been discussed, and demonstrate, with their formulation, how using substances maintains the cycle of negative emotional experience. Furthermore, once the link has been identified (e.g. 'Alcohol stops me feeling anxious in social settings') you could ask the client to explain how they think that would happen ('How does drinking make you feel less anxious when you're out with others?'). Conversations like this can lead to new information that helps advance understanding of the relationship between mood and substances (e.g. 'Alcohol seems to take my mind off worries about how I act when I'm with others') and may lead to alternative ways of coping without relying on substances (e.g. developing positive self-statements about social performance). Chapters 8 and 9 present detailed accounts of how to address any distortions in beliefs linking emotions and substances.

Identifying and labelling emotions

It is likely that you will have already identified some of your clients' emotional triggers and consequences in their formulation – this should be the case if, based on the formulation, you have decided to work with them on managing emotions. Different ways to identify emotions have been described in previous chapters, so the following section will recap this. It is useful to go over this again with your clients, as together you may identify additional emotions that can be added to their formulation.

As discussed in Chapter 5, your clients may confuse emotions with thoughts. Emotions (or moods) can usually be described in one word, whereas thoughts and beliefs reflect verbal statements (i.e. things we say to ourselves). As indicated in Chapter 5, you could refer to the exercise described in 'Mind over Mood' (Greenberger & Padesky, 1995) to help demonstrate the difference between moods, situations and thoughts. You can then help your clients identify their emotional triggers by using the worksheet in Appendix 5.1. Alternatively, you could simply ask your clients: 'What emotions do you think trigger your cravings?' or 'How do you feel [emotionally] before using?' You could ask these questions in general, or refer to a recent, specific situation when your client used or had a craving to use. Information about emotional triggers can also be gathered through drug/alcohol diaries as discussed in Chapter 5 (see Appendix 5.4).

To identify the emotional consequences of using, you could ask your clients: 'How do you feel [emotionally] after using?' It is helpful to break this question down into how they felt immediately after, a few hours after and later that day or the next day. Again, you could ask these questions generally, or refer to a recent situation when your client used or had a craving to use. Drug/alcohol diaries can be adapted to include a column about the emotional consequences of substance use; equally, the worksheet in Appendix 5.1 can be adapted for this purpose.

In addition to adding the identified emotions to your client's formulation, it can be helpful to compile two lists – one for emotional triggers and one for emotional consequences. The second list can be divided into immediate and longer-term consequences. The same emotions may be included in both lists, but this exercise can help make the distinction between emotional triggers and consequences clear, and can then be used to guide the strategies chosen to manage difficult emotions.

Strategies to manage difficult emotions

When working with emotions, cognitive and behavioural strategies can be used to help clients manage their emotions in ways that do not involve using substances. The interventions discussed below include those that have been described in previous chapters and we advise referring to the relevant section for guidance on using them. We also introduce two new interventions: emotion surfing and mindfulness. This section highlights which interventions we have found helpful in working with the following difficult emotions, which are common triggers and consequences of substance use:

- Low mood (feeling down, flat, depressed).
- Anger (irritability, frustration).
- Anxiety (fear, worry, apprehension, panic).
- Boredom.
- Loneliness.
- Stress.
- Guilt.
- Shame.

Which of the interventions you choose will depend on your client's own formulation and the emotions identified. When working with emotions, we recommend that you adopt an attitude of curiosity and a trial-and-error approach to finding out what strategy, or combination of strategies, works for each emotion and for a particular individual.

Attention-switching

When people are experiencing a particular emotion, there is a tendency for them to attend to information that is consistent with that emotion. For example, when feeling low in mood, they are more likely to focus on what they have not achieved rather than what they have. This biased focus can maintain their low mood. In contrast, when feeling angry, they are more likely to continue mulling over in their mind what someone has done that they consider wrong or unfair, which will exacerbate their anger. In these very emotional moments, especially if under the influence of a substance or when alone, it can be very difficult to step out of the mood or even challenge thinking. Therefore, in both examples attention-switching techniques can be a helpful short-term strategy to reduce the immediate emotional intensity of a situation. These quick techniques can sometimes help clients step out of the emotionally charged space and give themselves a moment to stop and think before acting. The list of activities described in Chapter 11 can be used to help people find ways to temporarily distract themselves from difficult emotions such as low mood and anger.

Relaxation

As stated earlier, emotions can manifest physically. Emotions such as anxiety, stress and anger can lead to people feeling tense and uptight. Relaxation techniques can be incorporated into clients' weekly timetables to help them experience periods of less physical pressure and tension. These periods of relaxation may help to improve clients' general well-being. The relaxation and self-soothing techniques outlined in Appendix 11.1 can be used as a foundation for these exercises. The techniques can also help clients manage low mood, guilt and shame, as they involve acts of care and kindness towards the self. It is also important to encourage your clients to have a regular sleep pattern and balanced diet, as these will help them feel more relaxed and can have a positive impact on their emotional state. These techniques become even more important and potentially useful with those clients who have had limited opportunity for daily routines or neglected emotional self-care due to their heavy reliance on substances.

Positive self-talk

Positive self-talk consists of positive statements that can help your clients manage difficult emotions without using substances. Positive self-talk statements can be used to counteract drug or alcohol-related thoughts that mediate the link between emotions and substance use. Positive self-talk reflects the control beliefs described in Chapter 5 and may include statements about confidence in managing emotional triggers, the negative emotional consequences of using and normalisation of the emotional experience. Examples include:

- Crack will lift my mood briefly but I will end up feeling more depressed from the crash.
- I can manage this anxiety without using heroin and have done so before.
- This anger will get less intense over time.
- Smoking cannabis makes me irritable the next day.
- Cocaine will eventually dampen my happy mood as I will be chasing the high.

Positive self-talk statements focused on managing emotions can be generated through the cognitive techniques detailed in Chapters 8 and 9. The statements each client finds most helpful will vary according to the individual. Again, it can be useful to ask your clients to write down these statements in your session. Some of the statements can be transferred to a flashcard. Positive self-talk can help tackle a range of difficult emotions, such as low mood, anxiety, guilt, shame and anger.

Problem-solving

Problem-solving can be used in a number of ways to help clients manage difficult emotions. As discussed in Chapter 11, avoiding addressing specific problems (e.g. by using drugs or alcohol) can increase stress, anxiety and worry. Therefore, the problem-solving approach can be used to reduce the intensity and duration of such emotions as it teaches people a way to tackle problems effectively. Problem-solving can also be used to help clients identify ways to reduce emotions such as low mood, boredom and loneliness. Again, the experience of these emotions is a warning sign that the individual needs to find something different to do. A problem-solving approach can be used to identify different solutions to these emotions. The steps outlined in Chapter 11 can be used in both these instances.

Activity scheduling

As previously noted, a lack of meaningful activity is an important trigger to and consequence of substance use, and is associated with low mood, boredom and loneliness. 'Meaningful activity' refers to activities that give enjoyment and/or a sense of achievement. Increasing positive daily activities strengthens an individual's sense of worth and belonging, and provides structure and purpose. It also increases opportunities to start building meaningful relationships. In addition, activities involving physical exercise release endorphins in the brain which lift the mood. Therefore, developing meaningful activity increases clients' experience of positive emotions as well as reducing their experience of more difficult emotions. When working with your clients on increasing their activity levels, the steps outlined in Chapter 11 can be followed, with the initial aim of identifying one activity for each day.

Behavioural experiments

Within the context of managing emotions without using substances, a behavioural experiment can be designed for the following three purposes:

1. To test beliefs about how helpful each strategy (discussed above) is in reducing the intensity and duration of an emotion.
2. To test beliefs about coping with emotions, such as 'I can't cope with/manage difficult emotions without using substances' and 'Difficult emotions are over-whelming/intolerable unless I use substances'.
3. To test beliefs about the emotional consequences of using and not using substances, such as 'If I stop using, I will feel more/less depressed/anxious/angry'.

Behavioural experiments can be used to test beliefs about all the difficult emotions previously listed. To identify alcohol and drug-related beliefs that relate to difficult emotions, similar questions to those outlined in Chapter 5, which aim to elicit general alcohol and drug-related beliefs, can be asked.

With regard to eliciting beliefs about emotional triggers you could focus on a recent situation when an emotional trigger was present (i.e. your client was feeling anxious/bored/depressed/angry) and ask:

*   How helpful might [a particular strategy] be in reducing the intensity of the [emotion]?
*   How well would you cope with the [emotion] if you did not use?
*   What would happen to the [emotion] if you did not use?

To elicit beliefs about the emotional consequences of using substances, you could talk about the substance use in general, rather than focusing on a recent situation, and ask:

*   If you stopped using, how would you feel emotionally?
*   If you continued using, how would you feel emotionally?

Remember to add any newly identified beliefs to your client's formulation to highlight the links between the beliefs, emotions and substance use. Once you have identified a belief to test, the steps outlined in Chapter 10 in setting up a behavioural experiment should be followed. Encourage your clients to test each belief and strategy more than once, and not to give up if their first attempt at using a particular strategy is not successful. In addition, prior to carrying out the behavioural experiment, you could examine with your clients the evidence for and against their beliefs, using the steps described in Chapter 8.

Emotion surfing

The focus on the behavioural and cognitive interventions described so far has been about changing difficult emotions by reducing their intensity. But it can be useful for clients to learn to stay with and tolerate difficult emotions, rather than always trying to change them, too. The idea of staying with emotions is known as emotion surfing.

Emotion surfing can be very powerful in reducing the fear many clients have about the consequences of experiencing difficult emotions and their ability to cope with them. By staying with the strong emotion rather than trying to get rid of it

Figure 12.5   Wave of Emotion

through using substances, clients realise that the emotional experience is not necessarily catastrophic. This intervention can be applied to all the difficult emotions described above.

Similar to urge surfing, the aim of emotion surfing is for your client to experience an emotion without fighting it or giving in to it. As described in relation to urge surfing, the analogy of a wave is useful when talking to clients about the duration of an emotion. As with cravings, explain to your client that emotions occur, peak and pass, like waves breaking on the shore. As a surfboarder surfs over the wave, the client's task is to 'surf' over the emotion. You could draw an 'emotion wave' to demonstrate the course of an emotion (see Figure 12.5). Your clients may choose to use a previously described strategy, such as positive self-talk, to help them 'surf' over the emotion.

Emotion surfing essentially involves your client taking a position of mindful awareness to help tolerate difficult emotions. Mindful awareness involves your clients learning to step back from their experience and observe their emotions, and the thoughts, physical sensations and urges or desires to act in a certain way that go with their emotions. You could encourage them to acknowledge their emotional experience and to normalise and accept this as non-judgementally as possible. Mindful awareness can also allow them time to stop and think before acting, rather than reacting to the emotion by using substances.

Mindfulness

Emotion surfing can be assisted by mindfulness practice. Mindfulness techniques have begun to be incorporated into cognitive therapy generally (Segal *et al.*, 2002) and in Chapter 2 we highlight how Buddhist thinking has influenced the development of thinking about relapse prevention. We include this section on mindfulness for your interest and awareness of these developments. It is not intended to equip you with the skills to integrate it in your practice. However, developing your own practice of mindfulness, which we believe is a necessary precursor to using it with your clients, is something you could attempt and we include an exercise for this purpose.

Mindfulness is an approach developed over many centuries as part of Buddhist practice. It can be understood as moving away from the *past* and the *future* so that you fully experience and live in the *present*. Mindfulness focuses on the richness of current experience without attempting to change or judge it. Mindfulness thus gives us the possibility of revealing life as transitory and naturally changing from moment to moment.

There are many reasons for developing mindfulness both as a specific practice and as a way of being in the world at every moment. Many people live in an automatic and unreflective manner, responding to the world in relation to their emotions or thoughts, yet, as we have stressed, such emotions or thoughts are not who we are. We can distance ourselves from them, thereby freeing ourselves from the need to react to them. Mindfulness can also shake up our scripted and habitual ways of responding to the world. We are not pre-programmed to respond in any particular way, but we act as if we were. Mindfulness can liberate us from the need to respond in habitual and unhelpful ways. Mindfulness can thus lead to a sense of freedom and freshness. Mindfulness can also lead to a true recognition of who we are and help to replace our idealised self-image with one that, although perhaps less flattering, is more realistic. Coupled with this is a more realistic appraisal of what the world is really like, rather than how we would like it to be.

We have found that many clients with addiction problems are sceptical of the value of mindfulness, but that once introduced to it find great value in it. There are a number of reasons for this. The most important reason for teaching mindfulness is that it allows clients to be anchored in the here and now without the need to change their response through alcohol or drugs. Second, it can serve as a distraction or relaxant for some clients even if they do not succeed in shutting off their thoughts completely. Third, it serves as a model of self-control and a small amount of exposure to this way of thinking and responding can bring enormous benefits. The essence of mindfulness in the context of substance misuse is about not being driven by emotions or cravings to use impulsively or automatically. Teaching mindfulness is a way of helping the individual to assume the stance of an impartial witness to become aware of his or her thoughts and feelings, learning to stand back from them and make a choice about whether or how to respond to them. Mindfulness gives choice and, in effect, disrupts old thinking, feeling and behaviour patterns, allowing the client to think, feel and act differently.

Mindfulness practice and you.   Before attempting to integrate mindfulness into your work with clients you need to practise it yourself. If mindfulness interests you, we recommend that you develop your own daily mindfulness practice. We suggest that you try the exercise in Appendix 12.1, along with any of the others found in the mindfulness literature. Where exercises do not feel right or do not flow, you can adapt them and develop new ones.

Case examples

The following case examples illustrate the use of behavioural experiments and the strategies described above in helping clients develop ways of managing difficult emotions without using substances.

Sally

For Sally, anxiety was often the emotional trigger that led to her alcohol use, particularly when she was planning to leave the house. Sally reported thinking that the anxiety would become increasingly intense if she went out without drinking alcohol and she believed there was nothing else she could do to manage this anxiety. Initially, various strategies were shared with Sally to help her manage the anxiety. She chose to practise progressive muscular relaxation before going out and attention-switching when she was out. A behavioural experiment was then designed to test her belief about the helpfulness of these strategies, as she held the belief: 'Only alcohol will reduce the intensity of the anxiety'. After carrying out this experiment a few times, Sally discovered that these strategies slightly reduced the intensity of the anxiety and she was able to go to her local shop without drinking alcohol, but no further than this. Sally decided to try some different strategies, including emotion surfing and positive self-talk (e.g. 'I used to go out without drinking alcohol', 'I can manage the anxiety without drinking' and 'The anxiety will pass'). Sally went to her local park to try out these strategies and reported finding them more helpful as the anxiety reduced further. She developed an alternative belief: 'Alcohol is not the only way to manage anxiety, other strategies are helpful'. This behavioural experiment could also have been framed to test Sally's belief that she can't cope with the anxiety without using alcohol.

Paul

Paul's drug use was triggered in part by boredom and low mood. Intervention was focused on activity scheduling to reduce the boredom and low mood by increasing Paul's engagement in meaningful activity during the week. However, Paul continued to feel bored when he was at home alone, and although he realised it was unrealistic to expect to be busy all the time, he reported finding boredom intolerable. At these times he often used drugs. Further exploration of what he meant by 'intolerable' revealed that Paul thought he would end up feeling depressed. Therefore, a behavioural experiment was designed to test Paul's belief: 'The boredom will become intolerable and I will feel depressed unless I use drugs'. The experiment involved Paul 'sitting with' the boredom for a set amount of time (at home) and not using drugs. This experiment was carried out over a number of weeks, in addition to the ongoing activity scheduling work. Over time, Paul developed an alternative belief: 'Boredom is unpleasant but I can tolerate it without using drugs and it won't lead me to feel depressed'. As in Sally's case, this behavioural experiment could have been framed to test Paul's belief that he can't cope with boredom without using drugs.

Simon

Simon had believed that if he stopped smoking cannabis he would feel irritable, and this had been his experience when he had tried to stop. After a couple of sessions, Simon acknowledged that he often felt irritable despite smoking cannabis and he began to consider whether irritability was a potential emotional consequence of using cannabis. Initially, a problem-solving approach was used to help Simon think of possible solutions to the problem of being unsure about the link between cannabis and irritability. Simon decided the best solution would be not to smoke cannabis for a few weeks and observe how irritable he felt. However, he identified cravings for both nicotine and cannabis as potential obstacles to this solution, as the cravings might lead him to use and could also make him feel irritable. Therefore, a longer-term behavioural experiment was designed to test his belief: 'If I stop smoking cannabis, I will feel more irritable'. Simon continued to smoke cigarettes and gradually reduced his cannabis use, using craving management techniques (as outlined in Chapter 11) to manage the cravings. Over time,

Simon noticed that he felt irritable when he was craving a joint, but that in general he felt less irritable since reducing the cannabis use (e.g. at work and with his girlfriend). Simon developed an alternative belief: 'If I stop smoking cannabis, I will feel less irritable'.

Summary

This chapter has highlighted how the interventions described in previous chapters can be used to help your clients manage difficult emotions. These emotions may act as triggers to substance use or be the consequences of substance use. The interventions outlined are best thought of as a 'toolkit' of strategies. Ideally, your clients need a number of well-rehearsed strategies so that they can select one or two to use for any given emotion. In general, the strategies described aim to help your clients manage and reduce the intensity of difficult emotions whenever they arise, without using drugs or alcohol. The strategies may also increase your clients' experience of more positive emotions. The different strategies can be framed as behavioural experiments to test your clients' drug or alcohol-related beliefs about difficult emotions and their ability to manage them without using substances.

Appendix 12.1: Mindfulness of your breath exercise

1. Adopt a comfortable dignified sitting posture. It is often helpful to sit slightly away from a chair so that your spine is self-supporting, and to let your shoulders drop naturally. However, if this is not possible, adopt any position that feels comfortable. Place your feet flat on the floor, with your legs uncrossed. Close your eyes if you feel comfortable with that.
2. Now become aware of your belly. Feel it slowly expand on the in-breath, and return on the out-breath. If you like, you can place your hand on your belly in order to feel the difference between the in-breath and the out-breath.
3. Retain your focus on your breathing and try to remain with each in-breath for its full duration and each out-breath for its full duration.
4. If during the exercise you find that your mind has wandered away from your breath, gently bring your focus back to the breath and the belly. No matter how many times your mind wanders simply bring it back to the in-breath and the out-breath.
5. At the end of 15 minutes open your eyes or look up and become aware of your surroundings. You may include some stretches or whatever you feel comfortable with.
6. Here are some tips to bear in mind about this exercise. Give up the idea that you are going to 'achieve' something whilst doing this exercise or even understand it. Instead, try to accept that you are going to find out what happens by simply doing it. Also don't think there is a 'right' way to do the exercise at which you may fail. Do it with an interested, open approach. Be aware and just accept whatever you experience.
7. If you become distracted by your surroundings, briefly notice what has distracted you and your responding thoughts or feelings and then return to the exercise.
8. Do not criticise yourself if this happens (e.g. you start to go to sleep, start making up shopping lists, forgetting what you are trying to do), these are your real experiences so just be aware of them.
9. 'Being in the moment', the expression practitioners use to describe mindfulness, is not as simple as it may seem. We live in an activity and goal-oriented society which leaves many of us uncomfortable with our own bodily sensations, thoughts and feelings. So, if possible, practise this exercise every day whilst becoming more mindfully aware of who and what you are in your day-to-day life.

Chapter 13

CBT and Pathways to Recovery

This book has given you a wealth of information on theory, techniques and skills to deal with thoughts, behaviours and emotions relating to substance use. It has also shown how these principles and techniques can be applied to the longer-term process of recovery management. Our principal aim is that it should be of practical use to you as a reader and ultimately benefit the clients you work with. It can be used in many ways:

- As a reference guide.
- As a brief overview of CBT for addictions.
- As a technical guide.
- As a recipe book.
- As a troubleshooting guide.
- As a resource to supervise others.
- As a resource for reflecting on your practice, attitudes and beliefs about working with substance use disorders and even as a resource to reflect on and initiate changes in your own substance using behaviour.

Although this book contains theory it is meant to be a practical guide. If it contributes to increasing your confidence to use CBT formulation and techniques and your overall understanding of CBT, then it will have achieved its objectives.

In this final chapter we place the ideas introduced in this book in a broader context and return to the concept of recovery introduced in Chapter 1. We also make some suggestions for how you can develop your CBT skills and integrate them into your practice.

Developing your practice

It is a truism that learning new skills is difficult. In this respect learning CBT is no different. There is good evidence that variation in therapist competence and performance is one of the most important variables in outcomes in psychosocial interventions (Okiishi *et al.*, 2006). Attention and planning about how you develop your practice is a necessary undertaking. This will be specific to your own learning needs and in Chapter 1 we outlined the ways in which you could use this book according to your role, knowledge and skill base. In this section we focus on factors in your environment that will facilitate your learning, consider some initial objectives for developing CBT skills and highlight the value of taking a competence-based approach as well as using routine outcome monitoring in your work.

Creating a learning environment

In learning anything new you may be aware that you have an optimal set of conditions for this to take place. These may be relatively simple for learning information, but are likely to be more complex for learning skills. It is our experience that the day-to-day working environment is rarely one in which these circumstances occur. Therefore, some initial attention to the learning context is important, at the very least to identify a minimum necessary set of resources – a place to see clients, time for yourself to reflect on your work, support to do this and a space in which you can share ideas and get feedback on your work. You also need to be attentive to your own mental well-being. Is this really the right time to be learning a new skill? Do you have the energy and time to commit to the process? With this in mind it is also better to start with clients with whom you have a good working relationship and whose difficulties are relatively straightforward. Whilst you may be tempted to tackle some of the more difficult issues, you can work up to these as your competence increases.

You might also want to consider the availability of training relevant to your specific needs. However, you may find that without attending to the context and ongoing support to develop your skills as outlined above, the initial enthusiasm and the skills gained through training are likely to decline over time. We would also advise you to give some thought to infrastructure issues, such as access to equipment to record your work with clients. There are good quality and relatively cheap audio devices (traditional tape and digital recording devices) readily available from high street and online retailers. We strongly believe that listening to your work and taking the brave step of sharing this material with a supervisor or in a peer supervision group is invaluable to learning CBT. Recording will enable you to reflect on your work in a number of ways. You may want to consider the use of the Cognitive Therapy Rating Scale (Young & Beck, 1980). You can use this as a reflective tool, but ideally you will have a CBT practitioner to evaluate your work and give you focused feedback.

Giving these issues due consideration will enable you to identify whether your current supervision is a place where some of this reflective work can be undertaken or whether you need to seek specific clinical supervision in CBT. If you are employed in an organisation, we recommend that you use your existing appraisal structures to support your learning, build the development of your CBT skills into your professional development plan and have this signed off by your manager. The more the development of your skills can be formalised and recognised by your organisation the more likely it is you will sustain your commitment and enlist the support of your managers in helping you to succeed. Are there like-minded individuals in your service? If so, you could organise yourselves into a peer support group focused on developing your CBT practice. The whole process of identifying the resources to support your skill development will inevitably raise some issues which won't be easily solved. In this case you may find the problem-solving framework described in Chapter 11 useful. We also encourage you to think about your responses to the difficulties presented. Identifying your beliefs and the assumptions that underlie the feelings may enable you take a different perspective and harness untapped resources. We strongly believe in the value of thinking as a CBT therapist about our own difficulties and suggest this may promote the development of your practice.

Setting objectives for your practice development

Once you have identified the resources to help you develop your practice it is time to focus specifically on what you hope to achieve and to articulate a clear plan about how you might do this. Your personal learning objectives will depend on your experience, but the need to specify them is relevant to everyone. Agreeing these with your mentor, coach, supervisor or manager will enable you to be realistic about your goals and set out the necessary steps for you to achieve them. Again, we believe that being as specific as possible and attending to how you will achieve them within a given time-frame will be associated with the likelihood that you will achieve them. Ideally, this will be in the form of a supervision contract which stipulates the expectations of both parties and includes a review.

What might these goals look like? We have stressed throughout this book the central role of formulation as an organising principle of doing CBT, so this may be the logical place to start when developing your practice. If you intend to use the cognitive techniques outlined in Chapters 7–10, then formulation is a prerequisite to doing this work as it is only by having a formulation that you will know why you have chosen a particular intervention. We recommend that you use the five-part cognitive model after sessions as a way of organising your thoughts about the information you have about your client. At this initial stage there is no need to share these ideas with your clients or bring them into the session; this is simply a way to get used to thinking formulation. You can add information over time and refine the formulation accordingly. Eventually, through appropriate supervision, you may wish to bring the formulation explicitly into your sessions with clients. There is no harm, however, in formulation being implicit (i.e. using it as an organising framework for understanding why you might want do certain things with clients). Some of the interventions described in Chapters 4, 11 and 12 can be used as brief, stand-alone interventions and may be more relevant to your specific role or particular settings. If this is the case, selecting one of these interventions to work on may be an initial goal.

Competency frameworks

Another way we believe is helpful to developing your practice is to think about your CBT practice in terms of learning a set of specific competencies. This is particularly relevant if you are new to CBT. The approach taken in the teaching and training of staff for the UK Improving Access to Psychological Therapies initiatives – is based on learning a set of competencies for each intervention. These are specified at four levels: generic competencies, basic competencies, specific techniques and meta-competencies. Generic competencies are common across psychological work and refer to having the ability to relate to and communicate with people. Basic competencies refer to the most commonly used interventions and specific techniques are specific to the particular intervention. Meta-competencies are the abilities therapists use to adapt interventions to specific client needs. Learning the use of formulation is useful for this – you will learn when and what to do and, importantly, when *not* to do things with clients. Applying a set of competencies is a very useful way to direct your learning and to specify what you need to focus on, step by step. It also enables you to be assessed on specific aspects of work and to recognise the achievements you have made. One of the key features and value of adopting a competency-based approach is that it allows for flexibility and adaptation for individual clients. This can be contrasted with a manualised approach in which the focus of therapy is dictated with little scope for interplay between therapist and client.

There are resources you can access to adopt this competency-based approach to learning CBT. One of these is the Psychosocial Interventions in Drug Misuse. A framework and toolkit for implementing NICE-recommended treatment interventions (Pilling, Hesketh & Mitcheson, 2009). Within this we would direct you to the competency frameworks for the low-intensity CBT interventions, CBT-based guided self-help and behavioural activation. These highlight the competencies relevant to socialisation to CBT in Chapter 5 and behavioural activation described in Chapter 11. For the interventions focusing more specifically on beliefs, you may wish to refer to the CBT competency sets for the high-intensity interventions available from the Centre for Outcome and Research Effectiveness website (www.ucl.ac.uk/core). It should be stressed that these are all CBT competency sets for common mental health problems and are not specific to the treatment of drug and alcohol use problems. However, there are enough commonalities for this to be a useful reflective practice tool and a framework for organising supervision.

Learning from clients and outcome monitoring

As we have stated, learning a new skill is never easy. Inevitably, you will encounter setbacks and things will not go as planned. However, we would encourage you to persist, to utilise the resources you have to hand, to get yourself back on track and to apply some of the ideas presented in this book to your own predicament and thereby enable you to identify and overcome any self-defeating thought processes.

Finally, we would encourage you to acknowledge that much of your learning is going to come from your clients themselves. As we hope you will appreciate by now, CBT is done *with* clients, not *to* clients. CBT is essentially a collaborative process. Approaching it in this way allows you to be curious and not to feel that you have to have all the answers all the time. It is our experience that clients with substance use problems are not hesitant in giving feedback. What is important is that you make sure it is elicited and responded to. In Chapter 3, we included seeking client feedback as part of the basic way of structuring sessions. Another important source of feedback is routinely to collect clinical outcomes. These may be specific to the goals set in therapy by using a simple rating scale or more formally by using standardised measures. Your service is likely to have some information requirements and we urge you to look at these and see if there is a way you can incorporate them into your work. One of these (for staff working in English drug treatment services) is the Treatment Outcomes Profile (TOP) (Marsden *et al.*, 2008). The drug use monitoring element of this will give you feedback about changes in quantity and frequency of substance use. Incorporating this valuable information into a discussion about goals and progress with your clients can be very helpful. It is our experience that staff can feel demoralised and stressed by the data they have to collect; the trick is to turn this process into something useful and relevant to what you are doing.

Summary

The task of embracing CBT and incorporating it into your practice should not be underestimated by you or your organisation. For your organisation, there will be demands to support practice development and delivery of CBT which will require investment and time. There is some evidence that adopting psychosocial interventions is good for organisational health and functioning so the organisation may benefit from supporting your CBT development (Simpson *et al.*, 2007). In a healthy organisation you may already be encouraged to make suggestions as to how services could be improved and which resources should be developed. We recommend that service users are also involved in this process. It is our experience that service users are pleased to support staff development and can see the benefits of having wider access to useful therapeutic interventions. Within your organisation, it might be useful to see CBT as defining a way of being with clients, curiosity, desire to understand the situation and a desire to help clients seek solutions from within their cultural background. If your organisation begins to 'think CBT', you should find that clinical meetings and care plan processes enable more sophisticated discussions about clients and give a greater range of potential solutions to their problems.

Integrating CBT for problematic substance use into your practice

In this book we have avoided being prescriptive about the timing and content of your work with clients. Your role and setting will dictate not only your work priorities but also the needs of your clients, which will vary over time. An important lesson learnt from experience is the ability to adapt your interventions appropriately. This is particularly relevant when we think about recovery from problem substance use. Is your goal to help your clients to initiate recovery and gain some initial control over substance use? Or are you helping them to overcome some of the obstacles that are impeding progress towards greater community reintegration? CBT will be helpful for both goals, but a map is useful to enable some thought about when to act and what you should be doing. In this section we develop the notion of stepped care and also give some ideas about how CBT can be integrated into standard elements of treatment in drug and alcohol services, including pharmacological interventions. This section concludes with some thoughts on getting started in your work with clients and how CBT can be integrated into standard assessment procedures.

Stepped care

We find the framework of stepped care (introduced in Chapter 2) a good way to see how interventions can be mapped across treatment pathways (Wanigaratne & Keaney, 2002). In an addiction-focused stepped care model the first two steps concern engaging clients and initiating early changes in substance use. The engagement strategies in Chapter 4 and the behavioural interventions in Chapter 11 may be useful here, so is encouraging your client to participate in a contingency management programme. For some clients this level of intervention may be sufficient, particularly if they have resources in their environment to sustain change. But many will need to move on to the next step and more focused work on the substance use behaviour itself, exploring in detail episodic drug and alcohol use as well as developing strategies to sustain any changes made. This can be seen as an early relapse prevention phase, helping clients understand lapses and actively work to gain greater control over substance use behaviour. At this stage, formulation and cognitive interventions are particularly relevant. In the final step, which can be seen as an aftercare phase or moving on to a recovery and reintegration phase, your use of CBT will be more focused on embedding robust relapse prevention strategies and helping clients develop resources in their lives to sustain recovery. This phase is examined below. As part of this work, and if you have the relevant competencies, this is an ideal time to initiate CBT for any co-occurring mental health issues. Within this stepped care framework you should be able to identify when to intervene and what you should be doing with clients, depending on their presenting issues. It is also possible to see the limits of your work and how different expertise and resources in treatment systems can be drawn on to help your clients initiate and sustain changes in their substance-using behaviour. We hope this book will add to your understanding of your clients' substance use problems and, at least at the level of formulation, see how associated mental health difficulties are caused, maintained or alleviated by substance use. However, this book is not intended to be a comprehensive CBT manual for all common mental health problems. Those commonly associated with drug and alcohol use include post-traumatic disorder, particularly multiple trauma associated with childhood physical and sexual abuse, depression and specific anxiety disorders, single-event trauma, obsessive compulsive disorder, generalised anxiety disorder, panic disorder and social anxiety. For these we recommend your client has access to a therapist trained in CBT and competent in working with these issues.

Substance use in therapy and pharmacologically assisted recovery

Pharmacological interventions are a common feature of drug and alcohol treatment services, particularly in the community (Sheridan & Strang, 2003). These may be used to assist detoxification or as part of a substitute prescribing programme. Clients with substance use problems are often excluded from talking therapies by virtue of the fact that they use substances, prescribed or otherwise. We agree that there is little point, and indeed there may even be dangers, in attempting CBT when a client is obviously intoxicated. At the very least it is unlikely they will remember anything. The same applies if a client is actively withdrawing. If your client is exhibiting withdrawal symptoms from alcohol or benzodiazepines, given the potential life-threatening consequences, your priority here should be to access immediate medical attention. We set ground-rules for therapy about not attending sessions while intoxicated and, when appropriate, address this behaviour by exploring beliefs, active problem-solving and reformulating goals. Nevertheless, you need to be interested in current and active substance use and this should form the content of sessions. Clients' attempts to stabilise on methadone or other substitute medication, or control or cut down drinking, should be the treatment focus. We believe it makes little sense to separate this part of care from psychosocial work. CBT therefore fits very well with pharmacological interventions. How it is used depends on where the client is in treatment (e.g. starting detoxification or seeking to stabilise on an opioid substitute). The goals of pharmacotherapy can also be mapped into the stepped care framework. Working with medication may already be part of your role, and part of the skill in integrating CBT into your practice may be managing the time so that discussion about medication does not dominate sessions. If this does happen, we recommend that you read Chapter 3 again to help you structure sessions and plan them more productively. Using CBT thinking to focus on how the client understands and engages with pharmacotherapy is important in helping clients, and indeed services, see medication as a means to an end rather than an end in itself.

Integration with other psychosocial approaches

Two psychosocial interventions fit particularly well with CBT: motivational interviewing (MI) and the International Treatment Effectiveness Project (ITEP) interventions. MI focuses on helping clients explore and resolve ambivalence about change. Using the stepped care framework, MI can be envisaged as a precursor to CBT and used to enable the client to move into an active treatment phase of CBT. MI can also be used as a fallback position. Ambivalence about changing substance use or about other aspects of treatment, such as completing homework assignments, is often an issue for our clients and the respectful, gentle enquiring approach of MI is invariably the best way to tackle these issues. (This is outlined in Chapter 4.) In Chapter 1 we refer to ITEP. We believe ITEP is a useful process tool to enable productive conversations with clients about their recovery and engagement in treatment. As such it can easily incorporate elements of CBT; here the use of visual maps and problem-solving fits well with the interventions described in this book. What we like about ITEP is that it familiarises both workers and clients with the basics – structuring sessions, defining problems, setting tasks, getting feedback, being collaborative and understanding in a simple and accessible way the connections between situations, feelings and thoughts. For clients, using the visual maps in ITEP is a good preparation for more formal CBT. For workers, maps can help break down some of the CBT interventions into simple stages and thus be an aid to learning CBT.

We have found that CBT offers a shared way of understanding the world and therefore of thinking about clients' problems. Integrating CBT into treatment systems and other interventions gives access to a language with which teams can begin to talk about the complex psychological and behavioural difficulties associated with problem substance use.

Getting started with your clients

In Chapter 1 we presented the case of Paul, in Chapter 5 of Sally and in Chapter 6 of Simon. We hope that you now feel both more confident and knowledgeable in dealing with clients like Paul, or indeed Simon and Sally. In our view CBT gives you choices and opportunities to do a number of different things and in that sense is more like an old-fashioned roadmap where you and the client decide the route, rather than a satellite navigation system which selects the route for you and can result in drivers being sent down byways. Indeed, flexibility and creativity are intrinsic to the way we use CBT when working in this area. This is particularly important as there is no evidence to suggest there is a validated, step-wise method to overcoming substance use problems; rather, it needs to be adapted to clients and the overall goal of recovery management.

In Chapter 6 we incorporated the key problem areas and interventions covered by this book in the five-part generic cognitive model (Figure 6.2). Again, this should not be taken as a rigid division between problems and solutions. Effecting change in one area will effect change in another, as each element is in interaction with the others and all sit within an environmental context. For some clients behaviour change may lead to changes in thinking; for others specific work may be needed on cognitions that lead to lasting behaviour change. Changes to environmental problems may lead to changes in both thinking and behaviour.

In addition to this map there are general principles. You would always do an assessment before an intervention, but what does this mean? What do you assess? Some services have structured assessments that cover the service's basic data needs and often contain elements of basic risk assessment. This information is important, but if the assessment is carried out rigidly it may immediately erect a barrier between you and the client. Needless to say, this initial contact is crucial and requires a great deal of skill on the part of the interviewer. A skilled and confident interviewer will gather all the information needed without going about it as if it were an interrogation. Basic counselling skills, such as warmth, empathy and unconditional positive regard for the client, are probably the most important therapeutic qualities you can develop (Rogers, 1967). In addition, this is the first opportunity to utilise the skills described in Chapter 4. If you get off to a good start, it is more likely that the client will give you the information required to make a full assessment and increase the probability of the client coming back. Reading Chapter 4 before you do your next new assessment and reading it again after you have done the assessment to evaluate yourself is a good way of putting CBT into practice.

Moreover, we hope that you will develop your troubleshooting skills and awareness of potential pitfalls before they occur as your CBT practice develops. Clearly, a number of things can go wrong – the client may be intoxicated, have clear but unrealistic expectations of you and the service, may be aggressive and demanding, or you may have very little time to get the information you need due to the pressures on the service. To improve your skills you need time to reflect on how you have performed. Supervision from a CBT practitioner to review your performance is ideal. If this is in place, your skills development and the increase in your self-efficacy can be rapid. In the absence of such a support system you could refer back to the chapters and reflect on your performance, or arrange to meet with a like-minded colleague to develop your practice together.

Ultimately, your clients will be your teachers, as the effectiveness of your way of working will be demonstrated in their attendance and changing behaviour. We actively encourage asking clients about the work you introduce them to as this not only helps them to remember the key points, but also emphasises the collaborative nature of your work.

Risk assessment is a critical and essential component of initial and ongoing assessment. It is defined as 'the systematic collection of information to determine the degree to which harm (to self or others) is likely at some point in time' (O'Rourke & Bird, 2001). With substance-using clients there are a number of risks that must be covered, both individual (overdose, withdrawal fits, TB and infection from blood-borne viruses, self-harm and suicide, self-neglect and being a victim of violence, particularly domestic violence), and harm to others (abuse and/or neglect of children or other dependants, violence towards others and spread of infection). This information can be obtained using an eliciting approach (Chapter 4) or in a CBT assessment style (Chapter 5). However it is obtained it is important that risk is assessed early in the assessment as it will determine the service priorities for interventions, which can then be incorporated into a shared agenda.

CBT work on formulating can begin once these initial stages have been completed. As we have said, formulation is generally a working hypothesis and alternative formulations should always be borne in mind, particularly when interventions, or ways of working, seem to be coming to a dead-end. This is particularly important since it may not be the technique that is wrong, or the motivation of the client or your therapeutic style; rather, you may have been focusing on the wrong thing. Sometimes things that seem highly important at first wane in importance during therapy. It is also worthwhile being attentive to what MI practitioners call 'premature closure', where something bears all the hallmarks of a problem with the result that you focus on this too soon or to the detriment of other areas. Clients who use substances or who are substance-dependent are rarely going to have a straightforward issue to deal with. Alcohol and drug problems not only often emerge in response to other difficult life experiences, but also generate a not insubstantial number in their own right.

When used appropriately, both cognitive and behavioural interventions allow us to keep on track and check with the client at all stages of treatment where we are and, crucially, adapt and change things if necessary. Technique for the sake of technique is as redundant as any unproven intervention and CBT techniques should not take precedence over other therapeutic factors. For example, if you ask a group of inexperienced therapists what they want to get out of their first meeting with a client they will perhaps say something about doing a good assessment. More experienced therapists just want the client to come back. Generally – and we are sensitive to the issue of risk – most information can wait. You do not need to get everything at once, although when training it can often seem that it does.

CBT and recovery management

In this final section we talk a little more about the broader issue of how CBT can be incorporated into recovery management. We address this by thinking about relapse prevention and client optimism, resilience, integration (or reintegration) and choice (ORIC), introduced in Chapter 1.

Relapse prevention and moving on from problematic substance use

Relapse prevention has a number of meanings. Almost 20 years ago one of the authors of this book co-authored the first British therapist manual on relapse prevention (Wanigaratne *et al.*, 1990), based on the Marlatt & Gordon (1985) model. The present volume builds on this and reflects over 20 years' clinical experience of applied relapse prevention and an accumulation of research as well as theoretical knowledge. This book takes a much broader approach to relapse prevention, integrating developments in CBT. In essence it is the sequel to that volume. The new dynamic model of relapse (Witkiewitz & Marlatt, 2004), described in Chapter 2, leads us from a simple, linear, stimulant–response way of understanding relapse to one that requires a number of factors determining the outcome (use/not use) to be considered at any given moment. In this new way of understanding relapse, clinical interventions such as those described in this book aim to enhance or strengthen the influence of particular factors (e.g. self-efficacy, mood), which then determine outcome (i.e. not use). Hence relapse prevention becomes an aim or philosophy of treatment rather than a treatment. On the other hand, all the interventions described in this book are useful for 'relapse prevention' as they are designed to assist clients to control and abstain from substances and move on in their recovery. In this definition relapse prevention *is* treatment. However, relapse prevention is also something to think about in the process of doing therapy, as well as something that would be explicit in conversations towards and at the end of therapy. These two aspects of relapse prevention are described below.

Relapse prevention and the process of therapy

Beck (1995) highlights how relapse prevention starts at the beginning of therapy. Right from the start it is important to normalise relapse or lapses for clients.

Practitioners working in the substance misuse field know that relapses happen, but it is our experience that anxieties surround talking about them, particularly if the client seems to be doing well. It is not uncommon for people to think that talking about relapse somehow gives clients permission to use. Whilst some reflection on your own thoughts will be useful, we also think it is important to discuss with clients how behaviour change takes place. Themes that may emerge from this conversation may include who is responsible for change, how change is often incremental, that setbacks are normal and that bringing episodes of substance use to therapy provides an opportunity to learn and do things differently. Through this discussion it may also be possible to identify cognitive distortions and beliefs that have the potential to undermine longer-term recovery, such as 'failure is not an option', 'I must be successful in everything I do 100 per cent of the time', 'I am weak, bad, etc.'. Time spent developing a set of more adaptive cognitions that are more forgiving to life's setbacks and compassionate about not always behaving as one would like to is time well spent and assists longer-term recovery. For some clients it will be important to stress that lapses are not a reason to disengage from therapy. Reflecting on setbacks within therapy also provides an opportunity to remind clients of specific techniques and strategies or adapt them so that things can be done differently. Judith Beck (1995) suggests that attributing change to the client is another important process to undertake during the course of therapy. The aim is for clients to become their own therapists. Highlighting how things that occur whilst in therapy are down to their own efforts and learning will help this process. This should be explicit if you use behavioural experiments in your work (Chapter 10). Normalising the experience of relapse, affirming your clients' use of strategies and modelling how to respond to setbacks are required throughout therapy.

Relapse prevention and ending therapy

Having frank conversations about relapse prevention towards the end of therapy is something that happens in CBT generally. This develops the idea of clients being their own therapists through reviewing what was learnt in therapy and thinking about how this will be useful for moving on in their recovery. We have developed a worksheet to help this process (see Appendix 13.1). Within these conversations the issue of relapse should be directly addressed. Again, as highlighted above, this may create anxieties for you as the therapist, but also for clients, who may believe that talking about relapse somehow increases the likelihood of it occurring. These can be addressed using some of the cognitive techniques described in this book and it may also be helpful to share the analogy of the 'fire drill' (see Chapter 2). In this, you describe how once a year your organisation requires you to undertake fire training, and fire drills are routinely carried out to test how efficiently people respond to hearing the fire alarm. You tell your client that you participate in these activities, not because you want there to be a fire, but because if there is a fire you will be clear about what you have to do (close the windows, leave the building, etc.). This increases the chances of managing the situation effectively so that the risks of a fire to you, your colleagues and clients are kept to a minimum. In this way talking through relapses is seen as a sensible act of preparation for an eventuality you do not want to happen.

Endings in therapy are an opportunity to address specific concerns clients may have about ending the relationship with you or your service. This is a complex issue and one that is useful to bring to supervision. Using the techniques described in this book to elicit and explore beliefs about ending is useful and it can be highly important and beneficial for clients to have a defined ending to formal treatment. How you work towards an ending is likely to vary, but as Beck (1995) suggests tapering off sessions by increasing the intervals between them can be helpful. This enables clients to experience life with less support and requires greater focus on self-management of any difficulties they encounter. Another way is to arrange booster sessions which are framed as opportunities to share good experiences of using CBT techniques, anticipate difficulties and articulate coping strategies. The feel of these sessions is more like coaching than formal therapy and they set the scene for clients to self-manage their longer-term recovery.

One of the reasons we believe it is important for clients to have an ending to therapy is that it may contribute to a shift in your client's identity, perhaps to being a person no longer defined by drug use. This should be actively encouraged as it may be significant in longer-term recovery (Maslin & Simons, 2009). However, for some clients recovery management can be a long-term process or even last a lifetime. With this in mind we would encourage some thought in your service to how extended periods of contact can be managed. We have had former clients drop in for a chat many years after discharge just to let us know how they are doing. They do not want, or need, therapy, but seem to want to check in for some validation or simply to get a perspective on the journeys they have made. This kind of contact could be formalised and for all ex-clients an invitation made for an annual recovery check-up (White, 2008). This frames the contact as something different from therapy and may even be better facilitated by peer advocates. This could be an opportunity to review progress in recovery plans and identify personal goals. At the very least a welcoming smile and an expression of support and gratitude for letting you know how they are doing will cost nothing but go a long way. In the final section of this chapter we develop the recovery theme and consider four qualities which we believe are integral to it.

Optimism, resilience, integration and choice

As clinicians it is gratifying to see specific problems and difficulties recede or sometimes disappear altogether, but there are four other factors that we believe are good indicators of an effective CBT intervention which we first introduced in Chapter 1. These are increased client optimism, resilience, integration (or reintegration) and choice (ORIC). Thus, even where we are contracted to work on a specific issue, we believe that it is the following principles that the clients learn through the process of CBT that will be the most salient for their future success and recovery. It is important to state that these four areas will be introduced in different ways by different therapists. Some will integrate them into all of their work, even whilst undertaking the more technical aspects of CBT. Some will feel more comfortable having specific conversations about these areas. There is no right or wrong way and one could argue that, in the spirit of CBT, a direct, transparent conversation about them best reflects the CBT approach. Again, as a therapist one has to judge when and how to introduce such topics. It may be more important to engender optimism than integration at the beginning of therapy, yet the idea of integrating, getting a job or partner perhaps, may be the very thing that engenders such optimism to change. Moreover, it is the concepts and the language that are used that are key here. Thus, optimism can be referred to as 'hope'; resilience as 'ability to recover'; integration as 'joining in' and choice as 'possibility'. The key is to ensure that, whatever language is used, it is consistent with the client's own.

Optimism

Optimism can be defined as hopefulness and confidence about the success of something or the future. This twofold meaning encapsulates both the confidence that we are seeking to instil in clients regarding their drug and alcohol use, whether this be sobriety or controlled use, and their lives more generally. Many clients come into treatment with a very bleak view not only of themselves, but of the world and the future. This triad of depression, which Aaron Beck (1967) has carefully analysed, clearly mitigates against optimism and propels clients inexorably towards a state of learnt helplessness or passivity. Thus, there are two key tasks facing the therapist when working with clients with drug and alcohol difficulties. The first is to engender optimism regarding the possibility of change with regard to their drug and alcohol use. The second is generating and sustaining optimism more generally so that life without drugs or alcohol or reduced usage feels worthwhile and meaningful. We shall deal with each of these tasks in turn.

How, then, does one go about engendering optimism in clients who present in therapy or at key working sessions? Whilst clients present as wanting things to be different, more often than not this is about *not wanting to do something*, rather than the more positive alternative of *wanting to experience something different*. This is paramount because simply stopping doing something that is so much part of one's identity and lifestyle is rarely successful on its own. AA uses the term 'dry drunk' to refer to individuals who have stopped drinking, but where no significant change has taken place. They have stopped, at least partly, doing what they still want to do and replaced it with nothing. This creates a vacuum of deprivation and often a sense of unfairness because alcohol and drug use, even where it leads to the most negative of consequences, has some sustaining property. CBT and MI remind us that clients' ambivalence is not so much an error of thinking as an unanalysed state. Addicted clients can get stuck in a cycle of self-frustration and physical and psychological damage because even in the most desperate state of addiction there is still something to be gained from it. Without helping clients to have a clear understanding of what this gain is, therapy is likely to proceed extremely slowly and may even stall altogether.

Once we are able to arrive at a shared understanding of the current function of using or drinking, it is possible to conceptualise any fears or concerns about stopping or changing use that may prevent the client from changing. As we saw in Chapter 2, reinforcement can be categorised as positive or negative. The former gives something pleasurable, whilst the latter helps us to avoid something unpleasant. Drug and alcohol use tends to flow through positive reinforcement to negative reinforcement, so that over time the reasons to drink or use are primarily in order to avoid psychological or physical pain. At the same time, there will be memories of the times when alcohol or drugs really did give the pleasurable sensation associated with early to middle use. This is the situation the clients often find themselves in. Intellectually, they know that they want to change because things need to be different, but they do not know what this difference will be like. Whilst CBT offers tools to undertake this change and to understand current motivation to use, what it cannot provide is direct knowledge or experience of what it will be like once this change has taken place. Research and our own clinical work may tell us that abstinence, for instance, is undoubtedly going to be the best thing that the client could ever do, but clients still have to want this themselves and also take it on trust that the change is going to be worthwhile. Cognitive distortions at this early stage may well be telling the client that it is not. Thus, we need the client to experience that internal state of optimism at the beginning of therapy in order to decide that change is worth undertaking. Once clients have been able to articulate what change will feel like to them and what they hope it will bring, we can use this throughout our work with them, particularly when they feel that change is pointless. It is also important to remember that clients will be all too aware of the difficulties of change in themselves and in others when it comes to changing addictive behaviour. Therefore, conversations about change are vitally important in creating the possibility of change, so it is worth looking at MI material on change-related conversations, particularly in the early stages of treatment.

The second task related to optimism is to generalise it from the specific problem area of drinks and drugs to life more generally. The fact that clients can be optimistic about changing their drink and drug use does not necessarily mean that they will become optimistic in other areas of their lives. Another way of thinking about this is to recognise that while our first task is to engender *situational* optimism (in that it related to a specific situation), the second is to generate *dispositional* optimism (dispositional being a characteristic or quality of the person). While the extent to which optimism is genetic and/or environmental is disputed, there are psychologists such as Martin Seligman who believe that just as we can learn to be helpless, we can also learn to be optimistic (Seligman, 2006). Indeed, Seligman argues that even if there is a genetic tendency towards pessimism, that does not preclude learning optimism. While Seligman specifically focuses on the first of the cognitive behavioural therapies – rational emotive behaviour therapy (REBT, also known as rational emotive therapy, RET) and Albet Ellis's ABCDE model of learning in order to do this – this approach will make sense to those coming to CBT through the work of Aaron and Judith Beck. It is worth looking at Seligman's books and his authentic happiness website based at the University of Pennsylvania (www.authentichappiness.sas.upenn.edu), as well as a more specific book on REBT and addictions (Ellis *et al.*, 1988).

It may also be worth sharing with clients who are showing dispositional optimism that this state is correlated highly with self-esteem as well as being protective against stress (Scheier & Carver, 1987; Segerstrom *et al.*, 1998). For those clients who are not showing optimism, such information should be avoided as it is likely to be perceived as burdensome and even somewhat bullying.

In summary, as CBT therapists we are ideally placed to work on optimism with our clients, both through the structured work we do with them and by highlighting and reminding them of what they have achieved and any of their intrinsic strengths.

Resilience

What is resilience? It is the ability to withstand or recover quickly from difficult situations and is characterised by persistence or adaptation to adversity. If optimism is a state of mind about the future and what it may hold, resilience is the cognitive and behavioural response to life's difficulties. Clients who habitually use drink and drugs tend either to underestimate their resilience or to ignore it altogether. This is perhaps not surprising. If you are dependent physically and psychologically on something external to you, then it is unlikely that you are going to focus on your inner strengths and abilities. It is probable that the development of resilience occurs early in life and that children who are insecurely attached may find it more difficult to sustain and develop inner coping mechanisms (Werner, 1982).

CBT, through its focus on our everyday cognitions and behaviours, is an ideal test bed for developing resilience. Each negative thought that is interrogated for its truth value, each automatic behaviour that is disrupted, reminds clients that they can define what happens to them. Siebert (2005) notes that one definition of resilience is being able to 'change to a new way of working and living when an old way is no longer possible'. This is a particularly useful way of thinking about the task for anyone who is trying to give up an old and well-entrenched behaviour, for it is not only the behaviour that needs to change, but also the way of living. *Living Sober* is the title of one of AA's books and we need to remind ourselves that symptom removal in and of itself does not promote sustainable change.

MI talks about being 'ready, willing and able'. Resilience is about being 'able'. We tend to spend a lot of time thinking about whether clients have the ability to stop or cut down their substance use and perhaps rather less about how they will be able to sustain any changes made. This is important because one of the facts about any change-seeking behaviour is that there is, of necessity, a form of built-in optimism as to what life will be like afterwards. On a simple cost–benefit equation, a judgement will be made that changing is better than not changing. This optimism can help sustain the process of change, but often when the difference that the client expects to see fails to materialise motivation dips and sustaining change becomes difficult. Indeed, we often wonder why so many clients relapse time and time again. It is possible that each relapse brings with it at least the possibility of future change and that then sustains another attempt. The development of resilience can help with such situations, not only because resilience strengthens the individual against difficulties and high-risk situations, but also because there is more likely to be a speedier recovery from stress or trauma in individuals who are resilient.

A good example of how resilience can work to the benefit of the client is to be found in one of the irrational beliefs identified in RET, namely, low frustration tolerance (LFT). Clients with LFT believe that they will not be able to stand their discomfort or frustration and that it cannot and must not be tolerated. Ellis *et al.*, (1988) call this 'discomfort anxiety' or 'discomfort disturbance'. For many individuals with substance misuse problems, intoxication thus becomes a means or method of coping with such impulses. Resilience, on the other hand, also provides a means of coping with LFT by reminding them that they can stand discomfort, and that whilst it is generally preferable not to experience discomfort, nothing awful happens when they do. Similar ideas can be found in the idea of surfing your emotions (see Chapter 12).

Whilst resilience perhaps even more than optimism is related to environmental factors, particularly early childhood experiences, there is much that can be done to promote and strengthen it. Thus, problem-solving skills, stress management skills, seeking help and adopting the belief that one can manage feelings are all recognised as important attributes or skills that lead to enhanced resilience. All of these do, or should, emerge during the course of CBT. Al Siebert, an American clinical psychologist, is Director of the Resiliency Centre, and his book *Resiliency Advantage* (2005) provides a number of exercises for building up resilience that you can use with your clients.

Finally, it is important to discuss with clients who attend AA, NA or any of the Fellowship programmes the relationship between 'powerlessness' and optimism and resilience. At first sight the idea of being powerless may appear closer to learned helplessness than to learned optimism, but the critical point is that 'powerlessness' relates to the drug or to alcohol and not to one's response to it. Thus, while one can have an illness such as diabetes which one is powerless over, one can still take considerable steps in how one deals with it, or how resilient one is.

Integration

Social integration or reintegration is a key goal of the 2008 UK drug strategy (Home Office, 2008). By social integration we are thinking about the opposite to alienation, of being on the outside. Substance use and dependence are all-consuming and often prevent people from developing alternative selves. Most people assume a myriad of roles and responsibilities in different walks of life, as a parent, employee, friend, or in terms of their interests and pursuits. Generally, none of these roles and responsibilities becomes ossified into sole definitions of who we are and what we can achieve. Substance use tends to do the opposite and becomes the defining characteristic of a person. This is not just stigma or labelling. There is a truth to the gradual restriction and loss of role and sometimes identity that comes with prolonged substance use. Living in an altered state of consciousness most of the time results in difficulties not just with simple tasks like cooking but more complex ones, involving social skills and negotiating emotions. Such skills may have been lost over time, or for some clients may never have fully developed due to the age at which their substance use took hold.

The majority of clients who use substance misuse services are startlingly ordinary in their aspirations and goals. Thus, a valued relationship, job, home of one's own and varied social interests with supportive friends and family pretty much sum up most people's goals. This is not to detract from the excitingly obscure or occasionally off the wall aspiration, but it does serve to remind us of the commonality of goals whatever people's backgrounds and experiences. While as therapists we may be sceptical when clients tell us that they want a mundane, 9–5 workaday existence, we should also be aware that this stands in a symbolic relation to their previous lives and activities and that there is something in the order and routine of such a life that the client may be seeking. CBT should allow clients to explore these goals and aspirations through such analyses as pleasure and mastery frameworks and other methods for constructing happiness and meaning. One such method we use to explore life enjoyment and life meaning is the Resources 4 Recovery Technique

(Psychosocial Interventions Resource Library on the UK National Treatment Agency website, www.nta.nhs.uk).

CBT is at best an extremely egalitarian and socially skilled activity which, when undertaken well, can promote and teach a whole range of higher-order social and executive-type tasks in a subtle and profound way. Thus, although a CBT intervention may appear to be focused on just one thing, it is also dealing with other, more complex phenomena. The end-point of CBT for those clients who have slipped out of the mainstream and who wish to rejoin it should be the possibility of doing so.

Choice

Adults take drugs and they drink. Unless there is some cognitive deficit related to decision-making, then they are simply exercising choice. One of the most useful things to remember about CBT is that it is essentially amoral. It is the client who is requesting to work on certain issues or behaviours, and although there is usually some criteria for engaging with services the exact nature of what is wanted remains the client's choice.

There may be many imponderables in working in the field of addictions, but one thing is certain: most drugs and alcohol over and above a very small quantity have negative physical and psychological consequences. Thus, clients whose goal is to drink or take drugs with impunity can be told quite clearly that this is a fantasy. The evidence does not support such a goal and realism dictates a different one. However, there are degrees of harm particularly in relation to drugs, from injecting crack or heroin into the groin to smoking cannabis occasionally. Therefore, it is important to remember that conversations about switching drugs or taking them in a more effective way should not be ruled out. If Paul wants to swap his crack habit and smoke more cannabis, then this is probably not only better for him, but is also more likely to help him in the long run through experiencing at least some degree of self-mastery. As therapists we would no more be suggesting this than we would be suggesting sobriety for clients with alcohol dependence. We work with the client's goals and correct these where we have information and the evidence to do so. For instance, the dream of many alcohol-dependent clients is to return to a position of controlled drinking. Should this therefore be our therapeutic goal? Yes and no. The therapist first has a duty to point out the evidence concerning the success of controlled drinking to those with a history of alcohol dependence (not good). There is also obviously a discussion to be had about the difference between wants and needs. But if the client, having heard, discussed and accepted this information, chooses to attempt controlled drinking, then we as therapists should help the client undertake a behavioural experiment that can test out the belief that it can be done, whilst trying to ensure the least possible harm if it does not work. This discussion should be transparent and we should make clear our concerns based on the evidence and the formulation that we have worked on with the client. It is, though, the client's choice what he or she is willing to risk in pursuit of his or her goal.

Clients are sometimes pleasantly surprised that, as therapists, we hold no particular view on whether or not they continue to drink or use drugs. Indeed, this impartiality can remind them of their own responsibility for what happens in their lives. This is extremely important given the power imbalance that lies at the heart of all patient–therapist relationships. Of course, the promotion of client choice can make the therapist feel uncomfortable, particularly if the client rejects our therapeutic interventions. Difficult though this is, we need always to bear in mind that therapeutic interventions are relational and a too rigid focus on technique, even where no objection is raised, may diminish clients' own capacity to determine what happens to them.

So whilst CBT gives us as therapists a number of tools to work with, it is also a wider project for long-term recovery. It is the emergence of these factors of client optimism, resilience, integration and choice that really indicate that we are on the right track in therapy.

A final thought. If you started reading this book from the back, then we congratulate you for exercising your choice; and to those who started at the beginning we congratulate you on your resilience. Whichever approach you adopted, we hope you have gained something and that you can take this into your work with clients so that addiction can be stripped of its mystery and a shared optimism about change given its rightful place.

Appendix 13.1: Treatment summary and relapse prevention plan

1. How did my drug/alcohol problem/s develop?
2. What kept them going?
3. What have I learnt in therapy that is useful?
4. What were my most unhelpful thoughts/assumptions/predictions that kept my drug/alcohol use going?
5. What are the alternatives to these unhelpful thoughts/assumptions/predictions?
6. What were the most important challenges and/or behavioural experiments that I faced and what did I learn from them (both in the sessions and outside them)?
7. What do I need to do to build on what I have learned and maintain my recovery?
8. What could trigger drug/alcohol use in the future?
9. What might be the early warning signs that I might be vulnerable to using again?
10. If I notice these early warning signs, what should I do?
11. If I do lapse, how can I deal with this setback?
12. What are the next steps for my recovery and who can help me?

References

Annis, H. M. & Davis, C. S. (1988a). Assessment of expectancies in alcohol dependent clients. In G. A. Marlatt & D. Donovan, eds. *Assessment of Addictive Behaviors*. New York: Guilford Press.

Annis, H. M. & Davis, C. S. (1988b). Relapse prevention. In R. K. Hester & W. R. Miller, eds. *Handbook of Alcoholism Treatment Approaches*. New York: Pergamon Press.

Arkowitz, H., Westra, H. A., Miller, W. R. & Rollnick, S. (2008). *Motivational Interviewing in the Treatment of Psychological Problems*. New York: Guilford Press.

Authentic Happiness. www.authentichappiness.sas.upenn.edu.

Baklien, B. & Samarasinghe, D. (2003). *Alcohol and Poverty*. Colombo: Forut.

Bandura, A. (1977a). *Social Learning Theory*. Englewood Cliffs, NJ: Prentice-Hall.

Bandura, A. (1977b). Self-efficacy. Toward a unifying theory of behavior change. *Psychological Review*, **84**, 191–215.

Bandura, A. (1982). Self-efficacy mechanism in human agency. *American Psychologist*, **97**, 122–147.

Bandura, A. (1986). *Social Foundations of Thought and Action: A Social Cognitive Theory*. Englewood Cliffs, NJ: Prentice-Hall.

Bates, M. E., Bowden, S. C. & Barry, D. (2002). Neurocognitive impairment associated with alcohol use disorders: implications for treatment. *Experimental and Clinical Psychopharmacology*, **10**, 193–212.

Beck, A. T. (1967). *Depression: Clinical, Experimental and Theoretical Aspects*. New York: Harper & Row.

Beck, A. T. (1976). *Cognitive Therapy and the Emotional Disorders*. New York: International Universities Press.

Beck, A. T., Rush, A. J., Shaw, B. F. & Emery, G. (1979). *Cognitive Therapy of Depression*. New York: Guilford Press.

Beck, A. T., Wright, F. D., Newman, C. F. & Liese, B. S. (1993). *Cognitive Therapy of Substance Abuse*. London: Guilford Press.

Beck, J. (1995). *Cognitive Therapy: Basics and Beyond*. New York: Guilford Press.

Bennett-Levy, J., Butler, G. *et al.* (2004). *Oxford Guide to Behavioural Experiments in Cognitive Therapy*. Oxford: Oxford University Press.

Breese, G. R., Chu, K. *et al.* (2005). Stress enhancement of craving during sobriety: a risk for relapse. *Alcoholism, Clinical and Experimental Research*, **29**(2), 185–195.

Burns, D. (1980). *Feeling Good: The New Mood Therapy*. New York: William Morrow.

Butler, G. (2006). The value of formulation: A question for debate. *Clinical Psychology Forum*, **16**, 9–12.

Carroll, K. M. (1998). *A Cognitive-Behavioral Approach: Treating Cocaine Addiction*. Rockville, MD: National Institute on Drug Abuse.

Carroll, K. M., Fenton, L. R. *et al.* (2004). Efficacy of disulfiram and cognitive-behavioral therapy in cocaine-dependent outpatients: A randomized placebo-controlled trial. *Archives of General Psychiatry*, **61**, 264–272.

Castellanos, C. & Conrod, P. J. (2006). Efficacy of brief personality-targeted cognitive behavioural interventions in reducing and preventing adolescent emotional and behavioural problems. *Journal of Mental Health*, **15**(6), 1–14.

Center for Substance Abuse Treatment. Treatment for Stimulant Use Disorders (1999). *Treatment Improvement Protocol (TIP) Series 33*. DHHS Publication No. (SMA) 99-3296. Rockville, MD: Substance Abuse and Mental Health Services Administration.

Charlton, B. G. (2000). The new management of scientific knowledge in medicine: a change of direction with profound implications. In A. Miles, J. R. Hampton & B. Hurwitz, eds. *NICE, CHI and the NHS Reforms: Enabling Excellence or Imposing Control?* London: Aesculapius Medical Press.

Clark, D. M. (1999). Anxiety disorders: why they exist and how to treat them. *Behaviour Research and Therapy*, **37**, 5–27.

Clark, D. M. & Wells, A. (1995). A cognitive model of social phobia. In R. G. Heimberg, M. R. Liebowitz *et al.*, eds., *Social Phobia – Diagnosis, Assessment, and Treatment*. New York: Guilford Press.

Cloninger, C. R. (1987). A systematic method for clinical description and classification of personality variants. *Archives of General Psychiatry*, **44**, 573–588.

Crews, F. T., Buckley, T. *et al.* (2005). Alcoholic neurobiology: changes in dependence and recovery. *Alcohol Clinical and Experimental Research*, **29**, 1504–1513.

Cummings, C., Gordon, J. R. & Marlatt, G. A. (1980). Relapse prevention and prediction. In W. R. Miller, ed. *The Addictive Behaviors*. New York: Pergamon.

Donovan, D. M. (1996). Marlatt's classification of relapse precipitants: Is the emperor still wearing clothes?' *Addiction*, **91**, 131–137.

Drummond, D. C. (2001). Theories of drug craving, ancient and modern. *Addiction*, **96**, 33–46.

Dudley, R. & Kuyken, W. (2006). Formulation in cognitive-behavioural therapy. In L. Johnstone & R. Dallos, eds. *Formulation in Psychology and Psychotherapy*. London: Routledge.

Edwards, G. (1987). Review of G. A. Marlatt and J. R. Gordon, eds. *Relapse Prevention*. British Journal of Addiction, **82**, 319–323.

Ellis, A., McInerney, J. F., DiGiuseppe, R., & Yeager, R. J. (1988). *Rational-Emotive Therapy with Alcoholics and Substance Abusers*. New York: Pergamon.

Epstein, D. H., Hawkins, W. E., Covi, L., Umbricht, A. & Preston, K. L. (2003). Cognitive behavioral therapy plus contingency management for cocaine use: Findings during treatment and across 12-month follow-ups. *Psychological of Addictive Behaviors*, **17**, 73–82.

Farrell, M., Howes, C. *et al.* (1998). Substance misuse of psychiatric comorbidity: An overview of the OPCS National Psychiatric Morbidity Survey. *Addictive Behaviour*, **23**, 908–918.

Franken, I. H. A. (2003). Drug craving and addiction: integrated psychological and neuropsychopharmacological approaches. *Progress in Neuro-Psychopharmacology & Biological Psychiatry*, **27**, 563–579.

Franken, I. H. A., Stam, C. J., Hendriks, V. M. & Van Den Brink, W. (2003). Neurophysiological evidence for abnormal cognitive processing of drug cues in heroin dependence. *Psychopharmacology*, **170**, 205–212.

Goeders, N. E. (2002). Stress and cocaine addiction. *Pharmacology*, **301**(3), 785–789.

Gorski, T. (1990). *Managing Cocaine Craving*. Center City, MN: Hazelden.

Graham, H. & Wanigaratne, S. (2000). Substance misuse. In N. Patel, E. Bennett *et al.*, eds. *Clinical Psychology, 'Race' and Culture*. Leicester: BPS Books.

Greenberger, D. & Padesky, C.A. (1995). *Mind over Mood: Change How You Feel by Changing the Way You Think*. New York: Guilford Press.

Grüsser, S., Mörsen, C., Wölfling, K. & Flor, H. (2007). The relationship of stress, coping, effect expectancies and craving. *European Addiction Research*, **13**, 31–38.

Harding, W. M. & Zinberg, N. E. (1977). The effectiveness of the subculture in developing rituals and social sanctions for controlled use. In B. M. du Toit, ed. *Drugs, Rituals and Altered States of Consciousness*. Rotterdam: A. A. Balkema.

Hill, R. G., Moran, P., Cooper, W. & Bearn, J. (2006). Early childhood maladjustment and adherence with inpatient drug detoxification treatment. *Journal of Substance Use*, **10**(6), 1–7.

Home Office (2008). *Drugs: Protecting Families and Communities*. The 2008 drug strategy. www.homeoffice.gov.uk.

Humphreys, K. & Weisner, P. (2000). Use of exclusion criteria in selecting research subjects and its effects on the generalisability of alcohol treatment outcome studies. *American Journal of Psychiatry*, **157**, 588–594.

Irvin, J. E., Bowers, C. A., Dunn, M. E. & Wang, M. C. (1999). Efficacy of relapse prevention: A meta-analytic review. *Journal of Consulting and Clinical Psychology*, **66**(5), 761–767.

Kabat-Zinn, J. (2001). *Full Catastrophe Living – How to Cope with Stress, Pain and Illness Using Mindfulness Meditation*. London: Piatkus Books.

Kabat-Zinn, J. (2004). *Wherever You Go There You Are: Mindfulness Meditation in Everyday Life*. London: Piatkus Books.

Khantzian, E. J. (1977). The self-medication of substance misuse disorders: a reconstruction and recent applications. *Harvard Review of Psychiatry*, **4**, 231–244.

Koob, G. & Kreek, M. J. (2007). Stress, dysregulation of drug reward pathways, and the transition to drug dependence. *American Journal of Psychiatry*, **164**, 1149–1159.

Koob, G. F. & Le Moal, M. (2006). *Neurobiology of Addiction*. London: Academic Press.

Kouimtsidis, C., Reynolds, M. *et al.* (2007). *Cognitive-Behavioural Therapy in the Treatment of Addiction: A Treatment Planner for Clinicians*. Chichester: Wiley.

Kushner, M. G., Abrams, K. & Borchardt, C. (2000). The relationship between anxiety disorders and alcohol use disorders: A review of major perspectives and findings. *Clinical Psychology Review*, **20**(2), 149–171.

Leahy, R. L. (2003). *Cognitive Therapy Techniques: A Practitioner's Guide*. New York: Guilford Press.

Liese, B. S. & Franz, R. A. (1996). Treating substance use disorders with cognitive therapy: Lessons learned and implications for the future. In P. M. Salkovskis, ed. *Frontiers of Cognitive Therapy*. London: Guilford Press.

Litman, G. K. (1974). Stress, affect and craving in alcoholics. The single case as a research strategy. *Quarterly Journal of Studies in Alcohol*, **35**, 131–146.

Manning, V., Wanigaratne, S. *et al.* (2008). Changes in neuropsychological functioning during alcohol detoxification. *European Addiction Research*, **14**, 226–233.

Marlatt, G. A. & Donovan, D. M. (2005). *Relapse Prevention: Maintenance Strategies in the Treatment of Addictive Behaviors*. New York, Guilford Press.

Marlatt, G. A. & Gordon, J. R. (1985). *Relapse Prevention: Maintenance Strategies in the Treatment of Addictive Behaviors*. New York: Guilford Press.

Marlatt, G. A. & Witkiewitz, K. (2005). Relapse prevention for alcohol and drug problems. In G. A. Marlatt & D. M. Donovan, eds. *Relapse Prevention: Maintenance strategies in the treatment of addictive behaviours* (2nd edn.). New York: Guilford Press.

Marsden, J., Farrell, M. *et al.* (2008) Development of the treatment outcomes profile. *Addiction*, **103**(9), 1450–1460.

Martino, S., Ball, S. A. *et al.* (2006). *Motivational Interviewing Assessment: Supervisory Tools for Enhancing Proficiency*. Salem, OR: Northwest Frontier Addiction Technology Transfer Center, Oregon Health and Science University.

Maslin, J. & Simons, I. (2009) Moving away from problematic substance use: The importance of 'identity shift'. *Clinical Psychology Forum*, **201**, 12–18.

May, J., Andrade, J., Panabokke, N. & Kavanagh, D. (2004). Images of desire: Cognitive models of craving. *Memory*, **12**, 447–461.

Miller, W. (1983). Motivational interviewing with problem drinkers. *Behavioural Psychotherapy*, **11**, 147–172.

Miller, W. (1985). Motivation for treatment: a review with special emphasis on alcoholism. *Psychological Bulletin*, **98**, 84–107.

Miller, W. R. & Rollnick S. (1986). *Motivational Interviewing: Preparing People for Change*. New York: Guilford Press.

Miller, W. R. & Rollnick, S. (2002). *Motivational Interviewing: Preparing People to Change Addictive Behaviour* (2nd edn). New York: Guilford Press.

Miller, W. R. & Wilbourne, P. L. (2002). 'Mesa Grande: A methodological analysis of clinical trials of treatment for alcohol use disorders.' *Addiction*, **97**(3), 265–277.

Miranda, J., Bernal, G. *et al.* (2005) State of the science on psychosocial interventions for ethnic minorities. *Annual Review of Clinical Psychology*, **1**: 113–142.

Morgenstern, J. & Longabaugh, R. (2000). Cognitive-behavioral treatment for alcohol dependence: a review of evidence for its hypothesized mechanisms of action. *Addiction*, **95**(10), 1475–1490.

National Institute for Health and Clinical Excellence (2007). NICE clinical guideline 51. *Drug Misuse: Psychosocial Interventions*. London: NIHCE.

O'Brien, C. P. & McLellan, A. T. (1996). Myths about the treatment of addiction. *Lancet*, **27**(347), 237–240.

O'Brien, C. P., McLellan, A. T., Childress, A. R. & Woody, G. E. (2009). Penn/VA centre for studies of addiction. *Neuropharmachology*, **56**, 44–47.

O'Rourke M. & Bird, L. (2001). *Risk Management in Mental Health: A Practical Guide to Individual Care and Community Safety*. London: The Mental Health Foundation.

Okiishi, J. C., Lambert, M. J. *et al.* (2006). An analysis of therapist treatment effects: Toward providing feedback to individual therapists on their service users' psychotherapy outcome. *Journal of Clinical Psychology*, **62**: 1157–1172.

Orford, J. (2001). *Excessive Appetites: A Psychological Review of Addictions*. Chichester: Wiley.

Orford, J., Johnson, M. R. D. & Purser, R. (2004). Drinking in second generation black and Asian communities in the English Midlands. *Addiction Research and Theory*, **12**(1): 11–30.

Padesky, C. A. (2003). *Harnessing Hope and Reducing Relapse. Engaging Clients in Cognitive Therapy for Depression*. London: London Workshop.

Padesky, C. A. & Mooney, K. A. (1990). Clinical tip: Presenting the cognitive model to clients. *International Cognitive Therapy Newsletter*, **6**, 13–14.

Peele, S. (1998). *The Meaning of Addiction: An Unconventional View*. San Francisco: Jossey-Bass.

Petry, N. M. (2006). Contingency management treatments. *British Journal of Psychiatry*, **189**, 97–98.

Pilling, S., Hesketh, K. & Mitcheson, L. (2009). *Psychosocial Interventions in Drug Misuse: A Framework and Toolkit for Implementing NICE-recommended Treatment Interventions*. British Psychological Society, Centre for Outcomes, Research and Effectiveness (CORE) Research Department of Clinical, Educational and Health Psychology, University College London. www.nta.nhs.uk.

Prochaska, J. O. & Di Clemente, C. C. (1983). Process and stages of self-change of smoking: Towards an integrative model of change. *Journal of Consulting and Clinical Psychology*, **51**, 390–395.

Prochaska, J. O. & Di Clemente, C. C. (1996). Towards a comprehensive model of change. In: W. R. Miller & N. Heather, eds. *Treating addictive behaviours* (2nd edn.). New York: Plenum.

Project Match Research Group (1997). Matching alcoholism treatment to client heterogeneity: Project Match post-treatment drinking outcomes. *Journal of Studies on Alcohol*, **58**, 7–29.

Robins, L. N., Helzer, J. E. & Davis, D. H. (1975). Narcotic use in Southeast Asia and afterward. *Archives of General Psychiatry*, **32**, 955–961.

Robinson, T. E. and Berridge, K. C (2003). Addiction. *Annual Review of Psychology*, **54**, 25–53.

Rogers, C. (1951). *Client-Centered Therapy*. London: Constable.

Rogers, C. (1967). *On Becoming a Person: A Therapist's View of Psychotherapy*. London: Constable.

Rollnick, S., Butler, C. & Stott, N. (1997). Helping smokers make decisions: the enhancement of brief intervention for general medical practice. *Patient Education and Counselling*, **31**, 325–334.

Rollnick, S., Mason, P. & Butler, C. (1999). *Health Behaviour Change: A Guide for Practitioners*. Edinburgh: Churchill Livingston.

Rollnick, S. & Miller, W. R. (1995). What is motivational interviewing? *Behavioural and Cognitive Psychology*, **23**, 325–334.

Rollnick, S., Miller, W. R. & Butler, C. C. (2008). *Motivational Interviewing in Health Care: Helping Patients Change Behavior*. New York: Guilford Press.

Ryan, F. (2006). Appetite lost and found: Cognitive psychology in the addiction clinic. In M. Munafo & I. P. Albery, eds. *Cognition and Addiction*. Oxford: Oxford University Press.

Salkovskis, P. M. (2002). Empirically grounded clinical interventions: Cognitive-behavioural therapy progress through a multi-dimensional approach to clinical science. *Behavioural and Cognitive Psychotherapy*, **30**, 3–9.

Scheier, M. E. & Carver, S. (1987). Dispositional optimism and physical well-being: the influence of generalized outcome expectancies on health. *Journal of Personality*, **55**, 169–210.

Segal, Z. V., Williams, J. M. G. & Teasdale, J. D. (2002). *Mindfulness-Based Cognitive Therapy for Depression*. New York: Guilford Press.

Segerstrom, S. C., Taylor, S. E., Kemeny, M. E. & Fahey, J. L. (1998). Optimism is associated with mood, coping, and immune change in response to stress. *Journal of Personal Social Psychology* **74**, 1646–1655.

Seligman, M. (2006). *Learned Optimism: How to Change Your Mind and Your Life*. New York: Vintage.

Sher, K., Bartholow, J., Bruce, D. & Wood, M. D. (2000). Personality and substance use disorders: A prospective study. *Journal of Consulting and Clinical Psychology*, **68**(5), 818–829.

Sheridan, J. & Strang, J. (2003). *Approaches to Community Pharmacy*. London: Macmillan.

Siebert, A. (2005). *The Resiliency Advantage*. San Francisco: Berrett-Koehler.

Simpson, D. D. & Joe, G. W. (2004). A longitudinal evaluation of treatment engagement and recovery stages. *Journal of Substance Abuse Treatment*, **27**, 89–97.

Simpson, D. D., Joe, G. W. & Rowan-Szal, G. A. (2007). Linking the elements of change: Program and client responses to innovation. *Journal of Substance Abuse Treatment*, **33**(2), 201–209.

Sutton, S. (1993). Is wearing clothes a high-risk situation for relapse? The base rate problem in relapse research. *Addiction*, **88**, 725–727.

Tober, G. & Raistrick, D. (2007). *Motivational Dialogue: Preparing Addiction Professionals for Motivational Interviewing Practice.* London: Routledge.

UK Drug Policy Commission Recovery Consensus Group (2008). A Vision of Recovery. www.ukdcp.org.uk.

UKATT Research Team (2005). Effectiveness of treatment for alcohol problems: Findings of the randomised UK alcohol treatment trial (UKATT). *British Medical Journal*, **331**(7516), 541–544.

Vaillant, G. E. (1983). *The Natural History of Alcoholism.* Cambridge, MA: Harvard University Press.

Volkow, N. D., Chang, L. *et al.* (2001). Low level of brain dopamine D2 receptors in methamphetamine abusers: association with metabolism in the orbitofrontal cortex. *American Journal of Psychiatry*, **158**, 2015–2021.

Wanigaratne, S. (2003). Relapse prevention in practice. *The Drug and Alcohol Professional*, **3**(3), 11–18.

Wanigaratne, S. (2006). Psychology of addiction. *Psychiatry*, **5**(12), 455–460.

Wanigaratne, S., Davis, P., Pryce, K. & Brotchie, J. (2005). *A Brief Review of the Effectiveness of Psychological Therapies in the Treatment of Substance Misuse.* London: NTA, DOH.

Wanigaratne, S. & Keaney, F. (2002). Psychodynamic aspects of relapse prevention in the treatment of addictive behaviours. In M. Weegmann & R. Cohen, eds. *The Psychodynamics of Addiction.* London: Whurr.

Wanigaratne, S., Salas, S. & Strang, J. (2007). Substance misuse. In D. Bhugra & K. Bhui, eds. *Textbook of Cultural Psychiatry*, Cambridge: Cambridge University Press.

Wanigaratne, S., Wallace, W. *et al.* (1990). *Relapse Prevention for Addictive Behaviours: A Manual for Therapists.* Oxford: Blackwell.

Weaver, T., Madden, P. *et al.* (2003). Comorbidity of substance misuse and mental illness in community mental health and substance misuse services. *British Journal of Psychiatry*, **183**, 304–313.

Werner, E. E. (1982). *Vulnerable but Invincible: A Longitudinal Study of Resilient Children and Youth.* New York: McGraw-Hill.

West, R. (2001). Theories of addiction. *Addiction*, **96**, 3–15.

West, R. (2006). *Theory of Addiction.* Oxford: Blackwell.

Westen, D., Novotny, C. M. & Thompson-Brenner, H. (2004). The empirical status of empirically supported psychotherapies: Assumptions, findings, and reporting in controlled clinical trials. *Psychological Bulletin*, **130**, 631–663.

White, W. (2004). Recovery: The next frontier. *Counselor*, **5**(1), 18–21.

White, W. (2005). Recovery: Its history and renaissance as an organizing construct. *Alcoholism Treatment Quarterly*, **23**(1), 3–15.

White, W. (2008). *Recovery Management and Recovery-Orientated Systems of Care: Scientific Rationale and Promising Practices.* SAMHSA. Northeast Addiction Technology Transfer Center, Great Lakes Addiction Technology Transfer Center, Philadelphia Department of Behavioral Health/Mental Retardation Services.

Witkiewitz, K. & Marlatt, G. A. (2004). Relapse prevention for alcohol and drug problems: that was Zen this is Tao. *American Psychologist*, **59**, 224–235.

Young, J. & Beck, A. T. (1980). *Cognitive Therapy Scale Rating Manual (unpublished manuscript).* Philadelphia, PN: University of Pennsylvania.

Zinberg, N. E. (1984). *Drug, Set, and Setting.* New Haven, CT: Yale University Press.

Index